Alcohol and Opium
in the Old West

WITHDRAWN

SCC

Alcohol and Opium in the Old West

Use, Abuse and Influence

JEREMY AGNEW

McFarland & Company, Inc., Publishers
Jefferson, North Carolina, and London

LIBRARY OF CONGRESS CATALOGUING-IN-PUBLICATION DATA

Agnew, Jeremy.
   Alcohol and opium in the Old West : use, abuse, and
influence / Jeremy Agnew.
      p.   cm.
   Includes bibliographical references and index.

   ISBN 978-0-7864-7629-9
   softcover : acid free paper ∞

   1. Alcoholism—West (U.S.)—History—19th century.
   2. Opium abuse—West (U.S.)—History—19th century.
   I. Title.
   HV5235.U5.A46 2014
   362.2920978'09034—dc23   2013036296

BRITISH LIBRARY CATALOGUING DATA ARE AVAILABLE

On the cover: The Fountain Saloon in Cripple Creek, Colorado
(Glenn Kinnaman, Colorado and Western History Collection).

Manufactured in the United States of America

McFarland & Company, Inc., Publishers
   Box 611, Jefferson, North Carolina 28640
   www.mcfarlandpub.com

For Tom and Terri,
who still carry on the traditions
of the Old West

Table of Contents

Preface

Whether justified or not, one popular image of the Old West revolves around gunfighters and frontier ruffians who drank constantly and whose behavior was worsened by drink. Another popular image, one derived mostly from motion pictures, is of the Western saloon populated with countless barflies who apparently have nothing better to do all day but sit around and drink while waiting for the inevitable gunfight between the villain and the hero to break out. A third striking image of the Old West from Victorian times is that of the opium den in an alley behind the red light district, a den peopled with sinister-looking Chinese skulking around among rows of emaciated dope fiends sprawled out on wooden cots in dark rooms filled with an aromatic haze of opium smoke.[1]

What is the truth of these perceptions? None of these three images of the Old West is totally accurate, though none of the three is totally inaccurate either. Heavy drinking, smoking opium, and swigging laudanum were indeed influences on mainstream life in the West in America during the last half of the nineteenth century.

Ingesting various substances, such as alcohol and opium, has been a form of social behavior throughout history. The production and consumption of alcoholic beverages has long been a part of human society and alcohol has been pervasive throughout history as Western civilization's favorite beverage. Like alcohol, opium was used in the Old West to provide an escape from reality and alter the perception of how the user viewed the world. Though many drugs have been popular throughout history for both medicinal and recreational use, none has had the influence of opium and its derivatives. It provided some users with welcome relief from the loneliness and harshness of life on the new frontier of the Old West and from the aches and pains that resulted from everyday working conditions. Patent medicines containing large amounts of both alcohol and opium were commonly found on the medicine shelf of most homes and ranches in the early West.

Excessive use of alcohol has been blamed for many of the gunfights and much of the violence that permeated the Old West. Opium was blamed for being the downfall of innocent young women and has been characterized over a broad spectrum, from serving as a useful medicine and the writer's innocent source of inspiration at one end to a terrible and evil drug at the other. The reality is that alcohol and opium were inherently neither good nor evil, but were used and regarded in different ways by different people.

Alcohol and opium operated on different ends of the spectrum, though the two went hand-in-hand in providing temporary escape from the Westerner's self-perceived hard lot. Alcohol solved problems externally by lowering the drinker's inhibitions and causing him to carouse, fight, run after women, shoot at other men, and break things. Opium, on the other hand, used for pleasure rather than for medical reasons, often solved the user's problems internally by producing inner calm and serenity. Author Frederick Powell, in *Bacchus Dethroned*, an eloquent 1874 tract in support of temperance, made a distinction between the two: "The paradise of the opium-eater is refined and spiritual; that of the alcohol-drinker coarse, sensual and devilish."[2] As Norman Kerr, a physician and contemporary author put it, "Opium exerts a soothing influence. Under its powerful sway, the cantankerous and quarrelsome are transformed for the moment into the most amiable and peaceful of beings."[3] Taking drugs or smoking opium for recreational use in the Old West were, however, considered to be different than heavy drinking. Smoking opium was considered to be deviant and was mostly associated with groups on the fringes of mainstream society in the West such as the Chinese, gamblers, pimps, and fallen women.

In his book, *This Drinking Nation*, author Jonathan Harris pointed out that "revealing insights into a nation's social history can be gained by tracing its drinking patterns."[4] The present work attempts to explain the roles of drink and opium in the history of the Old West and discuss their influence on the men and women who lived there. The Old West will be broadly defined here as North America west of the Mississippi during the last half or so of the nineteenth century, from the time of the emigrant wagon trains and the gold rush to California in the late 1840s to the closing of the Western frontier in roughly 1900.[5] This period was the first time in American history that heavy drinking and drug abuse became a major concern for society.

Both drinking and drugs have been subject to extremes of opinion. This work is intended to be neither for nor against the use of alcohol or opium, but tries to report the historical reality in the Old West without bias. This book confines itself to facts, and while every step has been taken to verify what is presented here, in the end, the author takes full responsibility for any errors that may have found their way into the narrative.

In some parts of this book I have chosen to use the convention of referring to modern states and towns that did not yet exist in order to conveniently place locations for the reader. And finally, readers may note that some of the material in the text (particularly regarding opium dens) would appear to relate more to cities in the East than in the West. However, a curious inconsistency existed in the Old West. As historian Thomas Noel has pointed out, "western cities were modeled on eastern ones and often had more in common with the urban East than the frontier West."[6] Thus any apparent paradoxical comparison is legitimate.

Timeline

1500s   The Portuguese use opium as a trade item with China.

1600s   Opium smoking increases in China.

1620   The *Mayflower* arrives in America with casks of "exhilarating spirits."

1630   Wine grapes planted in the future New Mexico by Franciscan missionaries.

1660s   Laudanum popularized by physician Thomas Sydenham in England.

1700s   Increased tea drinking in Britain boosts the opium trade with China.

1803   Louisiana Purchase adds large tracts of land to the West. Morphine is isolated as the primary active ingredient in opium.

1830s   First stirrings of the Temperance Movement. Mountain men trapping beaver in the Rocky Mountains and trading furs for whiskey.

1840s   Whiskey and medicinal opium come west with emigrant pioneers headed for Oregon and California.

1844   W.H. Smith's *The Drunkard* will go on to become one of the most successful of the temperance plays.

1846   War with Mexico annexes large parts of the Southwest, including the unopposed takeover of New Mexico.

1848   End of the war with Mexico adds California, Arizona, New Mexico, and parts of Colorado, Wyoming, and Utah to the United States.

1849   Start of the California "Forty-Niner" rush sparked by gold discoveries the previous year at Sutter's Mill in the Sierra Nevada.

1850   Increasing waves of Chinese immigrants used as laborers in the California gold camps bring opium smoking to the West Coast.

1854   Grattan Massacre in Wyoming sparks war with the Plains Indians for the next thirty-six years.

1856   First use of the hypodermic syringe in America by physician Fordyce Barker makes the administration of morphine easier and more effective.

1858   *Ten Nights in a Bar-room* spreads a message of the evil of drink to theatergoers across the country.

1859   Discoveries of rich ore in Central City, Colorado, and Bannack, Montana, reenergize gold mining in the West. "Uncle Dick" Wootton arrives from Taos in the brand-new town of Denver with a wagonload of whiskey to celebrate Christmas.

1860   Discovery of silver in the area of Virginia City leads to a mining rush to Nevada.

1861   Start of the Civil War between the Union and the Confederacy.

1862   Louis Pasteur shows that yeast is the catalyst for fermentation.

1863   Start of construction of the first transcontinental railroad from the East to California will eventually bring more than 8,000 Chinese laborers to work on the Central Pacific Railroad.

1865   End of the Civil War leaves many soldiers addicted to opium for medical pain control of wartime injuries.

1866   Start of the great cowboy cattle drives from Texas to railroad towns in Kansas. Start of the gunfighting era in the West.

1869   Meeting of the Central Pacific and the Union Pacific railroads at Promontory, Utah, completes the first transcontinental railroad across America.

1870s   The Chinese habit of smoking opium starts to be adopted by some whites.

1874   Discovery of gold in the Black Hills of South Dakota leads to creation of the town of Deadwood. Founding of the Woman's Christian Temperance Union (WCTU).

1876   Defeat of General Custer and the Seventh Cavalry at the Battle of the Little Bighorn.

1878   Boom in silver mining in the Colorado mountains leads to the town of Leadville.
        Peak year for the number of gunfights in the Old West.

1880s   Early understanding of opium addiction. Temperance workers campaign vigorously against the "demon rum" and other addictive substances.

1881   What is considered to be the classic Western gunfight occurs at the O.K. Corral in Tombstone, Arizona, a fight which pits the Earp brothers and Doc Holliday against the Clantons and the McLowerys.

1882   Passage of the Chinese Exclusion Act limits the number of Chinese immigrants to the United States.

1883   Robert Koch shows that the dysentery arising from cholera is caused by bacteria.

1885   End of the great cowboy cattle drives and the decline of the Kansas cattle towns.

1890   End of the Indian Wars in the West with the fight at Wounded Knee, South Dakota, between the U.S. army and a group of captive Sioux Indians. Discovery of gold behind Pikes Peak in Colorado leads to the last great gold rush of the Old West, attracting an estimated 30,000 to Cripple Creek. The WCTU grows to 150,000 members and 7,000 branches.

1893   Founding of the Anti-Saloon League.

1900   Opium smoking starts to decline as the Chinese Exclusion Act limits entry of new immigrants to the United States and many Chinese return to China. Essential end of the gunfighting era in the Old West. Carry Nation heeds her calling to smash saloons.

1906   The Pure Food and Drug Act requires accurate labeling of products that contain alcohol and narcotics.

1914   Passage of the Harrison Narcotic Act requires registration of manufacturers and distributors of opium and morphine.

1917   Passage of the Eighteenth Amendment to the Constitution of the United States heralds the start of Prohibition.

1920   The National Prohibition Act (the Volstead Act) starts the so-called "Noble Experiment."

1933   Ratification of the Twenty-First Amendment to the United States Constitution ends Prohibition.

CHAPTER ONE

The Demon Rum and
Other Drinks of Choice

"Whiskey! The mystery of the age; the curse of the United States; ever the first article of commerce on the borders of civilization."[1] This was the description of alcohol given by one early visitor to Colorado. Whiskey was all of these and more.

America has been a drinking nation since its birth. Alcoholic spirits arrived in Jamestown and Plymouth in the colonies with the early English and Dutch settlers. As early as 1609, Henry Hudson sailed into New York Bay with several casks of spirits. Even the *Mayflower*, aboard which the pilgrims sailed to America in 1620, carried exhilarating spirits. The first distillery was built on Staten Island, which lies between New Jersey and Long Island, in 1664.[2]

At that time, alcohol was regarded as a healthy and nutritious substance. A good stiff drink, among its other attributes, was considered to be a healthy food, a beverage, a medicinal drug, and an anesthetic. Because wines came from grapes, and beer and whiskey from various grains, early settlers felt that it stood to reason that alcohol would be a type of food. It was felt to strengthen the heart and improve the lungs. However, when excessive drinking was later considered to be a nasty addictive habit, alcohol became roundly condemned as the "demon rum."

Many men drank with meals, after meals, and between meals to help disguise the lack of taste in their food. Western settlers lived on a constant diet of bread and boiled or fried salt pork and beef that was monotonous, low on flavor, and laden with fat. Meat was generally boiled or fried because ovens to bake or broil meat were uncommon. Some felt that a drink before a meal prepared the stomach for food, and others believed that a drink after eating helped the digestion. This constant use of wine, beer, and whiskey with meals, along with an unbalanced diet, led to frequent stomach upsets and other digestive problems.

By the mid–1800s, many Americans were heavy users of strong drink, and alcohol was a common part of nineteenth century life. Much of the work performed by early pioneers, such as digging and planting crops, sluicing for gold, and logging, was dull and physically demanding. Alcohol was consumed in large quantities to provide relaxation and a temporary escape from these harsh realities of living on the frontier. Whiskey accompanied pioneer wagon trains to the West and emigrants brought plenty with them to ensure that it lasted for the entire trip. One popular formula for homemade shampoo consisted of a mixture of castor oil and whiskey, with lavender added to give it a pleasant scent.

A shot or two of straight whiskey gave a jolt to the drinker that was thought to toughen the body and prepare it to ward off disease. Even if it failed in this regard, strong drink was used to treat a variety of ailments from bad breath to heart problems. Whiskey was prescribed for colds, fevers, frostbite, broken legs, nervousness, as an antiseptic for wounds, and as an anesthetic for surgery. Self-proclaimed authorities on the subject of alcohol, who were to be found hanging around most saloons, said that whiskey was definitely good for treating a wide variety of complaints, such as bites from mad dogs, chills, malaise, palpitations, fevers, kidney ailments, and general debility.

Snakebite was an ever-present problem on the Great Plains and in the Southwest. One reported frontier antidote for a rattlesnake bite was to consume between a pint and a quart of whiskey within twelve hours of the bite. Beside dulling the pain, which may have made this a popular remedy, this "medicine" was reported to neutralize the poison.

One hotly debated theory in saloons was that, as alcohol would preserve the dead body of a heavy drinker, by a tenuous logical connection whiskey taken internally should also preserve a drinker's tissues and lengthen his life. Such reasoning was dubious, but undoubtedly the possibilities of this concept were enthusiastically explored by some. Even today a common expression for someone who has drunk a lot is that he is "pickled."

The results of using alcohol for preserving dead bodies were definitely dubious and had unfortunate consequences in the case of Jack Slade. Joseph Alfred "Jack" Slade was a mean gunman who was involved in several violent incidents in Colorado and Wyoming in the late 1850s, as a result of which he fled north to Montana. Slade was a heavy drinker and, in Virginia City, his violent ways exploded again in numerous fights. An intolerant vigilante mob finally lynched him at the Elephant Corral on March 10, 1864. Slade's wife placed his body in a zinc-lined coffin filled with alcohol, intending to transport it back to his birthplace in Illinois for burial. The usual winter snows that lie deep and heavy over Montana forced delays in her trip. By July, when the snows had finally melted enough for travel, she and the coffin had managed to journey only as far as Utah. The alcohol had not worked as a preservative as well as expected and after this length of time the body had decomposed so badly that she was forced by decency to bury him in Salt Lake City.

Many felt that whiskey was necessary to supply energy for hard physical labor and make outdoor work bearable in the cold northern climates of the Rockies and the Sierra Nevada.[3] No matter whether the weather was too hot or too cold, the use of alcohol was considered by Western pioneers to be part of the acclimatization process. At the two extremes, both sunstroke and the cold body temperatures of hypothermia were treated with strong drink. In the year 1898, during the height of the Klondike Gold Rush, 120,000 gallons of whiskey were reportedly shipped to Dawson in the Yukon Territory — presumably to take care of both of these problems.

There was, admittedly, a practical side to drinking whiskey and beer. Water along the emigrant trails could be dangerous, often containing a high level of naturally occurring alkali or germs left in watering holes by animals or previous wagon trains.[4] To offset any nasty tastes, travelers might add lemon juice or whiskey to the water sources found on the journey.

Water used for drinking purposes in the mining camps or other urban areas of the early West was often just as bad, being dirty, frequently laden with sediment and noxious natural minerals or mining chemicals (such as arsenic and lead), and frequently carrying diseases. Daylight Creek, which ran through the infant town Virginia City, Montana, became lined with corrals and barns soon after the town's founding. Pollution from horses, cows, and pigs stabled there obviously made the water unfit for human consumption. In the early 1860s, Virginia City residents had to purchase barrels of water taken out of the same creek further upstream and then hauled into the town on wagons. One early wit from Virginia City, Nevada, claimed that the town's poisonous water could be purified by diluting a spoonful of water with half-a-glass of whiskey.

As most local water sources in rapidly growing towns were contaminated and dangerous to drink, typically only water from fast-running springs, deep wells, and collected from rainfall was safe. But even then local springs were often laden with mosquitoes that transmitted malaria. Besides, in the minds of many imbibers, water was thought by self-proclaimed experts to dilute physical vigor and make the stomach cold. Alcohol, on the other hand, was known by the same experts to warm the stomach and thought to strengthen the body. Even milk was not always safe to drink as it might carry the germs of tuberculosis and undulant fever (brucellosis). Milk was also expensive, available only seasonally, and spoiled quickly without refrigeration. Whiskey, on the other hand, was cheap, didn't spoil, and the high alcohol content killed any germs contained in it. Drinking coffee or hot tea was relatively safe because the water was boiled during preparation and thus killed any bacteria that might be in it.

All these factors created the traditional view of the Old West that the American frontier was soaked in alcohol. And to some extent it was. Fur trappers who generally lived by themselves far from human society and the comforts of civilization were famed for their "rendezvous," or annual debauch of drinking and merriment. Whiskey was very profitable as a trade item at these events. In the early 1830s, a gallon of whiskey cost 25¢ in St. Louis. By the time it reached Fort Leavenworth in Kansas on the Santa Fe Trail, this same gallon sold for $34.[5] Diluted with water and sold by the drink at the rendezvous in Wyoming, the original gallon could bring in as much as $64.[6]

Cowboys who spent three months or more on the trail without liquor, driving cattle to market, made for the first saloon when they arrived in town at the end of the drive. The editor of the *Dodge City Times* estimated that the consumption of whiskey in the town in 1878, during the height of the cattle drives, was about 300 barrels. Soldiers who enlisted to fight Indians but spent their days at lonely frontier posts bored by endless rounds of drill and fatigue duty often drank heavily to relieve the monotony.

Stagecoaches in the Old West ran on copious amounts of alcohol. The drivers often drank and then drove like maniacs over precipitous mountain roads and through Indian Territory; in their turn, the passengers drank to calm themselves during the resulting wild ride. Drinking whiskey under these conditions in winter was not always the wisest idea, as the use of alcohol increased the risk of frostbite and death from exposure when traveling in unheated and drafty stagecoaches.

Stage stations, where horses were changed and passengers tried to grab a meal before the coach sped off again, might offer only whiskey to drink (besides the ubiquitous coffee) with the food. Passengers were usually advised to supply their own whiskey, as that sold at the stage stops was not of very good quality. Those who did bring a bottle were expected to be friendly and pass it around to the other passengers.

Miners drank to relieve the aches and pains from long hours spent panning for gold in creek beds and digging in underground tunnels. Despite the high cost of transportation and the remoteness of many of the gold mines in the high mountains of California in the 1850s, alcohol formed a major part of the cargo of the mule trains that brought in supplies. One can judge the importance of drink to the California Forty-Niners by considering that the gold rush spawned mining camps called Whiskey Diggings, Drunkard's Bar, Whiskey Hill, Brandy Bar, and even one named Delirium Tremens. In mocking deference to teetotalers one was called Temperance Flat. The lower portion of the mining town of Creede, Colorado, was named "Jim Town," but residents who knew about the large amount of spirits consumed there in the saloons nicknamed it "Gin Town" instead.

Empty whiskey bottles were often used as windows in the miners' primitive cabins and converted into candle-holders for lighting. Similarly, the early settlers on the Great Plains who built sod houses stacked their empty bottles horizontally and plastered them in place with mud to form primitive "windows." The left-over packaging, such as whiskey barrels and the crates whiskey and wine bottles were shipped in, was converted by thrifty California miners into useful items such as shelving and other furniture. Louise Clappe, the wife of doctor Fayette Clappe, lived at a mining camp called Rich Bar, on the Feather River in California, in 1851 and 1852. She described her toilet table in her cabin as being "a trunk elevated on two claret cases."[7]

An unusual use for alcohol in Dawson in the Yukon Territory of Canada during the great gold rush of the late 1890s was as a type of thermometer. If a conventional thermometer was not available, a bottle of Dr. Perry Davis' Celebrated Painkiller was placed in the window of a cabin. If this high-alcohol-content patent medicine froze, then the men knew that the temperature was at least -72°F. Even the hardy Canadian sleigh and stagecoach drivers considered this to be too cold outside for travel.[8]

Before local distilleries and vineyards reached the West, whiskey and wine had to be shipped for long distances by wagon. Whiskey came from the East or distilleries around Taos, New Mexico, and wine was shipped from Mexico, California, or as far away as France. To protect the precious cargo, bottles were packed in wooden crates and cushioned by wood shavings. After the bottles were emptied, they were reused and the empty crates were used as primitive furniture (author's collection).

These slices of life in the West were perpetuated by images such as that portrayed in one of the earliest motion pictures, *Cripple Creek Barroom* (1898), which supposedly took place in a saloon in the contemporary wild and woolly mining town of Cripple Creek, Colorado.[9] The brief plot revolves around a drunk who lurches into a saloon, gets into a fight, and is thrown out by the bartender. Part of the decoration of this static one-scene vignette is a large ceramic jug labeled "Red Eye" placed prominently in the foreground of the movie set.

Subsequent Western movies have perpetuated a similar image, with endless drinking sprees, fights, and shoot-outs in saloons located all over the West. In reality, this image was not inaccurate, as drinking to the point of not knowing what was going on was a factor in many of the gunfights that took place in the Old West.

Treaties Soaked with Alcohol

It has been said with some irony that every treaty with Native Americans was soaked in alcohol. Indeed, trading drinks to the Indians for buffalo hides and beaver pelts was a common practice. The principal supply of liquor to the Indians came along the emigrant trails with whiskey merchants. Some Navajo Indians called the kegs that whiskey came in "hollow woods."

As early as 1835, liquor was dispensed to the Oglala Sioux by traders at Fort William in Wyoming (the predecessor to Fort Laramie). Missionary Marcus Whitman, who observed this, noted that the Indians immediately got drunk.[10] The following comment described what happened when a keg of whiskey arrived in an Arapaho village: "The men began to hurrah and fight with each other, the women to reel about, and belabor their half tipsy husbands with tongue and fist, and be in turn, well pummelled themselves."[11] Some Indians were so passionate about liquor that there were reports of braves taking a drink of whiskey, holding it in the mouth for a few moments of enjoyment, then emptying it into a friend's mouth so that he could enjoy it also. In this way a mouthful was passed from man to man until it was all gone.[12]

Early trade with the Indians was characterized by friendly and peaceful negotiations. After the arrival of liquor, though, the goals and feel of the meetings changed. Part of the trading involved the exchange of gifts between traders and the Indians as a token of friendship and trust. Eventually the Indians came to expect these "gifts" as a prelude to trading. To nobody's surprise, whiskey featured prominently as a "gift." Traders had to guard their liquor supplies to prevent pilfering and in case the drinking and carousing got out of hand.

Some unscrupulous traders would start the drinking long before serious trading began, hoping to get the Indians in such a fog that they were not able to make any shrewd bargains. The warriors tended to barter away all their possessions for alcohol and it was their squaws who had to hold back some of their trade goods before they were all squandered for drink. The Osage Indians of Kansas were known to trade a good horse for as little as a bottle or two of whiskey.[13] One Indian squaw even offered to trade her four-year-old boy for some bottles of whiskey.[14] In 1841, at Fort Platte, a Brulé chief named Bull Tail offered his grown daughter Chintzille as trade for a keg of whiskey.[15] Even the trader balked at this offer, but this type of proposal was not uncommon.

Lieutenant Gaines Kingsbury commented that the Cheyenne "will sell their horses, blankets, and everything else they possess for a drink of it. In arranging the good things of this world in the order of rank, they say that whiskey should stand first, then tobacco, third, guns, fourth, horses, and fifth, women."[16]

With the genetic lack of tolerance for alcohol that occurred in some Indians, it did not take much whiskey for many of them to become drunk. Fighting, vomiting, and feelings of lust soon followed. Quite inappropriate behavior often accompanied the lowering of inhibitions among both men and women. Sergeant Hugh Evans witnessed one such revel and said, "All (or nearly all) men women and children were drunk ... filling their Bowls and horn spoons and hand it around with as much liberality as a candidate for office. Some reeling, stagering [sic] and hollowing [sic], falling down and raising up, frothing and naked, and such gestures and grimaces looked as if they came from the fields of the lower regions."[17] Some revels spiraled so out of control during trading that the traders felt threatened and feared for their lives.

It was a simple matter to get the Indians drunk and take advantage of them. A typical trade for a buffalo robe was three cupfuls of "whiskey." The trader would dilute the alcohol as much as he thought he could get away with. The drink that was finally delivered to the Indian doing the trading was so watered down that it was often equivalent to only about one-fourth of a cup of real whiskey. Some fur companies made even more profit by trading cheap or bootleg liquor instead of good whiskey for pelts. The more intoxicated the Indian became, the more the trader was able to dilute the alcohol and find similar methods of cheating. Other ways of shortchanging the Indians were for the trader to put his fingers into the cup when pouring the drink, or to use cups with thicker than normal bottoms in order to reduce the amount of alcohol in them.[18] Admittedly, these companies usually did not discriminate, but also treated the white trappers in the same manner.

Responsible traders did not participate in these practices and were critical of them. William Bent, for example, one of the early traders in Colorado who himself was married to an Indian bride named Owl Woman, was concerned that alcohol would undermine Indian society. To some extent, however, he had to participate in the whiskey trade or risk losing all his business to unscrupulous traders. Another of the honest traders' concerns was that if the Indians became sodden with alcohol they would not be in any suitable condition to hunt and the entire fur trade would eventually dwindle to nothing. But unscrupulous traders, who were often unlicensed, continued to make liberal use of whiskey. Often this whiskey was smuggled to avoid government inspection stations.

On their side, the Indians felt that if the American traders couldn't or wouldn't provide whiskey, they would take their trade to someone who did. When alcohol was barred in the fur trade in 1832, the American Fur Company complained that they were unable to compete successfully with their Canadian counterpart, the Hudson's Bay Company, because the latter was not bound by American law and was still able to use alcohol as a trade item if they needed to. This ploy, however, sometimes backfired. In 1830, a group of Indians who trapped for the Hudson's Bay Company was persuaded to give up their year's catch of furs to mountain man Thomas Fitzpatrick after he produced a barrel of whiskey for them in trade.[19] In the early 1840s, the Union Fur Company used alcohol to compete directly with the American Fur Company to try to draw in the Indian trade. One way that the reputable traders tried to ensure some degree of fairness for both sides was to withhold delivery of the bartered alcohol until after the trading was completed.

Laws passed in 1802, 1822, 1832, and 1847 prohibited trading or selling whiskey and other spirits in Indian country. Curiously, though, boatmen who plied the rivers into Indian Territory were excepted from the regulations. Accordingly, some traders applied for whiskey permits, even though they did not employ any boatmen at all, then sold or traded the whiskey to the Indians.[20]

A similar exception allowed drinking among the military. Technically, military installations in the West were not on Indian land, so they were exempt from liquor regulations. Indian agents often sold alcohol to Indians; and even military posts, such as Fort Riley in Kansas, regularly (but illegally) sold liquor to Indians.[21] Another loophole was that a group of Indians could travel off their reservation to a nearby town, purchase a barrel of whiskey legally (if a white businessman would sell it to them), and consume it before traveling back to the reservation.

Kegs of whiskey were routinely brought westward among other goods carried by wagons along the Santa Fe Trail. Liquor sales to the Indians went on as usual and the few prosecutions that reached the courts typically failed. Defendants were usually impossible to find and witnesses tended to be "unreachable" somewhere back in the hills.

Whiskey, either the genuine product or the homemade variety, was commonly bartered to the Indians for furs, such as this round beaver pelt and buffalo hide shown on the counter, at trading posts at Fort Laramie, Bent's Fort, or El Pueblo. Note the barrel at the right labeled "S. Turley," which refers to Simeon Turley, an early distiller of fiery whiskey in Arroyo Hondo, New Mexico (author's collection).

From the Distant Past

The Bible contains many references to wine and there is evidence of beer and wine being drunk in the Middle East thousands of years ago, but the origin of fermented beverages is lost in antiquity. Archeological evidence, however, shows that wine and beer were consumed in the Stone Age, with some beer containers dated at 10,000 years old.[22]

The word "alcohol" is derived from the Arabic *al kohl*. *Al* is the equivalent of "the." *Kohl* was originally the name for powdered antimony sulfide that was used as eye makeup for women. The term referred to the creation of the antimony from the mineral stibnite, and thus the reduction of this naturally occurring material to its "essence," or "spirit." The name continued into ancient English to describe a powdered substance. The change of meaning to apply to distilled spirits occurred with later European usage as distillation produced alcohol, or the essential essence, of a fermented drink.

Pottery jars used for alcoholic drinks in northern China have been dated from around 9,000 to 8,000 B.C. Wine production and trade were an important part of commerce in the Mediterranean around 3,000 to 2,000 B.C. The Greek god of wine, Dionysus, was honored annually with a four-day orgy of drunkenness and subsequent sobering up.

Some Romans tended to overdo their drinking. On more than one occasion, Marc Antony, Cleopatra's lover, drank so much at night that when he gave a public speech the next day he threw up on his sandals. Reportedly, a helpful friend delicately held his robe up out of the way to avoid contamination.[23] Apparently some things never change. Contemporary woodcuts of early American taverns usually include in the background the figure of some helpless drunk throwing up.

Strong Drink

When speaking of "drinking" and "alcohol" most people are referring to ethyl alcohol (ethanol), the type of alcohol commonly drunk as an intoxicating beverage.[24] Among the other simple alcohols, methyl alcohol, also known as methanol, is not safe to drink. Other names for methanol are "wood alcohol" and "wood spirits," because it used to be made by burning wood.[25] Methanol is widely used in the manufacture of plastics, paints, varnishes, and adhesives. It is also used as an industrial solvent, and as a component of antifreeze for automobile radiators. Methanol is very volatile and has been used as a fuel for rockets. Another of the simple alcohols is propyl alcohol, also known as propanol. Propanol is used as a solvent for plastics and is used in cosmetics, such as shampoo, hair spray, aftershave, and mouthwash. Isopropyl alcohol, or rubbing alcohol, which has a slightly different chemical structure, is used as a paint thinner and in antifreeze. In 70 percent concentration, it is used as an antiseptic and as a soothing liniment for rubbing and massaging. Ethanediol, or ethylene glycol, is used as an antifreeze in car radiators, as a deicing fluid, and in manufacturing plastics. None of these alcohols are suitable for drinking and consuming them leads to serious toxic side-effects, such as blindness, kidney damage, and death. Any further generic references to "alcohol" here, then, should be understood to mean ethyl alcohol, or the alcohol which mankind commonly drinks for pleasure.

Ethyl alcohol, or beverage alcohol, is obtained from the fermentation of plant material that contains sugar, such as molasses, or from any similar substance that can be chemically broken down into sugar, such as the starch in various grains. The number of plants that can be, and have been, used to produce drinking alcohol is very large. Practically all grains, fruits, berries, and vegetables can be fermented and at one time or another almost all have been used.

During fermentation, yeast is added to start the process and chemically break down molecules of sugar into two molecules of ethyl alcohol and two of the gas carbon dioxide. Yeast commonly used for fermentation is *Saccharomyces cerevisiae*, which is a type of microscopic fungus that feeds on sugar with alcohol as a by-product. This is the same yeast that is commonly used for baking bread. Though yeast is nearly always added to the sugar solution to induce fermentation, it is not essential to the process. As Antonio Escohotado pointed out in *A Brief History of Drugs*, "To manufacture a coarse beer, all one has to do is chew some fruit and then spit it into a container; spontaneous fermentation of saliva and the plant will produce a low-grade alcohol."[26] Louis Pasteur in France in 1862 was the first to understand fermentation when he discovered that yeast was responsible for the conversion of sugar to alcohol. Before his discovery, nobody knew how the process worked and many thought that it was due to divine intervention.

What most people refer to as "alcohol" is not the chemist's version of pure ethanol, but is a mixture of ethyl alcohol with added substances that create the flavor and color of the particular beverage. At room temperature, pure ethanol is a colorless, clear liquid with a rather unpleasant taste. Dilution with water makes pure alcohol taste better. What really provides the flavor in alcoholic drinks is the addition of other substances during later processing. The characteristic flavor of gin, for example, comes from the berries of the juniper tree. Whiskey is made from several cereal grains, including wheat, rye, oats, and barley. Adding peat and "aging" the ethanol in barrels that were previously used to store sherry produces the flavor and color of Scotch whiskey. Kentucky bourbon is alcohol made from corn mash that is distilled and aged in oak barrels to create its characteristic flavor. Beer is made from various grains and is flavored by hops. Rum, which was popular on the early Western frontier, is derived from molasses. Vodka, on the other hand, is almost pure alcohol, so the best vodkas are essentially colorless, odorless, and almost tasteless.

Alcoholic Beverages

Alcoholic beverage drinks can be considered in three very general categories: beer, wine, and liquor (distilled spirits). All of them were very popular in the Old West. The strength of the alcohol produced in the particular type of drink depended on the strain of yeast used, the type of material used to provide the sugar for fermentation, and the temperature of the process.

BEER

Beer was brewed through the action of brewer's yeast (*Saccharomyces cerevisiae*) on malted barley or other cereal grains, with hops (ripe dried cones from the hop plant) added for flavor. The barley was soaked in hot water to allow the grain to germinate and sprout. The resulting product, called malt, was dried and ground up. Brewer's yeast was added and the mixture allowed to ferment. Malt contained diastase, which was an enzyme that helped to break down the carbohydrates in the grain and convert them to sugar that could be fermented. The carbon dioxide gas generated during the fermentation process produced the carbonation.

Barley was commonly used for brewing beer, but beer could also be made from rye, wheat, or rice. Most beers brewed in the Old West contained 3 to 6 percent alcohol, but some beers contained up to 10 percent alcohol by volume.[27] Brewer's yeast could tolerate only a 5 to 6 percent strength of alcohol, thus the natural ceiling on the alcohol in beer that used this strain of yeast was around 6 percent.

In the late 1860s, many Germans immigrated to the United States and brought with them their taste for lager beer. *Lager bier* in German literally means "stored beer," because in the German method the beer was aged by being stored in a warehouse for several months after it was brewed. By the late 1880s, rapid expansion had taken place in the brewing industry and, by 1890, beer was the largest-selling alcoholic beverage in the country. Working in a brewery was a popular job because employees in many breweries were allowed to drink as much beer as they could manage.

The Germans were quite serious about their beer-drinking. At the celebration ball of the German May Feast that was held in Weaverville, California, in May of 1859, sixty ten-gallon kegs of lager were consumed. In describing the event, one of the participants innocently added, "but it isn't intoxicating, you know."[28] Some drinkers seemed to believe this misconception. A serious question posed by a reporter for the *Idaho World* newspaper in 1866 was, "Does Lager Beer Intoxicate?"

Meanwhile, back in Weaverville at the May Feast of 1860, after the participants had drunk the last keg of lager, they placed it on a bier covered with black cloth. While a band played a suitable funeral dirge, six men — followed by 500 or so somber "mourners" — carried the empty keg out to one of the mines, where they ceremonially buried it with the appropriate farewells.[29]

WINE

Though wine could be fermented through the action of a strain of yeast that occurred naturally as a fungus on the surface of ripe grapes, brewer's yeast was usually added to produce reliable and uniform fermentation. The flavor of the wine came from the type of grape used. Other sources of material used to produce wine were as diverse as apples, cherries, plums, pears, and dandelions. The strength of the alcohol in wine varied, but was generally about 12 percent.

As part of the preparation process, the grapes had to be crushed. For white wine, the pulp and skins were removed before fermentation. Yeast then converted the sugar to alcohol. To produce red wine, the skin, pulp, and juice were all fermented together.

The strain of yeast used for making wine was often the same as that for making beer, though other strains could be used. The yeast *Saccharomyces cerevisiae* has been widely used for fermentation of wine for thousands of years. When the concen-

Wine was a popular drink in the Old West. This example was a domestic variety that was shipped from the East to a remote mining camp in Idaho. Some wine was even shipped from as far away as Bordeaux, France. In the 1630s, wine was shipped to Santa Fe from vineyards south of El Paso before Franciscan missionaries planted grapes in New Mexico and California for sacramental use (author's collection).

tration of alcohol in wine rose to between 10 and 15 percent (typically about 12 percent with an upper limit of 18 percent), the yeast was inhibited by the alcohol it had produced and died, thus halting further production of alcohol. Ironically then, the yeast's own success in producing alcohol killed it off and placed a natural ceiling on the strength of the alcohol in wine.

DISTILLATION AND STRONG SPIRITS

Serious drinkers soon found that by concentrating the alcohol in their beverages through a process called distillation they could get a faster and stronger feeling of intoxication. Alcoholic beverages produced by fermentation and then distillation were called "spirits." Whiskey, for example, was distilled from a fermented mixture of grain (mash) to produce a high alcohol content. As another example, the high alcoholic content of brandy was produced by distilling wine.

Distillation to produce brandy or other spirits worked because the boiling point of alcohol occurred at a lower temperature than that of water.[30] In making brandy, for example, a closed container of wine was heated at a low enough temperature that the alcohol in it boiled but the water did not. The alcohol evaporated like steam. This vapor was condensed back into a liquid by cooling it and collecting the resulting spirits. In this way much of the water was removed from the original wine and the resulting liquid was concentrated to a level of 40 to 50 percent ethanol.

Like beer, the primary raw materials used as the basis for spirits are the cereal grains, such as corn, rye, and barley. It has been said that the ingenious and thrifty residents of Scotland could make whiskey with only corn, water, a fire, a kettle, and a wet towel to condense the evaporated alcohol back to a liquid.[31] The ethanol-soaked towel was wrung out to recover the alcohol. Because of its common origin in barley, whiskey was sometimes referred to in the Old West as "barley water" or "John Barley Corn." Albrecht's Saloon in Manitou Springs, Colorado, for example, advertised on the outside of their building "Barley Water & Bad Cigars." Some of the early spirits were so raw that Colonial Americans called alcohol produced by distillation "ardent spirits," with the adjective "ardent" meaning "burning" or "on fire."

The "proof" of spirits is twice the alcohol content, thus 80 proof is 40 percent alcohol by volume. Most spirits today, such as whiskey, gin, and vodka, are 80 proof. In the United States, for simplicity 100 proof is 50 percent alcohol content. In England, 100 proof is 57.1 percent alcohol, because that is the percentage at which alcohol burns steadily.

The term "proof" originated in the eighteenth century when British sailors were paid partially with 100 proof (57.1 percent alcohol) rum. To ensure that the rum was not diluted with water, it was "proofed" by pouring it on gunpowder and setting the mixture on fire. If the gunpowder did not flare up and produce a steady blue flame, it was presumed that there was too much water in the rum and it was considered "under proof."

The origin of distilled spirits is lost somewhere in ancient history. Distillation of alcohol was known to have been used in China, Japan, and India as long ago as several thousand years. The Greek philosopher Aristotle described wine distillation in his writings. Distilling was also known to the ancient Egyptians and to Arabian scientists though, ironically, Arabs were prohibited from drinking fermented beverages and distilled alcohol for religious reasons. The process was refined in Europe and was commonly used in the eleventh century, then became widespread by the 1400s and 1500s. Spirits were initially distilled for medicinal use before drinking them expanded to recreational use.

After distillation and concentration, the resulting alcohol was flavored with various herbs and spices, including sage, lavender, angelica, ginger, cinnamon, and nutmeg, to disguise the taste of the raw alcohol. Distillers in Holland made gin, which was flavored with the berries of the juniper. The original name for gin was *geneva*, from the French word *genièvre* for the juniper berry or juniper tree. Gin was drunk extensively by fighting men of the time, hence the expression "Dutch courage" for one who obtains his bravado from drink. Scotch whiskey was distilled from barley malt. Bourbon was made from corn, rum from sugarcane or the left-over material from making molasses, brandy from distilled wine, tequila from the agave cactus, and vodka from potatoes.

Early alcoholic drinks appeared in the Old West mostly in the form of distilled spirits such as whiskey and rum, as the distances to economically transport other forms of alcohol were too great. Distilled spirits could be easily transported because they were concentrated and could be freighted relatively cheaply by wagon. Beer barrels and kegs were bulky, heavy, and expensive to ship over long distances until the arrival of the railroad, so beer tended to be brewed at local family breweries. Beer was later shipped all over the West in railroad cars. Wine generally had to be brought in from Mexico, California, or France because the grapes required specific growing conditions to provide a quality product.

Before the arrival of the railroad, most liquor came to the West by wagon. In the northernmost states of the West, shipments started in April and ended around mid–November when the heavy snows started to fly. As winter approached, merchants who were located north of Colorado increased their orders to ensure that customers would not run out over the winter, which was considered to be a dire situation. On the last day of November 1864, for example, a wagon train carrying 1,600 barrels of whiskey arrived in Denver to replenish supplies for the winter.[32] The dilemma of Denver running out of whiskey and possibly spending a long, hard winter without liquor was satirized in the Western motion picture *Hallelujah Trail* (1965).

The Effects of Drinking Alcohol

Once alcohol enters the body via the mouth and is swallowed down the throat into the stomach it is absorbed by the lining of the stomach into the bloodstream, and thence journeys to the brain. Drinking a modest amount of alcohol, whether it is beer, wine, or whiskey, produces a feeling of euphoria in the drinker. Physiological changes include a rise in pulse rate and blood pressure. An accompanying problematic disadvantage is the intake of additional fluid and the effect of alcohol on the kidneys of an increase in the output of urine.

On a more positive note, alcohol is thought to cause a chemical substance called dopamine to be released into the brain, which increases the drinker's brain activity and induces pleasurable feelings.[33] As a result, in this early stage of intoxication many drinkers become happy, enthusiastic, relaxed, and talkative. Joking and laughing is common. Nineteenth-century physician Benjamin Rush described the symptoms of drunkenness as "singing, hallooing, roaring, imitating the noises of brute animals, jumping, tearing off clothes, dancing naked, breaking glasses and china, and dashing other articles of household furniture upon the ground or floor."[34]

Overindulgence in whiskey made drunkenness, fighting, and general mayhem seem like the normal behavior in many saloons and low-class brothels of the Old West. In the booming mining town of Deadwood, South Dakota, the *Black Hills Daily Times* of September 5, 1877, complained about the number of women in the local dance halls who appeared with black eyes and bruises.[35]

Having a few drinks might be referred to by the cowboys as "bending an elbow" or "painting your tonsils." The cowboy expression for becoming blind drunk was getting "roostered" or "alkalied." One of the related expressions was that a man who had imbibed too freely "couldn't hit the ground with his hat in three throws." The delightfully vivid cowboy expression for vomiting after drinking was "airing the paunch." Louise Clappe described a drinking orgy she saw at Rich Bar in California during the Christmas season of 1851: "They were dancing when I went to sleep, and they were dancing when I woke up the next morning. The revel was kept up in this mad way for three days, growing wilder every hour. Some never slept at all during that time. On the fourth day they got past dancing, and, lying in drunken heaps about the barroom, commenced a most unearthly howling."[36]

Drinkers also usually experienced increased feelings of power and amorous intent. Whiskey was considered by patrons of saloons and other drinking establishments of the Old West to be a stimulant because of the sensations it produced. In reality, alcohol does not stimulate this excess of outgoing feelings, but depresses the part of the brain that controls them, thus decreasing inhibitions and shyness, allowing the more primitive instincts to manifest themselves freely. The alcohol reduces what would be considered awkwardness and restraint.

Alcohol in sufficient amounts suppresses moral inhibitions and control, and allows lusty feelings to come to the surface. What the men of the Old West did not realize was that excessive use of alcohol diminished the body's level of testosterone and sexual function. Instead of improving their performance, they suffered from what is euphemistically called "brewer's droop." In women, three or more drinks a day caused reproductive problems and could suppress ovulation.[37] For prostitutes who drank frequently and continuously with their customers, this could be an unexpected benefit.

Whiskey was also considered to be a stimulant because it produced a warm glow in the throat and stomach, and produced a feeling of heat in the skin as it dilated the blood vessels. This led to the erroneous idea that alcohol should be given to individuals who had been out in the cold in order to warm them. In reality, this level of drinking caused the muscles at the surface of the skin to relax and allowed the blood vessels in the skin to dilate further. Thus the individual lost even more heat as the flow of blood underneath increased, making the drinker appear flushed and red. This dilation of the capillaries in the skin also caused the drinker to lose more body heat, thus making him susceptible to dangerously low core body temperatures if he was exposed to the cold of winter. This could be a serious problem in the mining towns in the mountains or in the cold northern states of the West, such as Montana or Wyoming. If a man passed out behind a saloon after a serious bout of drinking, he could easily freeze to death. Women were not immune; in 1877, prostitute Cad Truckee passed out in a snowbank after drinking in Gold Hill, Nevada, and had to have both feet amputated as a result of frostbite. Another woman, whose working name was Irish Mary, died as a result of a combination of drink and exposure to the cold.

As the drinker tried to increase her initial sensations of pleasant euphoria by continuing to consume alcohol, the result was that emotions soon went in the other direction and produced feelings of depression and maudlin sentiments. Mood swings became evident. Other, more significant, effects that occurred as drinking progressed were an impairment of reaction time, slurred speech, a disruption of coordination, a staggering gait, and a lack of the ability to maintain proper balance. Some heavy drinkers could not even stand or walk by themselves. Too much whiskey also impaired reasoning, self-control, and good judgment. Anger and aggression rose to the surface, which led to many of the saloon gunfights of the Old West.

Continuing to drink in this condition resulted in nausea, vomiting, and blackout. In these large quantities, whiskey and other drink caused slowed brain activity, drowsiness, and impaired motor functions. If sufficient alcohol was ingested, the result was depression of the respiratory system to the point of coma, followed by death from a failure to breathe and paralysis of the heart.

Bogus Booze

Whiskey in the Old West was not always the legitimate product. Though saloon liquor was sold as bourbon whiskey, its true origin might have been in the backroom of the saloon. The liquor might be homemade because of a shortage of real whiskey or, in many cases, due to the desire of an unethical saloon owner to increase his profits. Sometimes genuine distillery whiskey was simply watered down to make it go further and then colored with a little tea or tobacco juice to bring it back to a semblance of its original color. This practice extended the number of servings and could yield drinks at the bar of three or four times the original quantity of alcohol, hence raising the profits for the saloon owner.

Bogus whiskey was made by starting with raw ethyl alcohol, then adding various adulterants to flavor and color it until the result could fool inexperienced drinkers. Some of the additives used to give raw alcohol the general appearance and taste of whiskey were chewing tobacco, tea, coffee, red pepper, prune juice, gunpowder, and tree bark. In addition, burnt sugar, molasses, sagebrush, black bone meal, or dried peaches might be added to give color and flavor. The ingredients for some of these homemade whiskeys were bizarre. Even less-conventional chemical ingredients, such as tartaric acid, sulfuric acid, ammonia, strychnine, turpentine, or creosote, might find their way into the brew to give it a little bite. Though these additives may sound humorous, the side effects of drinking them could cause serious harm to the unwary recipient, and drinkers occasionally even died as a result of ingesting them.[38] The practice of adding noxious chemicals became so common and so bad that on June 6, 1857, *Frank Leslie's Illustrated Newspaper* (one of the leading national newsmagazines of the time) reported that the Ohio legislature had banned the use of strychnine in manufacturing liquor.

As a result of these peculiar mixtures, counterfeit booze packed a powerful jolt, leading to a variety of colorful names that were attached to them (see Illustration 1–1). Among the pet names for whiskey on the frontier was "forty-rod." This peculiar name came from the belief that the drinker could expect to travel about forty rods (220 yards, or an eighth of a mile) before the booze took hold and he collapsed.

ILLUSTRATION 1–1

You Drank *What?*

Of the many names applied to liquor in the West, these are a few of the more colorful ones.

busthead	pop skull
bug juice	sheep dip
coffin varnish	skull bender
corpse reviver	snake poison
dust cutter	stagger soup
gas remover	sudden death
gut warmer	tangle-leg
jig juice	tarantula juice
leopard sweat	tongue oil
nose paint	tonsil varnish
phlegm-cutter	widow-maker

Other "drinks" might be counterfeited in a similar manner. One recipe described how to produce fine "Irish whiskey" by adding a half-pint of creosote to a barrel of raw alcohol. Bogus "wine" might consist of watered-down alcohol with the appropriate coloring and flavoring, such as cherries or prunes. "Brandy" could be made from a half-barrel of alcohol, with grape juice, burnt sugar, sulfuric acid, and tobacco added to provide color and flavoring. Some "brandies" were produced by simply adding grape juice to a raw alcohol base. In Leadville and Denver, in Colorado, in 1879, some drinkers became quite inebriated on a low-alcohol mixture of brown sugar, water, and yeast that was sold as "champagne cider" for five dollars a quart.[39] One of the more peculiar additives to "whiskey" was rattlesnake heads. Some peddlers of bogus booze and patent medicines were known to add a half-dozen or so to a barrel of counterfeit whiskey in order to "add power to the liquor." The resulting brew was sometimes known as "snakehead whiskey."

Because drinkers could not be certain what was in the fancy bottles at the bar, customers applied a series of tests to determine if the brew was true. Liquor "experts" knowingly ordered "sink-taller whiskey," because they believed that a piece of tallow (beef or mutton fat) would float in whiskey that had been diluted or had a low alcohol content but would sink in liquor with a high alcohol content. Others felt that they were able to determine the strength of the liquor by studying the bead, which was the bubbles that formed at the surface when the liquor was shaken. When whiskey of good quality was shaken, it produced a bead at the top. The longer the bead was present, the higher the proof. Real experts knew that half of a true bead would stay in the liquor and half would float on top. If all the bead floated on top it was probably due to soap, which was often added to counterfeit whiskey to produce the appearance of a good bead.[40]

Another test for quality was to throw a little of the liquor onto a fire to see how high the flames flared, similar to the British seaman's test for proof. This test was the origin of the Indian name of "firewater" for whiskey with a high alcohol content. This was indeed a reasonable test, but had to be performed with care. On June 22, 1881, a bartender inspecting the inside of a barrel of whiskey at the Arcade Saloon on Allen Street in Tombstone, Arizona, inadvertently brought a lighted cigar too close to the fumes. The whiskey must have been good stuff because it ignited. The resulting fire destroyed four city blocks of the downtown area and leveled sixty-six businesses.[41]

Unfortunately a frequent recipient of many of these strange "whiskeys" was the Native American. Whiskey was one of the prime bartering tools in the fur trade, despite a prohibition by Congress and the presence of the U.S. Cavalry, who were supposed to prevent the sale or trade of whiskey to the Indians. Because liquor was legally banned on Indian reservations, the demand was often met by illegal producers who smuggled their so-called whiskey to an eager and lucrative market. Unscrupulous traders knew that they could bargain a cheap bottle of homemade liquor for a prime buffalo robe.

The Indians had their own ideas about whiskey and as long as the "whiskey" they traded for met these expectations, the drink was considered to be good. One preconceived notion was that they felt liquor had to be strong enough to make them throw up, and they figured that it wasn't any good unless it did. Unscrupulous white traders soon realized that various additives could make the Indians just as sick without wasting good alcohol. To achieve this when they made their "whiskey," they added a bar of soap — which also produced a good bead at the surface — or some tobacco, both of which induced vomiting in the drinker. Traders developed various recipes of their own for Indian "whiskey." One consisted of a gallon of raw alcohol, three gallons of water, and a pound of tea or black tobacco to give the mixture the correct color. Ginger and a handful of red peppers went into the mix to give it a kick. One variation was to add a quart of blackstrap molasses to the mixture and call the resulting mixture "rum." As well as trading with the Indians, the same traders foisted this "rum" off on the mountain men at their annual rendezvous.

If no legitimate alcohol was available, the early fur trappers in the Rocky Mountains sometimes prepared a curious drink called "bitters" that was concocted from water mixed with ox-gall.[42] This was described as being an "exhilarating drink," but unless the drinker stuck with it, the drink was reputed to cause vomiting. In the words of Rufus Sage, "To a stomach unaccustomed to its use it may at first create a slightly noisome sensation, like the inceptive effects of an emetic; and, to one strongly bilious, it might cause vomiting;—

but on the second or third trial, the stomach attains a taste for it and receives it with no inconsiderable relish."[43] It is surprising that the results were not more spectacular, as purified ox-gall was recognized and sold as a legitimate medicine. Its use was as a cathartic (a really strong laxative!).

A rather peculiar drink brewed up by the old mountain men was made by soaking a section of the bark from an aspen tree in sarsaparilla.[44] The bark was removed after a suitable period and the resulting liquid was mixed with an equal measure of whiskey and then drunk. This odd beverage was described by its drinkers as being "an invigorating tonic." Another recipe for "Indian whiskey" started with a barrel of water. Added to this were two gallons of raw alcohol, two ounces of strychnine to give the drinker a jolt, half a pound of red pepper to give the mixture some spice, five bars of soap to produce a good bead, and three plugs of tobacco to make the Indians sick. Shepherds in Idaho brewed a homemade liquor called "sheepherder's delight." It consisted of raw alcohol, a plug of tobacco, some prune juice for color and taste, and a dash of strychnine to give it a kick.

Bootleggers and Moonshine

As well as making counterfeit liquor by adding various substances to raw alcohol, making the raw ethanol itself was popular in the West. The manufacture of homemade brews in America came from a long tradition of the illegal distilling of spirits in Europe.[45] During colonial times distilling whiskey for home use was not illegal and was carried out on thousands of farms. It was not until 1862 that making whiskey without a federal license (which was really a tax to help pay for the Civil War) became a federal offense. Distilling whiskey illegally continued to be popular as, in that way, bootleggers could avoid paying liquor taxes. Consequently, this dubious material of doubtful heritage was lower in cost than the legitimate product, which made it popular for purchase by unscrupulous saloon owners who wanted to make additional profit on drinks.

The making of illicit alcohol was called "bootlegging" because the illegal product was carried in bottles hidden in the tops of the boots of whiskey smugglers. The alcohol was also called "moonshine," because the illegal liquor was made in the dead of night, by the light of the moon, to avoid local law enforcement agents. The names "moonshiner" and "bootlegger" are often used interchangeably, but Dabney has pointed out that, strictly speaking, the moonshiner was the manufacturer of the illicit alcohol, whereas the bootlegger was the individual who transported and sold it.[46] During the Revolutionary War, bootleggers were called "blockade runners" because they shipped their illegal products through and around coastal blockades.

In the West, illegal stills became the source of running battles — sometimes literally — between moonshiners and law enforcement officials who sought to shut them down. Some stills were located under thick stands of pine trees deep in the forests of the West or buried in the ground to avoid detection by revenue agents who worked for the government. To counter these tactics, law enforcement officials sat on high ridges and watched for smoke curling up from the forest. This would be their tip that an illegal still was being heated.

Illegal liquor was produced mostly from corn. In making alcohol, the basic brew (mash) was a mixture of corn or barley, water, sugar, and yeast. The corn was ground into meal and soaked in hot water, then malt might be added to start fermentation. One formula called for a barrel of water filled with corn or barley, a gallon of barley malt, a pound of yeast, and sixty to eighty pounds of sugar. The mash usually fermented in three to four days if

Illegal stills for making moonshine liquor, such as this one in the mountains of Colorado, were sometimes buried underground to avoid detection by government agents. The stills were further concealed by being located under a thick cover of trees. Revenue agents defeated this tactic by sitting on high ridges and watching for columns of smoke rising from the forest, which often indicated that a moonshine still was being heated (author's collection).

the mixture was kept warm. If yeast was not added, the spores of wild yeast that occurred naturally in the air would start the fermentation process, but colder temperatures and the absence of sugar and yeast lengthened the process to two or more weeks. The mixture had to be stirred frequently during this stage, so moonshiners often slept out near the cooking pots. Even today dilapidated mattress springs may often be found near the remains of old stills. When fermented, the mixture became a type of beer called "corn beer" or "distiller's beer." The result was distilled in a homemade still. Forty gallons of mash would produce six or seven gallons of ninety-proof whiskey. When the bootleg corn alcohol was fresh from the still and unaged, it was clear and colorless like water, which gave it the name of "white lightning" or "white mule." Some moonshiners then diluted and aged this pure product in charred oak barrels that gave the resulting liquor the amber color and some of the taste of bourbon whiskey.

In one area in central Colorado where moonshining was popular, some of the "white lightning" was traded for food and other supplies during hard economic times. Much of this illegal booze, however, went to the saloons of nearby Cripple Creek, where it enhanced the profits of some of the saloon owners.

CHAPTER TWO

The Convoluted
History of Opium

Along with whiskey, the other major substance that was used to provide a temporary escape from the harsh realities of frontier life was opium. The origin of opium dens in the Old West and the eventual addiction to opium by many respectable women started with what the drug was and where it came from. The immediate origins in the Old West were as a medicine to relieve pain and then its later introduction for recreational smoking by Chinese workers who arrived as laborers in California. But the story started long before that.

Raw opium is dried sap that is collected from the unripe seed capsules of the poppy *Papaver somniferum*. The name "opium" comes either from the Greek word *opion*, which means "poppy juice," or from the Greek *opos*, which means "vegetable juice" and describes the hardened, dried juice of the poppy. This juice contains a collection of substances that are used as drugs. These chemicals are called alkaloids, which is the name for a group of complex organic compounds that are derived from plants. One characteristic of an alkaloid is that it turns litmus paper blue, which is a characteristic of an alkaline chemical substance and which gave rise to the name. More than fifty alkaloids have been identified in the dried juice of the poppy. When taken by mouth as medicines, these alkaloids typically have a characteristic bitter taste and their effect is toxic in relatively small amounts.

The most important alkaloid present in opium, and the one that produces the strongest effect, is the powerful narcotic morphine. In the Old West, the concentration of morphine in opium varied depending on where and how the plant was cultivated, but it was typically in the range of 3 percent to 20 percent.[1] Opium grown in China usually contained less than 7 percent morphine and that from India rarely reached 8 percent, whereas opium grown in the Mediterranean region often contained 16 percent.[2]

Four other alkaloids found in opium that have medical applications are codeine, noscapine, papaverine, and thebaine. These have medicinal uses,

32

but not enough narcotic properties to be relevant here. Other alkaloids present in opium are nicotine, narcotine, atropine, cocaine, and mescaline. Why the opium poppy created these substances is not known, though several theories have been proposed. The most reasonable one appears to be that the plant produced these noxious chemicals to discourage animals that might want to eat the poppy for food. Another theory — which seems less likely — is that prehistoric humans cultivated the poppy to try to grow plants with the most opium in them through a process of selective propagation.[3]

The Poppy of Joy

The opium poppy, *Papaver somniferum*, is part of a large botanical family that grows in the wild and in cultivated settings around the world. Most of these poppies grow in the temperate and subtropical regions of the northern hemisphere. Of all the varieties of poppy that have been cultivated by man, only *Papaver somniferum* and *Papaver bracteatum* produce opium in any significant amount. *Papaver bracteatum* is not used as a commercial source of opium, so the rest of this book will refer only to *Papaver somniferum.*

The opium poppy is a tall, thin, annual plant that grows to a height of between three and five feet tall, with a growth cycle of approximately 120 days. For proper growth, the plant requires rich, well-cultivated soil. The poppy can be cultivated with relative ease in a temperate climate that is warm and sunny with low humidity and moderate rainfall. As a result,

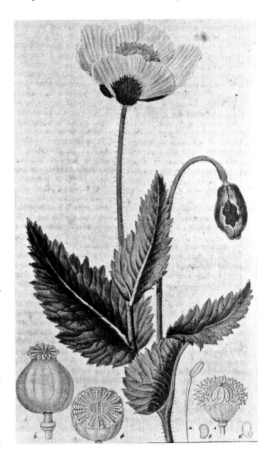

Opium was derived from the seed capsules of the opium plant (*Papaver somniferum*), which was three to five feet tall with white flowers. When the petals dropped off, the seed pod (shown at the bottom) was scored with a knife to allow the opium juice to ooze out. After collection, the dried opium was rolled into balls, flattened into cakes, or molded into blocks for storage and shipment (National Library of Medicine).

opium has been cultivated widely in China, India, and the Near East, though the plant also grows wild in many countries with a similar suitable climate. At least twelve hours of daylight per day are required for proper growth.

Somewhat surprisingly, opium has even been grown in the United States and has been extracted from white poppies cultivated in Vermont, New Hampshire, Connecticut, Florida, Louisiana, California, and Arizona.[4] In colonial times, opium was freely administered by physicians as a cure-all to relieve pain. Many colonists, therefore, cultivated opium poppies in their gardens and mixed the dried juice from the seed pod with whiskey to relieve coughs, aches, and pains. During the Civil War, opium poppies were cultivated for medicine in both Union and Confederate territories, including Virginia, Tennessee, South Carolina, and Georgia.

The flowers of the opium poppy are traditionally white, so the plant is sometimes referred to as the "white poppy," but the blooms can also occur as pink, crimson, blue, or purple. The flower lasts for only two to four days, then the petals drop off and the remaining seed pod grows to the size of a golf ball. This pod is known as the capsule, bulb, or poppy-head. After the petals are gone, the capsule can be tapped to extract the opium. The alkaloids are produced in the plant only during a period of ten to twelve days when the pod is ripening. Then alkaloid production stops. If the juice is not collected soon after this, the alkaloids start to disintegrate and eventually disappear.

In the 1800s, harvesting the drug was performed by hand in a labor-intensive procedure that essentially hadn't changed in hundreds of years. The grower tapped, or scored, the pod with a series of shallow vertical knife cuts. The opium resin seeped out of the pod as a runny, opaque, milky sap. When the sap came into contact with the air, it turned into a dark-brown viscous substance that was sticky and had a distinctive odor.

Cutting the pod was a delicate process that had to be performed correctly. If the cut in the pod was too deep, the sap flowed out quickly and dripped to the ground where it was lost. A deep cut also damaged the pod and the plant could not be tapped again. If the cut was too shallow, on the other hand, the juice could not ooze out sufficiently freely, the opium dried out, the flow stopped, and the cut sealed itself. If cutting the capsule was performed correctly, the pod could be tapped several times during the growing season — perhaps up to a half-dozen times.

Several hours after tapping the pod, the grower returned and scraped off the dried resinous gum with a knife. This yielded a dark-brown, sticky substance with the consistency of paste. To prevent the gum from sticking to the knife blade, the harvester usually wetted his knife by licking it. As a result of doing this, he constantly ingested a small amount of opium and eventually became addicted to his own crop. After the season's opium was collected, the rest of the plant was harvested. As well as the opium, which is contained in only the outer layer of the capsule, the pod contains a thousand or so seeds. Curiously, these seeds, which are also used to grow new plants, contain so little of the narcotic substances that they are edible with safety and are commonly used as a garnish for food or for decoration on the top of cakes and bread.[5] The seeds are often crushed to make poppy-seed oil, which is used for salad dressing and for cooking oil. This oil does not contain opium. Poppy-seed oil has also been used as lamp oil, in the manufacture of perfumes, and as a drying oil in paints for artists. The remaining leaves and stems of the plant are used for cattle feed.

Raw opium at this point in the collection process was a dark-brown, bitter tasting, gummy substance. After it was dried, it was rolled into balls, flattened into cakes, or molded into blocks for storage and shipment. It could be eaten as a granular powder, smoked, mixed into drinkable form as a tincture (opium dissolved in 10 to 20 percent alcohol) or syrup, or made into pills. Eating opium was technically called "opophagia."

The Dim Distant Past

Opium was probably the first medicinal drug to be discovered and the white poppy is certainly the oldest drug-containing plant to be cultivated. Poppy plantations in Mesopotamia, Egypt, northeast Africa, and Greece are among the oldest known. The origin of opium as a drug goes far back into antiquity. The date of its earliest use is not known, but it is thought to predate even the fermentation of grain into alcohol.[6] Certainly, opium has been recognized for its medicinal properties for thousands of years.

Around 3400 B.C. opium was cultivated in lower Mesopotamia between the Tigres and Euphrates rivers by the Sumerians, one of the world's earliest civilizations. References to the poppy have been found on Sumerian tablets that date back to 4000 B.C. The Sumerians called the plant *hul gil*, which means "joy plant," so the narcotic properties of opium were obviously recognized.[7] The Egyptian *Therapeutic Papyrus of Thebes*, a medical treatise dating from 1552 B.C., described the use of opium for the relief of pain.

The white poppy was handed down from the Sumerians to the Assyrians, to the Babylonians, and eventually to the ancient Egyptians, who had more than 700 medicines that contained opium. It has traditionally been suggested that opium spread from Egypt to Asia Minor then back to the rest of the Old World. Newer historical discoveries, however, show that it probably originated in eastern Europe and then spread to the south and west, before eventually being taken to western Europe.[8]

Opium's narcotic properties were described around 400 B.C. by the Greek physician Hippocrates, who is generally considered to be the leader of ancient medicine. The drug was used in ancient Greece both for religious ceremonies and to heal illness. The opium plant was a symbol for Demeter, the Greek goddess of fertility and the protector of marriage. Married women who were childless often wore jewelry shaped like the seedpod of the opium plant, hoping by this to induce pregnancy. Around A.D. 150 the Greek physician Galen recommended the use of opium to take away pain, to stop coughing, to relieve stomach problems, and to induce sleep. He called it the strongest of the drugs that stupify the senses and induce sleep.

The Romans used the opium poppy for recreational purposes, as well as for medicinal applications. One of their methods of ingestion was to crush the entire pod and mix it with water and honey or with wine to disguise the bitter taste of the raw opium. After the fall of the Roman Empire, much of the existing medical knowledge of the time was temporarily lost to the Western world, although Arab physicians continued to maintain and use the knowledge of Roman and Greek medicine, including the use of opium.

Opium is believed by many to have been introduced to China by Arab traders around A.D. 700. This is debatable, however, as there are earlier references to opium being grown in China. By the time the Arab opium trade flourished, the Chinese were already cultivating their own opium, as well as importing the drug from India.[9] It is probable that the plant arrived in China with itinerant traders who visited in the first century B.C. Opium was used by the Arabs as an international trading commodity, thus it is more likely that the Arabs organized the opium trade better than previously was the case and traded the drug in larger quantities. By the eighth century, opium was being carried throughout Asia by caravans of Arab traders, who were certainly selling large quantities of opium for medicinal and recreational use to China, where it was known as "smoking dirt."[10] Arab traders controlled the opium trade for the next 800 years.

Trade in the Middle Ages

Though opium had been in casual use in the Far East for a long time, it was the Europeans who organized the opium trade into a large-scale industry. The Portuguese were the first to realize the value of opium as a trade item. In the 1500s, Portugal controlled a trade monopoly with India; and one of their trade items that was in high demand was opium. By 1516, the Chinese and East Indians were consuming large quantities of opium, and there was an established market across Europe for the drug. Initially the Portuguese traded Chinese silk for tobacco from the Americas, but they soon realized that opium was a better business tool and an ideal trade good as it was light in weight for ease of transportation and could be bartered for a very high value due to demand. The Portuguese traded opium for pepper and other valuable spices or sold it for silver.

Opium smoking increased in China in the 1600s among the rich as a means of relieving boredom and among the poor to temporarily escape the drudgery of their everyday lives. The Chinese originally used much of their opium for medicinal purposes and ingested it by mouth. This changed around 1620 when Portuguese and Dutch sailors who visited China introduced the new habit of smoking tobacco. Around 1650, sailors started to mix opium with tobacco in the belief that this practice prevented malaria. Tobacco smoking became so popular in China that the Chinese emperor Tsung Chen prohibited it. Unfortunately the ban backfired. The Chinese continued to smoke, but because they now couldn't use tobacco, they smoked plain opium instead. By the time the ban was repealed, the damage was done and the habit of smoking opium was established.

By the late 1600s, smoking opium had become rampant. The Dutch bought cheap opium from India through the Dutch East India Company and traded it with China. In 1699 the trade involved eighty-seven tons of opium.[11] Ironically, then, the habit of smoking opium was first introduced to China by Westerners, but then, as we will see later, Chinese laborers introduced smoking opium to the Old West when they immigrated to California.

The British, seeing a lucrative trade opportunity, formed the British East India Company in 1600 and started trading in China in the 1670s. As a result, the Dutch, the French, the Portuguese, and the British all struggled to gain control of the opium trade. The eventual winner was the British East India Company, which grew massive amounts of opium in India and exported it to China.

The Chinese Tea Connection

The British wanted Chinese tea and silk, and the Chinese wanted opium. The conquest of India by the British allowed a three-way trade that was controlled by the East India Company. Opium grown in India was traded to China for tea, which was shipped to Britain for consumption. But opium had now become a problem for the Chinese government. Seeing the potential for harm, in 1729 Emperor Yung Cheng prohibited the smoking of opium except as a medicine and mandated severe penalties (including execution) for those who were caught. The Emperor's prohibition on opium trading with Europeans was an attempt to stop the trade of tea, spices, and silk for opium, which was now draining the Chinese reserves of silver.

Tea drinking had been introduced to Europe by the Dutch in the 1660s and it rapidly became an important part of British culture. Tea was drunk by all social classes — at breakfast, dinner, and supper, and as a refreshing drink between meals. Chinese tea was considered to be the best. By 1830 the British East India Company was importing 30 million pounds of tea to Britain each year.[12] Perversely, tea drinking became a problem for the British government because almost all the imported tea came from China. This placed Britain at a trade disadvantage, as tea imports had to be paid for in cash, which caused a large imbalance in trade.

The problem was simple, but troublesome to the British. The Europeans, and later the Americans, wanted goods from China. This consisted mainly of tea and silk, but also porcelain and spices. China, however, did not particularly want to trade for Western goods. China already had plenty of its own resources and did not lack for much. The result was that the British had to pay for their tea with silver, which drained the British reserves of bullion. Emperor Ch'ien Ling stated his view: "The Celestial Empire possesses all things in prolific abundance and lacks no product within its borders. There is therefore no need to import manufactures of outside barbarians in exchange for our products."[13] This, however, was not strictly accurate, as the Chinese exported silk, tea, sugar, paper, mother-of-pearl, bamboo, and porcelain. In return they received raw cotton, items manufactured from cotton, iron, tin, lead, and other goods — including opium. Indian opium brought to China by the British was considered to be better quality than the homegrown Chinese product.

Tea preparation was a complicated process, a secret closely guarded in China, in spite of British attempts to duplicate it. Tea was also a popular drink in the United States and was even imported to such remote places as Bent's Fort in present-day Colorado, which was a distant outpost on the Santa Fe Trail during the 1830s and early 1840s.

Mountain men commonly carried among their supplies black tea leaves compressed into tiny "bricks" about a half-inch thick by two inches square. For use, they scraped a small portion into a mug of hot water with their knives.

Silk was also a major export from China, and Chinese silk was very expensive. Around 1900, a pair of opera-length, striped silk stockings cost around $6 in New Orleans.[14] Adjusted for inflation, this would be equivalent to around $150 in 2010 dollars. Only the very rich and some of the high-class prostitutes in the most expensive bordellos could afford this price. Because silk was so expensive, most women used it only for ribbons or trim. Besides, silk stockings held up through only one or two washings.

To the advantage of the Chinese, silkworms lived primarily on the mulberry bushes that grew naturally in China. The silk business was so important to the Chinese that they guarded the secrets of silk production very closely and the punishment for exporting mulberry seeds was execution. Even if mul-

Tea from China was considered to have the best flavor and was therefore in high demand, thus draining the British treasury of silver and leading to the opium trade and the two opium wars of the 1840s and 1850s. Chinese tea was popular on the Western frontier in the 1830s, even in remote places such as Bent's Fort on the Santa Fe Trail (author's collection).

berry seeds were available outside the country, however, they wouldn't grow properly in the cool, wet climate of northern Europe. The British tried to produce silk for over a hundred years, but weren't able to overcome the problems of Britain's cold winters.[15]

The trade deficit problem was resolved in part by selling opium produced in India to China. By 1773 the British East India Company had taken over the opium trade from the Dutch. The governor-general of Bengal drove out all the competing sources of opium production and trading in India, thus leaving the British government as the sole grower and supplier of Indian opium. By the end of the 1700s, through this monopoly, Britain controlled the cultivation, processing, export, and sale of opium to China. The opium was molded into balls, then packed into chests that contained forty balls of crude opium and weighed between 130 and 160 pounds.

In 1799, Emperor Kea King (Kia King or Chia-ching, depending on Western spelling) made another attempt to stop the trade. He prohibited the importation and local growing of opium in China and took a more aggressive stance towards the traders. This merely shifted opium from a legal trade to smuggling. As a result, the opium trade increased a hundred times between the mid–1700s and the mid–1800s. China became concerned again with the drain on its silver reserves, while the British were pushing even more supplies. The British East India company promoted this trade so well that by 1804 the balance of trade in paying for Chinese tea had reversed, and the sale of opium was a major source of income for Britain. In addition, the tax on the flourishing business in tea was very important to the British government as a source of revenue. By 1830, there were more than three million Chinese opium addicts and Britain was selling almost five million pounds of opium a year to China. At one point, one-seventh of the revenue of British India came from China as payment for this habit-forming drug. In the words of one British official, this situation was "one of the most unique facts that the history of finance affords."[16]

By 1838 China's balance of trade had become so unfavorable that the Chinese emperor started another war on opium. He increased the penalties for growing, selling, or smoking opium and eliminated many of the prominent opium dealers. But this still did not eliminate the opium trade. Finally, in desperation, the emperor wrote to Queen Victoria and requested that she take steps to stop the trade, but she either ignored the letter or it was never passed on to her by the British government.[17]

The Chinese wanted the smuggling stopped, but the British wanted it to continue, so tension between the two countries escalated. As a next step, in an attempt to limit the opium trade, the Chinese blockaded the port of Canton (Kwangchow), which was the only legal port for trade with foreigners. When negotiations failed, the Chinese seized and destroyed the British stockpile of 20,000 chests of opium, which was a year's supply. Furious at this attempt to disrupt their very lucrative trade, the British declared war in 1839 and sent warships to China, starting what has been called the "First Opium War," which continued with sporadic skirmishes from 1840 to 1842. The outcome was that the British defeated the Chinese and forced them to sign the Treaty of Nanking in 1842. The treaty made the Chinese open up four more ports to foreign trade, to pay reparations, and to cede to the British control of the island of Hong Kong, which was used to stockpile opium on the way to China. Smuggling and corruption increased. The economic pressures on the tea trade were so great that British spies in China, after some diligent research, learned the process. In 1851 the British were able to start growing tea in India and Ceylon (the present Sri Lanka), thus relieving some of the trade imbalance with China.

The opium trade persisted, however, and tensions soon mounted again between Britain and China, which led to the Second Opium War in 1856. Active fighting in this war was, however, very short-lived. The British stormed the port of Canton and, in the resulting fierce battle, killed or captured an estimated 10,000 Chinese in the space of ten minutes. Even in the face of this defeat and massive loss of lives, the Chinese did not surrender, so the British advanced towards Peking. To avoid a repeat of the massacre at Canton, the Chinese finally capitulated. On June 26, 1858, both countries signed the Treaty of Tientsin, which legalized the traffic in opium in China. The predictable result was, of course, a further spread of addiction.

Opium Haunts Britain

Opium was important for Britain in their overseas economy. The British East India Company, however, supplied not only China but also Britain with opium. During the eighteenth century the working class in Britain was awash in gin. Gin was easy to make and was therefore cheap. This provided a panacea for people who wanted to escape the grim realities of life during the industrial revolution. With some irony, gin was called "mother's milk" or "mother's ruin." At the same time, however, drink was considered evil and a sign of degradation and moral turpitude among the common masses.

The British Parliament passed gin acts in 1729, 1733, 1736, 1738, and 1751, all basically aimed at trying to raise the price of gin and thus lower the amount of drinking. This increase was accompanied by various penalties for noncompliance, but people still drank. Prodigiously so. In 1751, approximately seven million gallons of gin were taxed. But the general population was only compliant to a point. When gin prices rose too much, many turned to opium.

By the sixteenth century, the use of opium had become well established in western European medicine. Opium had become an essential commodity in Europe, and opium use increased across Europe and Asia. It was freely available on the flimsiest of medical advice and by the 1800s the use of opium was widespread for pain, coughs, and diarrhea, and was sold by pharmacies, as well as shoemakers, tailors, and grocery stores. It was combined with liquor and sold in bars. It was used for such diverse ailments as cholera, dysentery, toothache, flatulence, insanity, and menopause. It was only a short step from using opium as a medicine to treat cholera and dysentery to using it for recreation. As a result, the habit of using opium spread rapidly.

Opium was not seen as a dangerous drug but was viewed as a mildly addictive, pleasant substance. It could be taken more discreetly than gin and did not produce aggression and violence. It could be freely purchased over the counter or drunk as a medicine. The poor class, who lived under appalling conditions of grinding poverty and worked long hours in the coal mines or cloth factories and at other menial jobs, found that opium was cheaper than gin or beer. In the industrial northern part of England, where opium provided an escape from the drudgery and misery of working-class life, the drug received the nickname of "Elevation."

Author Adam Hart-Davis reported that an estimated five families out of six in Victorian times used opium for medicinal purposes.[18] Godfrey's Cordial, for example, consisted of opium in a thick sugary syrup to disguise the bitter taste. It was used to treat colic and to quiet fussy babies, even to the extent of unattended babies being dosed with it to keep them sedated while the parents worked. In 1827, Britain imported 17,000 pounds of opium from Turkey and by 1859 this amount had become almost four times as much.[19] Because of the problems caused by the drug habit, Britain passed legislation in 1860 to try to control opium.

The background for opium in the Old West, then, was set by its use in China, Britain, and Europe for the preceding hundreds of years. In America, the immigrants who spread westward brought opium with them from the East Coast for medicinal and recreational use. On the other side of the continent, thousands of Chinese laborers came to the West Coast in the 1850s and 1860s to work in the gold fields of California and on the transcontinental railroad, and they brought with them their habit of smoking opium. These Chinese immigrants have been blamed for bringing opium use to the United States, but this is not correct, as opium had been used previously for over a hundred years in American medicine. It had been used as a therapeutic agent since colonial times and was used as a medicine for pain relief for wounded soldiers by both the American and British forces during the War of Independence.

Smoking opium, however, as was practiced on the West Coast, was a new method of ingesting the drug. The harsh working conditions and the strain of physical labor for the Chinese workers, coupled with a new life in a strange country and the lack of Chinese women for companionship, made opium a suitable vehicle for temporary escape from reality. Opium use was generally tolerated by employers because it kept the Chinese workers happy and willing to continue as slave labor. A more pragmatic side to the issue was that opium distributors profited from its importation, the government profited from taxes on sales, and business owners saw the use of opium as a form of control over their workers.

CHAPTER THREE

A Motley Mix
of Indigenous Brews

Alcoholic drinks that were brewed and drunk in South America and Central America before the arrival of European invaders and settlers eventually worked their way north during contact with native civilizations. As a result, the use of intoxicating and mind-altering substances was not unknown to the indigenous Native American cultures before white pioneers from the East brought the use of alcohol and opium with them to the Old West in the 1840s and 1850s.

Except for a few tribes in the Southwest, however, most native North American Indians had no fermented beverages before the arrival of the white man. Among the few who produced and drank alcoholic beverages were the Apache and the Zuni Indians of Arizona and New Mexico. The Pima and Papago (now called the Tohono O'odham) tribes of south-central Arizona used fermented drinks in religious ceremonies, though only sparingly. It is not known why the use of alcohol was not universally present in Native American tribes, as there were many available wild and cultivated plants that could have been fermented.

Intoxicating Beverages

As the Spanish moved north from their conquests in Mexico in 1539 in search of the legendary Seven Cities of Gold that were thought to lie somewhere in New Mexico, they found that intoxicating beverages had preceded them. The local natives were making fermented drinks from various fruits and cactus plants (notably the agave cactus), and even the seeds of the mesquite tree. Maize, which was an important local cereal crop, was commonly used to make a type of beer.

PULQUE, TEQUILA AND MESCAL

The alcoholic beverage that was the most popular was pulque, a drink handed down to Native Americans from the Aztecs. Pulque was the fermented sap of the agave cactus, which was also known by the Spanish generic name of mescal or maguey. The agave grows throughout the Southwest, but was found particularly in the high desert country of southern New Mexico and Arizona and the Mojave Desert of California, where it was used by local Indians and early Hispanic settlers to make an intoxicating beverage.

The Aztecs in Mexico drank pulque that fermented naturally when exposed to yeast spores that drifted into it from the air. The alcohol content was typically 3 to 4 percent. The agave was also commonly called the "century plant" because pioneers originally thought that the plant took a hundred years to produce a flower. Depending on the species, most agave plants take only four to five years to bloom, though some of the larger plants can take up to forty or fifty years.

There are 120 species of agave, with twelve species in Arizona alone. Some species of the plant, such as Parry's agave (*Agave parryi*), look similar to the common yucca plants of the West, with spiky, narrow leaves that end in a sharp spine but with a very tall flowering stem. Others species, such as *Agave chrysantha*, have fatter leaves that serve as vast reservoirs of liquid. The desert agave (*Agave deserti*) has a flower stalk that reaches thirteen feet high and can contain as much as forty pounds of liquid. When the agave plant matures, which may take anywhere from five to twelve years depending on the species, a single large bud forms in the center to create a flower. The plant's energy goes into producing one giant flower-stalk, so it blooms just once and then dies.

American Indians extracted sap from the plant by cutting a hole in the bud and letting the liquid inside drain out. When the bud was cut open, the cavity could produce several gallons of liquid before the plant died. This juice, from which pulque, mescal, and tequila were made, was called *agua miel*, or "honey water," by the Spanish because of its sweetness. Pulque was made primarily from six of the species of agave plant, but particularly the *Agave americana*.

The extracted sap was fermented by sealing it in a pot for several days. This step yielded an alcoholic beverage similar to beer or hard cider. The resulting brew, named pulque, remained viable for only about twenty-four hours, so it had to be drunk right away. When fresh the brew smelled sweet, but when it went bad it smelled horrible. One Spanish observer said that it smelled like a dead dog. Fresh pulque was sometimes mixed with a type of local chocolate (cocoa solids), which has been a popular central American additive to many foodstuffs and drinks since at least 1000 B.C.

This type of drink had historical precedent in a type of beer called *chicha* made by the Incas of the Peruvian Andes. The Incas used it for rituals and drank it in large quantities during religious festivities. Mills discovered in the Andes for processing chicha have been dated back to the 1500s. This drink, fermented with human saliva, was made from corn but could also be made

There are more than 120 species of agave plant. Six of them were commonly used to produce the beer-like drink called pulque, which was also distilled to make the fiery liquors mescal and tequila. This is the golden-flowered agave (*Agave chrysantha*) from Arizona, which produces a tall flowering stem and a fat stalk that could be tapped to produce liquid. The roots of agave plants were roasted and stored as a source of food by Native American Indians (author's collection).

from various fruits and berries. Chicha had a pale straw color, a milky appearance, and a slightly sour taste. Like pulque, the brew spoiled within a week.

Fresh pulque could also be distilled into two intoxicating spirits. Tequila was distilled specifically from pulque made from the blue agave (*Agave tequilana*). The name is reputed to have originated in Tequila, Mexico, which supposedly made a superior version of the drink. Mexican law says that tequila can only be made in Jalisco, Mexico. The first mescal distillery was licensed to José Antonio Cuervo in Jalisco, Mexico, in 1821.[1] The other fiery spirit produced from pulque was mescal, which was distilled from the fermented product of several different species of agave. The final product varied somewhat depending on the particular agave used, and some mescals had a smoky taste that came from the original plant. Mescal was distilled only once, which left it as a rather rough drink. Tequila was distilled twice, which gave it a smoother taste. Old-timers in Arizona aptly called both of the resulting liquors "cactus juice."

It should be noted that references to "mescal" in various books and other places can be the source of some confusion. The name "mescal" has been variously applied to the agave plant, the peyote-producing cactus plant, and to any clear, fiery liquor made from the agave cactus. Most dictionaries will give these three meanings to the word. Some authors use the names mescal, pulque, and tequila interchangeably for the fermented and distilled maguey sap, which leads to even more confusion. Sometimes the word is spelled as "mezcal."

All the species of agave were roasted or boiled and stored for food by Native Americans; the word mezcal itself means "oven-cooked agave." Other uses were for soap and fibers for making sandals and cloth. Agave also served as a medicine and was commonly used by the Indians to treat arthritis. The Hualapai Indians of northwest Arizona used pulverized agave as a facial cream.[2]

The baked root of the agave served as an important food source for the Apache Indians. One of the subtribes, the Mescalero Apaches of southern New Mexico, received their name because of their extensive use of this plant. They roasted the bud at the center of the flowering agave plant in a pit and stored it for food. It was said to taste like a sweet-potato, but with a smoky, molasses-like flavor.

Mescal was a common drink around and south of the Mexican border. In 1880 a popular drink at the Cosmopolitan Bar in Tucson, Arizona, was mescal mixed with an equal amount of whiskey. At army posts in the Southwest, where whiskey was at times hard to obtain, soldiers might drink locally made mescal, sometimes called "Indian firewater" by the troops.

TISWIN

The Apache Indians of the Southwest also brewed an intoxicating beer-like drink called tiswin (sometimes spelled tizwin), that was made from fermented, maize, wheat, or mesquite beans. For obvious reasons, tiswin was sometimes called "Apache beer." Blevins, in the *Dictionary of the American West*, on the other hand, claims that tiswin was a sweet Apache drink made from corn, whereas the fermented version was a type of beer called *tulapai*.[3]

Hallucinogenic and Narcotic Substances

Along with alcoholic beverages, Native Americans used several hallucinogenic beverages and substances to alter their state of consciousness. These were typically used in religious ceremonies. The hallucinations were also enjoyed for themselves and some Navajo Indians claimed that the effects were similar to drinking too much of the white man's whiskey.[4]

Several plants were used by American Indians for their narcotic properties. The paper mulberry (*Broussonetia papyrifera*), for example, was used by several of the Apache tribes as a narcotic. The fruit of the Christmas cactus (*Opuntia leptocaulis*) was crushed and made into a beverage by the Chiricahua and Mescalero Apaches, who enjoyed its narcotic properties. The root of the Colorado four o'clock (*Mirabilis multiflora*) was chewed by Hopi shamans (medicine men) to bring on visions to assist in making a diagnosis of illnesses. The Zuni Indians of New Mexico claimed that a beverage made from the touristplant (*Dimorphocarpa wislizeni*) loosened their tongues and made them talk like drunken fools. They claimed that for this reason they did not want women to drink it.[5]

DATURA

One of the common hallucinogens used by Native Americans in ritual and religious ceremonies was the datura plant, *Datura meteloides*, more commonly known as Jimson weed. This plant is arguably the hallucinogenic plant most used by humans, as its ingestion made it possible for a shaman to induce dreams and visions in order to give advice to his followers. The Utes, the Navajo, the Zuni, the Hopi, and the White Mountain Apache all used powdered datura root in their ceremonies and as a narcotic drug.

The name was given to the plant in 1676 when a group of soldiers at Jamestown were poisoned by the weed. They originally called it "Jamestown weed," a name which eventually became corrupted to "Jimson weed." Other popular names for the plant are thorn apple, devil's weed, loco weed, and hell's bells. Slightly different, but in the same botanical family, are *Datura wrightii* and *Datura stramonium*, both commonly known as sacred datura or sacred thorn apple, and also commonly known as Jimson weed. Sometimes these names are all used interchangeably. Because the plant has a very strong smell, it is also less-affectionately known as "stinkweed."

Datura typically grows in warm areas in valleys alongside streams in the West from western Texas to southern California. The plant grows to a height of between one and three feet tall and it has large leaves and large trumpet-shaped flowers several inches long that vary from white or pale violet to purple in color.

To prepare datura for use, the Indians either pulverized it into a liquid or dried and powdered it. When ingested, datura produced hallucinations, the source for which was a series of poisonous alkaloids similar to those found in the *Solanaceae* family, which includes the deadly nightshade group. Random variations in toxicity of the datura plant, depending on the age of the plant and local growing conditions, made ingestion of datura very hazardous. Effects included an inability to differentiate reality from the hallucinations and a tendency towards bizarre behavior, both of which could last for days. Less pleasant were other side effects, such as convulsions, vertigo, dimming of the vision (which could be temporary or permanent), and even possible respiratory arrest.

On the plus side, smoking Jimson weed mixed with tobacco or the leaves of the mullein plant was a legitimate use by Native Americans and white pioneers for relieving asthma and bronchial spasms. Datura was also used as a poultice or liniment to reduce pain and inflammation. More humans have been poisoned by Jimson weed than have animals, which apparently do not like the taste of the plant. In spite of this, as cowboy movie star Gene Autry rides the range he croons about "Where the longhorn cattle feed / On the lowly Jimson Weed," in the popular Western song "Back in the Saddle Again" (1939).

PEYOTE

Another drug used to produce narcotic and hallucinogenic effects by American Indians was peyote. The name was adapted from a similar substance called *peyotl* that was used by the Aztecs. The use of peyote in ceremonial rituals to induce visions eventually spread north from Mexico to the North American Plains Indian tribes. The use of peyote buttons in Texas has been dated back to around 4000 B.C. Peyote was used in various ceremonial and religious rituals involving singing, chanting, meditation, and prayer by the Apache, Navajo, Comanche, Kiowa, Sioux, and other Plains Indians.

Peyote came from a small, spineless pincushion cactus named *Lophophora williamsii* that looks somewhat like a small gray-green carrot top sticking out of the ground. The plant grows in the Chihuahuan desert of Mexico and is commonly found in a wild state in the desert country of the lower Rio Grande Valley of southwestern Texas. The small button-like part that grows at the top of the cactus was cut and dried in the sun. The resulting wrinkled brown disc was called a mescal button (remember the confusion of names, as the name "mescal" is also used to describe intoxicating drinks made from the agave cactus). When the button was peeled, dried, and chewed it caused brilliantly colored hallucinations that were interpreted in native cultures to be spiritual and religious visions. The button was also boiled in water to make a beverage somewhat like tea, but with psychoactive properties. In the Southwest, so-called cactus wine was made from tequila with peyote added, a combination that must have induced curious results when it was drunk.

One later investigator experimenting with the effects of peyote described the following vision: "From the edge of the field of vision there crept across the green carpet beasts like the monsters from a fairy tale stretching out tongues and claws.... Scarcely had this thought passed through my mind before the eyes of the beasts glittered with green or red lights.... Somewhat later I fixed my eyes on a point on the ceiling on which were a few small flies in the web of a spider. Suddenly the flies began to multiply lit up by beautiful colors within the ever-changing form of the spider's web."[6]

Like opium, the use of peyote did not stimulate debauchery. The visions were reported to be pleasant and were accompanied by extraordinary displays of light and brilliant colors. Mescal buttons were reported to taste bitter and have a nauseating odor. Chemists later isolated nine alkaloids from the button, of which the most active was mescaline.[7] Peyote was also used by American Indians to treat arthritis, tuberculosis, intestinal ailments, and influenza.

Early Spanish priests in the Southwest gave the cactus the Spanish name of *raiz diabolico*, which translates as the "devilish root," because the church didn't like its use in native religious ceremonies. The actual root of the plant was more potent than the button and was generally not used for chewing.

The Early Liquor Trade

Emigrants on the Oregon and California trails in the 1840s and 1850s brought opium with them as a medicine. They also carried with them plentiful supplies of alcohol for their own consumption. They sold or traded any excess to Indians along the way, even though this was a violation of the 1832 federal law that made it illegal to provide alcohol to Indians anywhere in the United States. Some politicians, however, did not condemn this practice and felt that whiskey might be one way to rid the country of Indians. Benjamin Franklin had said earlier, "If it be the design of Providence to extirpate these savages in order to make room for the cultivators of the earth, it seems not improbable that rum may be the appointed means."[8]

Early explorers in the West had always brought spirits with them, both for their own use and to trade with local Indians when they needed supplies during their travels. Trading companies, such as the American Fur Company, for example, brought casks of whiskey to the West to trade with the Indians for beaver pelts. In spite of the liquor ban, when contact with native tribes showed that the desire for alcohol could be manipulated to advantage in the fur trade, unscrupulous traders and military personnel augmented the flow of whiskey. When white traders introduced whiskey to the West the results were profound and many Indian tribes embraced liquor widely. The Teton Sioux, for example, when they first tasted whiskey, called it "sacred water." Not all of the tribes liked this white man's drink, however. The Arikara Indians, for example, refused to drink whiskey because they realized that it made them act like fools.

An early priest who observed the use of alcohol by the Indians reported, "Lewdness, adulteries, incests, and several other crimes which decency keeps me from naming, are the usual disorders which are committed through the trade in brandy, of which some traders make use in order to abuse the Indian women, who yield themselves readily during their drunkenness to all kinds of indecency." He added that "injuries, quarrels, homicides, murders, parricides are to this day the sad consequences of the trade in brandy."[9]

But even this was not the first arrival of alcoholic drinks in the West. The Spanish brought strong drink to Mexico in the 1500s. Franciscan missionaries trying to expand the church's influence in the New World brought grapevines for sacramental wine to New Mexico and California as they pushed colonization efforts north from Mexico in the 1600s. They produced a wine for church masses that was fermented by a wild yeast that occurred naturally on the skin of the grapes. Before these grapevines were planted and harvested, wine for church purposes was brought from Spain by ship in stone jugs, then was carried north to Santa Fe and Taos (then in Mexico, now New Mexico) from Chihuahua in Mexico in wooden-wheeled wagons. Some wine was also grown around El Paso del Norte (south of modern El Paso) just south of the Mexican border on the Rio Grande River and the Camino Real highway from Mexico to Santa Fe.

Some of the oldest wineries in the United States are located in New Mexico. Wine grapes arrived in New Mexico in 1630 when Franciscan friars planted some of the first vines near present-day Socorro in the Rio Grande Valley of New Mexico. This was probably the first vineyard in the United States. Grapes of this variety, which still grow in New Mexico today, were known as "mission grapes." In 1776 a monk named Francisco Dominguez noted that the Indians of the Isleta Pueblo, just south of present-day Albuquerque in New Mexico, were growing grapes and drinking wine.

By the mid-nineteenth century, more wine was produced in New Mexico than in California. By 1884, over 3,000 acres of grapes were providing about a million gallons of wine a year. Processing included crushing the grapes in

Some of the first grapes grown in the United States for wine were planted in 1630 by Franciscan friars near Socorro, in central New Mexico. The juice was fermented by a wild yeast that occurred naturally on the skin of the grapes (author's collection).

the traditional European way, by women who walked on the ripe fruit in their bare feet in a large wooden vat. Fermentation was carried out in wooden kegs or large ceramic jugs. Small glass bottles were scarce at the time, so wine was typically served from a *bota*, which was a traditional wine bag made from leather and lined with a goat's bladder. In more affluent households, large glass vessels that were used for shipping olive oil from Spain were reused for bulk storage of wine.

As the friars moved northwards from Mexico during the eighteenth century to establish a series of church outposts along the California coast, they also took with them grapes that they planted at the missions. In 1820 a Mexican woman named Maria Felix planted a vine in Santa Barbara, California, that eventually grew to be a foot in diameter at the base and yielded 1,200 pounds of grapes at each harvest.[10] Until 1860, California white and red wines were made from the original grapevines that the missionaries had brought with them. After the mid–1860s other varieties of grapes were also planted.

The first grapes were used by Spanish missionaries to make sacramental wine. Because of this origin they were commonly known as "mission grapes." Descendants of these first grapevines still grow in New Mexico today (author's collection).

TAOS LIGHTNING

In the Old West, early distilleries in northern New Mexico produced a raw, fiery liquor called *aguardiente de Taos*, otherwise known as "Taos lightning" and affectionately known by its drinkers as "Old Towse."[11] The name came from combining two Spanish words, *agua* and *ardiente*, which mean "fiery water." Various ingredients were used to spice up the raw alcohol and give it some flavor. Typical additives were pepper, chili powder, or even a touch of gunpowder. Not that such a raw taste put off the mountain men who wanted to drink it. During the 1830s and 1840s Taos lightning was a popular barter item for obtaining beaver pelts and other valuable furs.

Eventually the name *aguardiente* was applied to any kind of raw spirits. Those who drank the Taos variety insisted that after two glasses the drinker felt like he had been struck by lightning — hence the nickname. The early distillers in the area around Taos, New Mexico, never seemed to get the process quite right and the resulting alcohol was said to be somewhat rough. The drink was very potent, but was (like other strong liquors in the West) highly recommended by locals as an antidote for rattlesnake bites. And reportedly the drink was very popular at parties, being drunk freely by both men and women — sometimes too freely. Nancy Fitzhugh described a dinner that she attended in Denver at Christmas of 1859 at which Taos lightning was served. She recalled that everyone passed out, except for her and the man who brought the liquor to the party.[12]

Taos lightning was first produced in 1824 by Thomas Long Smith (later better known as mountain man Peg-Leg Smith) and three partners. Smith constructed a distillery in the upper Rio Grande River Valley of New Mexico, where he distilled local corn and grain into a high-proof alcohol. This powerful drink was so popular that it was soon produced by other local merchants such as Simeon Turley, who owned a two-story mill, granary, barns, and a still about two miles west of Arroyo Hondo on the Rio Hondo ten miles north of Taos. Turley was one of the pioneers in the Taos liquor industry, starting his business in the 1830s. He grew his own grain, ground it in his own mill, and processed it in his distillery. The resulting "whiskey" was distributed to the local pueblo Indians and mountain men in nearby Taos. It was also carried

The residents of the trading post at El Pueblo in southern Colorado celebrated Christmas of 1854 with a little too much Taos Lightning, didn't stay on their guard, and were massacred by a local band of marauding Ute Indians. Fifteen men and one woman were killed (author's collection).

north by wagon in five-gallon barrels to forts along the North Platte, South Platte, and Arkansas rivers, and traded there for beaver pelts, buffalo skins, and Indian-made items. The going price was $4 a gallon.

In 1842 Turley established a store for selling whiskey and trading furs at an adobe fort called El Pueblo, which was located at the junction of Fountain Creek and the Arkansas River in south-central Colorado.[13] Unfortunately, in 1854, the occupants of the fort celebrated Christmas with too much Taos lightning and in their befuddled state were overrun and massacred by a marauding band of Ute Indians.[14] Fifteen men and one woman were killed. Turley himself met a similar fate on January 21, 1847, during the Taos Rebellion, when a heavily armed group of Mexicans and Pueblo Indians attacked his mill.[15] Turley and eight mountain men held out initially, but they were overrun on the second day of the siege when their ammunition ran low. Turley and six of the others were killed. They were buried in a common grave in Kit Carson Cemetery in Taos.

A similar type of powerful brew was another so-called whiskey named Valley Tan or Mormon Whiskey, which was made in the Henry Mountains of southern Utah. The drink was so raw that it was appropriately nicknamed "leopard sweat." This powerful brew was the basis for a popular rhyme of the time:

> Valley Tan, Valley Tan,
> Maketh glad the heart of man.[16]

Whiskey and other distilled spirits like it were always present at frontier celebrations, as drinking to excess was considered to be a measure of having a good time. At a celebration at Rich Bar in September of 1851, Louise Clappe described the refreshment as being a "twenty gallon keg of brandy ... with quart-dippers gracefully encircling it, that each one might help himself as he pleased."[17]

CHAPTER FOUR

Medical Use of Opium
and Alcohol

Through the 1800s, opium was an important medicine with three principal uses. One was for the relief of acute or chronic pain, another was as a cough suppressant for lung diseases such as tuberculosis, and the third was as a medicine to treat dysentery and diarrhea. Nineteenth-century physicians held opium in such high regard as a medicine that it was regarded as a miracle. Physician William Osler in Canada, for example, writing in the late 1800s, called opium "God's own medicine."[1] The spreading use of opium as a recreational drug and the associated problems of addiction were an undesired element of its use.

Medical Practice in the 1800s

The widespread use of opium as a medicine in the Old West had its origin in the way medicine was practiced in the early nineteenth century. The causes of illnesses were not understood, surgery was risky due to the high likelihood of infection, and anesthetics had not yet been discovered. Much of frontier medicine dealt with diseases such as malaria, typhoid, and cholera. Certainly no cure for these diseases was available and medical treatment consisted mostly of supportive care until the patient either recovered by himself or didn't. Opium was one of the few drugs available to relieve the pain of diseases and to treat the resulting stomach and bowel upsets, so its use became widespread. In this manner physicians could often relieve the symptoms of a disease, but they could not necessarily cure the disease itself.

In the early 1800s, medical practice had not progressed much beyond the humoral theories that Greek physicians were using around 400 B.C. The Greeks believed that the body contained four fluids called "humors." These were blood, phlegm, yellow bile, and black bile. These disgusting-sounding substances corresponded respectively to the four material elements of air, water, fire, and earth, and to combinations of the four conditions of hot, wet, cold, and dry. Greek physicians thought that good health depended on the proper balance of these four humors, and disease was thought to occur when the humors were out of balance.

The humoral theory evolved into what came to be called "heroic medicine," which was refined in Europe before coming to the United States. Medical treatments consisted primarily of methods to flush the supposed "bad stuff" out of the body and presumably restore the balance of the humors. Common methods of achieving this were bleeding from veins, purging the intestinal tract, blistering the skin, and inducing vomiting and sweating. Sweating was supposed to allow excess bad humors to escape through the skin. A doctor's black bag contained sweating-producing drugs (in the medical world called sudorifics or diaphoretics), emetics to produce vomiting, and purgatives to flush out the supposed disease-causing agents.

Bleeding continued as a treatment in the Old West well into the second half of the nineteenth century. It was performed by using a special knife called a fleam and making a small cut in a vein near the site of the pain or illness. In bleeding, typically if a little was good, more was considered to be much better. The sicker the patient the more blood was removed, as excess blood was thought to cause fevers, excitement, and irritability. Sweating was induced by administering a dose of Dover's powder or sweet spirits of nitre (ethyl nitrite). Vomiting was achieved by drugs such as ipecac or tartar emetic. The purgative drugs were legion and included calomel, jalap, colocynth, and croton oil, with enemas commonly used to produce the same effect. Much contemporary medicine consisted of various treatments for the stomach and bowels, as the intestinal tract was readily accessible through natural openings from both ends.

Not unusual was what happened to twenty-three-year-old Francis Parkman from Boston as he was exploring the Oregon Trail and the West. As he later recorded in the book that detailed his travels, he consulted a doctor after he suffered from debilitating diarrhea for most of the summer of 1846. After pondering the problem, the medical man came up with the following: "'Your system, sir, is in a disordered state,' said he, solemnly, after a short examination. I inquired what might be the particular species of disorder. 'Evidently a morbid action of the liver,' replied the medical man; 'I will give you a prescription.'" The doctor gave him some medicine. "'What is it?' said I. 'Calomel,' said the doctor."[2] The doctor was using the most modern medical thinking of the time, as calomel was a drastic purgative that was used as a universal cure-all. But from Parkman's standpoint it was probably not the most desirable or pleasant course of treatment.

Diarrhea and Dysentery

One of the primary uses for opium in medicine was to treat cases that involved diarrhea and dysentery. Typhoid, dysentery, and diarrhea were common and often fatal. The standard remedies were emetics and laxatives, along with whiskey and morphine. The distinction between diarrhea and dysentery was a fine one, but it was an important one. Diarrhea was the name for a series of frequent and uncontrolled evacuations of the bowel. It was a symptom of an intestinal disorder or of some infectious disease. Dysentery, on the other hand, was the name applied to a collection of intestinal diseases and disorders that caused diarrhea and that resulted from various viral or bacterial infections, such as cholera or typhoid, or parasites in the intestines.

Dysentery was characterized by an inflammation of the bowel wall. As one physician vividly described it in 1836, "This is an affection or inflammation of the alimentary canal, characterized usually by nausea, pain, fever, tensemus, with fetid mucus, or bloody evacuations, and is sometimes contagious."[3] One of the symptoms of cholera, for example, was violent diarrhea. In reality, however, the disease was caused by the bacterium *Vibrio cholerae*.

The name "cholera" was sometimes used as a generic term to describe any dysentery or diarrhea rather than what is now considered to be a specific disease. Typical of the medical texts of the 1830s was the following obscure statement: "Dysentery may be caused by whatever obstructs the perspiration. Morbid humors are thrown with the blood upon the intestines, causing all the phenomena of the disease.... It may depend on a putrid acrimony generated in the system."[4]

As late as the mid–1800s, diarrhea and dysentery were often confused with each other and were thought to be the same problem. With a lack of understanding of the causes of many diseases, physicians were not able to tell the difference. During the Indian Wars in the West in the second half of the nineteenth century, when disease, unsanitary living conditions, and poor nutrition often caused diarrhea, military surgeons made few attempts to distinguish between the two. In 1893, the Army Medical Corps reported that almost 10 percent of frontier troops were suffering from diarrhea and dysentery.

Though diarrhea and dysentery arose from various causes in the Old West, the commonest were improper preparation of food and poor sanitation practices. Dysentery often resulted from toxic organisms such as typhoid or giardia in contaminated water, or salmonella in spoiled food. The result was violent diarrhea, accompanied by severe abdominal cramps and frequent stools of blood, pus, and mucus, due to damage to the intestinal wall and internal bleeding. Because of these symptoms, dysentery was known colloquially on the frontier as the "flux" or "bloody flux." It was not until the late 1870s and

1880s that the true culprits of many of these intestinal diseases were understood. The cause of bacillary dysentery, for example, was not explained until 1898, when Kiyoshi Shiga discovered the *Shigella* bacterium.

Opium as a Medicine

Throughout the nineteenth century, opium was widely prescribed in America because of its seemingly miraculous ability to relieve pain and to check diarrhea. Opium and its derivatives were the drugs of choice to treat dysentery and diarrhea because they relaxed the smooth muscles of the abdomen that propelled material through the intestinal tract. Both cholera and dysentery killed by dehydrating the victim with diarrhea, so opium had a high success rate for helping to stem these diseases by stopping the dehydration. As one frontier physician succinctly put it, opium tended to "lock up the bowels."

ILLUSTRATION 4–1

Recommended Doses for Opium-Based Drugs Used for Medicinal Purposes (1895)

Opium as powder: ¼ to 1 grain
Laudanum: 5 to 15 drops (up to 25 drops)
Paregoric: ½ to 1 teaspoon
Morphine: ⅛ to ¼ grain

(Pierce, *The People's Common Sense Medical Advisor*, 31).

One contemporary medical text commented that "A woman generally requires a less dose than a man, being generally of weaker constitution" (Gardner, *The Domestic Physician and Family Assistant*, 27).

Opium was commonly used to treat stomachache, headache, typhoid, tuberculosis, rheumatism, syphilis, joint inflammation, pneumonia, and asthma. Though doctors could not cure these diseases, opium relieved the patients' symptoms. Opium was also the perfect cure-all for treating diseases accompanied by pain, such as the difficult complaint of neuralgia, which was severe pain associated with a nerve.

A druggist usually purchased opium in raw form. He, in turn, made up various medicines containing opium, such as laudanum (tincture of opium, an alcohol-opium solution), paregoric (tincture of opium with camphor added), and Dover's Powder (a mixture of ipecac and opium). Opium appeared in such diverse forms as elixirs to treat coughs, lozenges to calm the nerves, laudanum to treat colic, cigars and cigarettes to create a euphoric feeling (and — of course — to stimulate repurchase of the product), and tea fortified with the drug to treat insomnia.

A soothing treatment for irritations of the throat was morphine dissolved in glycerin. A combination of morphine and cocaine was used for treating "catarrh," which was an older generic medical term that was used to describe any inflammation of the mucus membranes of the breathing organs, such as in the nose, throat, or lungs. This combination of drugs was also widely used to treat hay fever because the cocaine shrank inflamed and congested nasal tissues. Opium or one of its alkaloids was used to treat insomnia, and a mixture of opium and tartar emetic was used for delirium. Rectal suppositories of opium were used to check diarrhea and dysentery. Vaginal suppositories of opium were used for uterine complaints and painful menstruation.

American patent medicines, most of which were laced with opium and alcohol, were at their peak in the 1880s and 1890s. It was estimated that 60 to 70 percent of women between the ages of twenty-five and fifty-five used some form of opiate tonic for menstrual distress.[5] Many women took their "medicine" in private, and not even their husbands knew what they took or the amount. These medicines were reported to cure anything and everything from yellow fever to asthma. Patent medicines containing opium were used to ease the pains of teething for infants. Unfortunately, such medicines were used as a cheap babysitter by women who worked outside the home. They would give the baby a large dose in the morning so that it would sleep through the day while the mother was at work.

The use of opium, however, even as a medicine, was not without serious side effects. Opium produced flushing, sweating, itching skin, nausea, sleepiness, restlessness, anxiety, and shortness of breath. Opium also quickly induced constipation, which was the desired result when treating diarrhea, but not so desirable when treating pain or lung diseases.

Morphine

In 1803, Friedrich Wilhelm Sertürner, a twenty-one-year-old pharmacist's assistant in Germany, isolated in pure form the substance that was the principal active ingredient in opium. He named the new substance *morphium*, after Morpheus, the Greek god of dreams. The substance also became known as morphia, morphinum, morphin, and sulfate of morphia. It is now known as morphine. It was previously thought that opium was acidic, but Sertürner's work showed that it also had alkaline qualities. As a result he called the active substances in opium "alkaloids."

Morphine is the primary alkaloid present in opium and the one that gives the drug its seemingly miraculous ability to relieve pain. However, prescribing opium in the 1800s was essentially guesswork because the morphine content of a specific batch of opium was not known to the physician. Depending on where the opium was grown, the morphine content varied anywhere from 3 to 20 percent. Thus, intending to prescribe ¼ of a grain of morphine could require the equivalent of administering anywhere between 1½ and 7 grains of opium, depending on the origin and purity of the opium plant. Sertürner first published his results in 1806, but his work was largely ignored. He published further results in 1814. This time, in 1817, it attracted the attention of two French chemists, Joseph Cavento and Pierre Joseph Pelletier, who developed a process for producing morphine in useful quantities.[6] In 1827 E. Merck & Company in Germany started manufacturing morphine commercially and the drug became widely available.

Morphine was a white crystallized salt that could be dissolved for use in medicines that were swallowed or injected. The use of morphine was a substantial improvement for treatment, as a physician no longer had to guess at the unknown level of morphine that might be present in a particular batch of opium. The concentration of morphine was always the same. Purity of the drug could be maintained, and the administered dosage was exact.

After morphine became readily available, it was quickly hailed as the new drug of choice. Morphine controlled pain, coughing, and vomiting, but it also induced euphoria and sleepiness. Though morphine induced sleep in most patients, in some it caused insomnia. It also tended to reduce the appetite. Its effect on the gastrointestinal system was to relax overactive muscles in the intestines and reduce bowel movements. On the negative side, few substances created dependency like morphine. It was — and remains — one of the most powerful sleep-inducing, dream-making drugs ever discovered. Ironically, Sertürner, who made the initial discovery, was addicted to opium and became a morphine addict towards the end of his life.[7]

How Opium and Morphine Work

The human nervous system performs two important functions. One is that it operates as a command system that sends orders via chemical messengers called neurotransmitters to different parts of the body to perform various actions. When these neurotransmitters bind to receptor sites on cells, they cause the body to perform the required action, such as a muscle contraction or an increase in heart rate. Receptor sites on cells are very specific in the neurotransmitters that they recognize and allow to bind to them. Some chemical molecules, known as agonists, bind to the site and cause an action. Other molecules, called antagonists, bind to the site and block the action of the neurotransmitter.

The second important function of the nervous system is that it acts as a receiving system that sends information back to the brain from areas containing nerves that transmit feelings of pain. To reduce or relieve the pain of an injury or disease, the human body produces a series of natural narcotic substances called endorphins.[8] Endorphins occur predominantly in the brain, but also in the intestines. The reason that opium and morphine are able to suppress pain is that the body recognizes morphine molecules as having a similar chemical structure to its natural endorphins. Thus the alkaloids in opium can interact with these specific receptor sites to mimic the action of the natural opiates. When morphine attaches to the receptors on the nerve cells, they inhibit the reception of pain and produce a state of inner calm.

Drugs that affect the central nervous system may also have a major effect on the gastrointestinal tract. Thus opium alkaloids produce a constipating effect. This process is reversed once the opium is withdrawn, but a number of the symptoms of opium withdrawal are due to a rebound effect on the functions of the gastrointestinal system. During withdrawal from heavy opium use, the entire nervous system is upset as it readjusts to its original drug-free state.

Though opium affects the perception of pain, opium users have reported that the drug didn't necessarily stop their pain. Instead they stated that either the severity of the pain was more bearable or that they simply had the feeling of not caring about it any longer. In practice, the pain-killing effect of opium appears to be a combination of some reduction of the pain through the blocking of pain receptors, along with some level of suppression of the anxiety that is a result of the expectation that the person will experience pain. Combining these effects leads to a better ability of an individual to tolerate pain.[9]

Opium, once used as commonly as we now use aspirin, is rarely prescribed today in medicine. The isolation of morphine and the use of newer synthetic narcotics have made its use obsolete. Today's powerful painkillers include oxycodone and hydrocodone. Oxycodone, a morphine derivative, is used today for short-term control of moderately severe pain, such as that from dislocated joints and broken bones. Hydrocodone, similar to codeine, is also used for the relief of moderate pain.

Other Medicinal Preparations of Opium

As well as raw opium and morphine, nineteenth-century physicians prescribed opium or opium extracts in several other preparations.

DOVER'S POWDER

A medicine based on opium that was used extensively in the nineteenth century was Dover's powder. Dover's original formula consisted of an ounce each of opium, ipecac, and sugar of milk (lactose). This powerful concoction was developed in 1732 by Thomas Dover, a British physician, and was used until World War II. It was used as a medicine to induce sweating, for example to treat gout. But, perversely, it was also used to treat cases of night sweats.[10] Dover's powder was administered as forty grains of powder in a glass of white wine. Some physicians prescribed up to seventy grains — a massive dose. The action of Dover's powder was so powerful that even Dover said "some apothecaries have desired their patients to make their wills before they venture upon so large a dose."[11]

LAUDANUM

Physicians soon realized that the alkaloids of opium dissolved more readily in alcohol than in water. One of the popular preparations of opium that took advantage of this was laudanum, a solution of opium in alcohol that was also known as "tincture of opium." Laudanum was used as a medicine to dull pain and to suppress the severe coughing that occurred in cases of consumption (now known as tuberculosis). It was used so commonly as an aid to sleeping that it was nicknamed "sleepy stuff" or "quietness."

One of the widest uses of laudanum was for "female complaints," the delicate Victorian term for menstrual pain and other pelvic aches and pains suffered by women. The use of this drug, however, was not without its perils. As one 1837 medical manual warned, "the habitual use of tinctures and essences is full of danger. Many an invalid has unconsciously formed intemperate habits by means of these seductive medicines."[12] A flowery way to say that addiction could result from its use. The formulation of laudanum was typically a solution of 10 percent opium in alcohol, made by dissolving 2½ ounces of opium powder in a quart of spirits. Laudanum was strong medicine and, in most preparations, twenty-five drops were equal to one grain of opium — also a hefty dose. Medical author Lydia Child commented that "considerably less will affect those unused to it; fifteen drops would probably be the safest medium."[13]

Laudanum as a name for a mixture of opium, alcohol, and other additives dates from 1527. Its invention is generally credited to Swiss scientist and physician Paracelsus (1493–1541; real name Philippus von Hohenheim).[14] Though the ancient Greeks had previously used opium dissolved in wine, Paracelsus dissolved opium in brandy to create a mixture that he named "laudanum." He derived the name from the Latin verb *laudare*, meaning "to praise," because he thought the drink was so effective it was worthy of praise.

Seen as an almost universal medicine, it was used in the treatment of many ailments and was prescribed for such diverse complaints as headaches, toothaches, neuralgia (nerve pain), sore eyes, and coughing. Benjamin Franklin took laudanum regularly for the pain of kidney stones during the last few years of his life.[15]

The popularity of laudanum is usually attributed to seventeenth-century English physician Thomas Sydenham, who is now generally recognized as the founder of clinical medicine. The mixture that Sydenham concocted in the 1660s consisted of two ounces of opium and an ounce each of saffron, cinnamon, and cloves, mixed into a pint of port, sherry, or strong red wine to disguise the bitter taste of the opium. Sydenham prescribed massive doses of laudanum for vomiting and diarrhea. Among other patients, he treated the British regent Oliver Cromwell and the monarch Charles II with it. Sydenham believed so fervently in his mixture that he personally took twenty grams of it every day.

Drinking laudanum became a fashionable pastime for the middle and upper classes. As it was inexpensive and commonly available, vast quantities were sold in England during the 1600s. Addiction was recognized to occur in some individuals, but any resulting problems were generally ignored. The use of laudanum spread quickly to continental Europe, where it was mixed with other exotic ingredients, such as camphor, honey, benzoic acid, and licorice. Fifteen drops of essence of peppermint mixed with fifteen drops of laudanum was recommended to treat convulsions and stomach cramps. Peppermint was often added to medicines to cover any disagreeable taste and to relieve symptoms that were delicately described as "wind, spasmodic pains, nausea, &c."[16]

A typical treatment for a case of diarrhea was to take twenty-five drops of laudanum, and repeat the dose every three, four, or six hours. For dysentery, the patient was told to start with a good dose of Epsom salts as a purgative then to take laudanum, followed by more laudanum six hours later. The process was the same the next day. Another dose of salts, followed by laudanum, then salts again every day. The length of time before ending this sequence was not specified. Presumably the patient stopped when he felt better, though in light of today's medical knowledge this violent treatment of the bowels would seem to be somewhat exhausting.

In cases of "mountain fever," the cure was even more drastic. The patient took a large dose of calomel, then forty drops of laudanum (compare this to the dose of five to fifteen drops of laudanum recommended in Illustration 4–1). Subsequent doses of twenty-five to forty drops of laudanum were repeated in order to keep the patient sedated for the next forty-eight hours — and surely it must have done so. This was followed with more purging and more laudanum.[17] Laudanum diluted with water was recommended for application to fresh wounds, where it would be easily absorbed into the flesh to lessen any associated pain. Similarly, it was applied to sprains and bruises, and poultices of laudanum and hot water were used to treat skin inflammation.[18]

The substance was used to treat the lung ailments of various types common in the West. Mining and smelting towns, such as Blackhawk and Leadville in Colorado, and Butte in Montana, had dense black clouds containing arsenic, lead, and soot permanently hanging over them from the smelters, which led to a collection of lung diseases then called "phthisis."[19] Another serious lung disease was consumption, now known as tuberculosis, or TB. The disease was also known as the "White Plague," because when the disease became sufficiently advanced, the lungs filled with white material similar in appearance to cottage cheese.

In the early 1880s, tuberculosis was still thought to be caused by factors such as diet, lifestyle, the local climate, and the patient's mental state. In reality, tuberculosis was spread by droplets that contained bacteria when a TB patient coughed. Bacteria breathed into the lungs then caused destruction of the tissue. Fever, night sweats, cough, and weight loss followed, with the result eventually being massive lung hemorrhage and death. Various medical therapies, including drinking whiskey, kerosene, or creosote proved to be ineffective. TB patients were treated with opium or laudanum, as these drugs at least relieved their symptoms and suppressed the coughing.

Popular destinations for "lungers," as TB sufferers were nicknamed, were the high, dry mountains or the deserts of the Southwest in Arizona, Colorado, and New Mexico. Tuberculosis seemed to improve with altitude, outdoor living, eating healthy food, fresh air, a dry climate, sunshine, and exercise. Though some relief was often obtained and spontaneous cures did occur, the disease couldn't be truly cured. After German bacteriologist Robert Koch showed in 1882 that the cause of tuberculosis was a specific bacillus called *Mycobacterium tuberculosis*, successful treatments for the disease became possible. Before then, the change in climate felt good and often stopped the cough, but the patient eventually died anyway.

Some doctors also prescribed whiskey to men with consumption, partly to cheer their spirits and partly to provide some relaxation from their gloomy ordeal. As a result, whiskey manufacturers promoted whiskey as a "cure" for tuberculosis — when taken purely for medicinal use, of course. Many "lungers" became alcoholics after reading glowing advertisements in the local paper that promoted whiskey as a positive cure.

One of the best known of the tubercular patients who lived in the Old West was Doc Holliday, the gunfighter friend of Wyatt Earp who participated in the famous shootout at the O.K. Corral on October 26, 1881. According to a Chinese woman who lived in Tombstone, Holliday took opium regularly for his tuberculosis. He also drank heavily to dull the pain of his cough and consumption. He started drinking early in the morning and usually drank around two quarts of whiskey a day. Drink got him going and kept him going in spite of his wracking disease.

In his later years, Wyatt Earp recalled that "perhaps Doc's outstanding peculiarity was the enormous amount of whiskey he could punish. Two and three quarts of liquor a day was not unusual for him, yet I never saw him stagger with intoxication. At times when his tuberculosis was worse than ordinary, or he was under a long-continued physical strain, it would take a pint of whiskey to get him going in the morning, and more than once at the end of a long ride I've seen him swallow a tumbler of neat liquor without batting an eye and fifteen minutes later take a second tumbler of straight whiskey which had no more outward effect on him than the first one. Liquor never seemed to fog him in the slightest, and he was more inclined to fight when getting along on a slim ration than when he was drinking plenty, and was more comfortable, physically."[20]

Lawman and gunfighter Bat Masterson recalled that Holliday "had a mean disposition and an ungovernable temper, and under the influence of liquor was a most dangerous man.... He was hot-headed and impetuous and very much given to both drinking and quarreling, and among men who did not fear him, was very much disliked."[21] One suggested medical treatment that Holliday would probably have approved of if he had known about it was the recommendation that "weakened and consumptive patients are benefited by being washed in warm white rum."[22]

PAREGORIC

Paregoric, also called camphorated tincture of opium, was a weaker form of opium. It consisted of tincture of opium with camphor added. It was used to treat asthma, to soothe teething babies, and to check diarrhea in children. Paregoric was first used as a medicine for asthma by chemistry professor Jakob Le Mort at Leiden University in the Netherlands.[23] The drug was described by one contemporary medical authority as "a pleasant elixir used to allay coughs, and quiet nervous wakeful people."[24] Because the opium in the medicine was effective in suppressing coughs, paregoric was commonly used as a treatment for individuals with tuberculosis and the other common lung diseases of the time.

CODEINE

Codeine, first isolated in 1832, was one of the weaker alkaloids of opium but was chemically a close relative. As such, it also had useful properties as a pain reliever, though it was not as powerful as morphine. Codeine achieved its narcotic effect because about 10 percent of the chemical was metabolized into morphine by the liver. It was used as a cough suppressant and for the pain of toothache.

Opium Marches into the Old West

Common injuries, such as knife cuts and stab wounds, gunshot wounds, broken bones, and mishaps due to animal or wagon accidents, were the leading reasons to require medical attention in the Old West. All of these typically required opium or morphine for treating the resulting pain.

Unfortunately, ranches might be forty or fifty miles from any town and isolated from the nearest doctor. If someone had to travel to summon medical assistance, it might be several days before the messenger and the doctor returned to treat the ill or injured patient. That assumed that the weather and travel conditions were not severe. In addition, doctors' fees were expensive. The charge might be as high as 50¢ a mile to visit a patient on an outlying ranch, and another dollar or two for any prescribed medicine. As a result, many people in the Old West doctored themselves or each other at home.

ON THE EMIGRANT TRAIL

A few of the wagon trains traveling to Oregon and California had a doctor with them, but most medical problems were treated by the emigrants themselves or by wagon masters who had a smattering of medical knowledge that they had picked up by practical application. The typical medicine chest carried on the trail included quinine, opium, whiskey, cathartic pills, castor oil, laudanum, sulfur pills, and morphine.[25] Sometimes the whiskey and quinine were combined to treat or (the pioneers hoped) prevent malaria. Emigrants on the Oregon Trail and soldiers at forts close to malaria mosquitoes' breeding grounds often took a daily dose of three grains of quinine in an ounce of whiskey as a preventative.

ILLUSTRATION 4–2

Recommended Contents of a Medicine Chest When Traveling on the Oregon Trail

Half a drachm of calomel
Half a drachm of blue mass
Eight ounces of paregoric
Four ounces of laudanum

Life was perhaps simpler for the pioneers. The first two were strong cathartics to open the bowels. The second two, besides relieving pain, were opium-based medicines to stop them up again.

The common need for opium or laudanum was to treat the constant diarrhea and dysentery that came with disease or followed long months of a poor diet of salt pork and flapjacks. About 90 percent of fatalities on wagon trains traveling to the West in the 1840s and 1850s came from diseases characterized by diarrhea, with cholera being the leading culprit. It is estimated that over 2,500 emigrants died of cholera during their journey to the California gold fields in 1849 and 1850. Some emigrant groups lost two-thirds of their people during the journey, and the graves of the victims of disease were common alongside the Oregon Trail and the Santa Fe Trail.

Cholera did not strike only on the trail. In California, epidemics of cholera swept many of the gold camps in 1850 and 1852, and again in 1854. Symptoms included diarrhea, vomiting, cramps, thirst, and prostration. During severe outbreaks, at least half of those who contracted the disease died. Cholera could kill with frightening speed. Most victims died within a few days, or even within as little as twenty-four hours. A man might seemingly be in good health in the morning, but by nightfall he might die in convulsions.

In 1832 people believed that cholera attacked those who weakened themselves by overeating, intemperate drinking, and other such habits that were considered to be sinful. Outbreaks came and went with no apparent cause. Doctors noted that the disease seemed to mostly strike in areas where filth and poverty were present, which reinforced their theory that it was a disease associated with degenerate people and their degenerate lifestyles. Contemporary medical thinking was that the disease was carried by miasmas, which was the name for foul or unpleasant gaseous exhalations or terrible odors which typically came from places such as swamps, privies, and garbage heaps. The accepted view was that anyone who breathed these smelly gases was in danger. Among other atmospheric origins, it was believed that the cause might be a lack or excess of electricity in the air — or an excess of nitrogen — or a deficiency of oxygen. Nobody knew. At one time it was even thought that dried beans were responsible for cholera, so many wagon trains discarded them alongside the trail as a safety precaution.

In reality, cholera spread easily in the crowded conditions of the wagon trains and through water supplies contaminated with unseen microorganisms from the passing of previous travelers. Emigrants were told to purify water, but most did not bother and filled their canteens and coffeepots directly from polluted rivers and springs.

There was no cure, no real treatment, and no clear idea of how the disease was spread. Treatments to get rid of the infection were by purging and flushing out the intestines and then inducing sweating through medicines such as Dover's powder to try to perspire out the rest of the toxins. Other people tried cures that ranged from drinking laudanum to dosing themselves with hot pepper sauce.

It was not until 1883 that German physician and bacteriologist Robert Koch identified the cause of cholera as a bacterium that attacked the intestine and then was excreted in human feces. In the early 1900s, attention to the purity of water and food and the control of insects that transmitted diseases began to check outbreaks of typhoid, cholera, yellow fever, and malaria, and death rates from these diseases dropped dramatically.

Opium and laudanum were commonly used to treat intestinal diseases, such as the frequent diarrhea and dysentery caused by contaminated water sources on the Oregon and Santa Fe trails. A typical danger would be this watering hole of murky water that contained fecal bacteria left by horses, oxen, and previous wagon trains. Further contamination of drinking water (such as by the organisms of *Giardia lamblia* or *Cryptosporidium*) would be produced by the animals living in the conical mud-and-stick beaver lodge seen at the far edge of the pond (author's collection).

Opium in the Home

With the high cost of a doctor's visit and the problems of the distance to medical care, illness was typically treated at home. Hospitals in the Old West further spread sicknesses among their patients because people ill with contagious diseases were often placed in beds that were close to each other. Typhus, for example, was nicknamed "hospital fever" or "jail fever" because that was where it was commonly found. When the disease spread among patients, chills, fever, and headache were followed by peeling skin, loss of sight, and eventual death. The few hospitals that were available in the Old West were considered to be places to go to die instead of places to recover health.

In addition to prescription and patent medicines, opium was often one of the ingredients mixed into homemade remedies. Kitchen recipe books and homemakers' manuals of the mid-nineteenth century often contained simple remedies for the pain and fever that accompanied diseases. Some of these cures were based on herbal remedies. Many, however, were based on opium. People took opium for pain, colds, coughs, fevers, pleurisy, and inflammation of the lungs. In what would seem to be overkill, a combination of morphine and cocaine was a home remedy to relieve colds.

In 1872, the Third Annual Report of the Massachusetts State Board of Health reported that "opium and morphia are not only freely used in patent and commercial medicines, but they have now become common ingredients in many family remedies, which were formerly made at home from simple herbs and roots,— such as cough mixtures, tooth washes, lotions, liniments, enemas, poultices, healing tinctures and decoctions."[26]

ILLUSTRATION 4–3

Two Housewives' Recipes with Strong Concentrations of Alcohol and Opium

(1) ALCOHOL: *A recipe for making Hydragogue* Drops*
   Add one gill† of dwarf elder berries to one pint of Holland gin. Let the mixture stand. Shake it once a day until the berries are dissolved. Strain and keep it corked. The dose is from half a teaspoonful to two spoonfuls. With great understatement the author commented that "these drops possess very active properties" (Gardner, *The Domestic Physician and Family Assistant*, 55).

(2) OPIUM: *A recipe for White Poppy Syrup*
   "Take of the capsules, or pods of white poppies, eight ounces, water one pint; infuse them twelve hours; then boil fifteen minutes; then strain, and add sufficient sugar to preserve it. Dose: from 10 to 15 drops. Use: this syrup forms a good anodyne‡ for infants, as it contains less of the narcotic properties of the poppy than when prepared in spirits. It relieves pain, causes sleep, similar in its effects to paregoric" (Gardner, *The Domestic Physician and Family Assistant*, 52).

*A hydragogue was a drug that produced copious watery evacuations of the bowel.
†A gill was an older measure for wine which equals ¼ of a pint.
‡A soothing medicine for relieving or lessening pain.

ACHES AND PAINS

Much of the population of the Old West, like the rest of the country, suffered from various aches and pains which were treated with opium. These conditions were brought on or aggravated by factors such as cowboys sleeping on damp ground in the open and working in the frigid winters of the Rocky Mountains; stress on muscles due to working in cold, wet environments such as those encountered trapping beaver or in Western mines; carrying heavy packs and loads in the military; or wrestling railroad ties and rails into place for a living. What was then commonly called "miner's rheumatism" was probably what would now be called osteoarthritis, or degenerative wear and tear in the legs, arms, and back that produces aching and painful joints.

Injuries and accidents that resulted in pain of various degrees were part of the way of life of the Old West. Cowboys received sprains, fractures, and dislocations from being thrown from horses, burns from branding irons, wounds and broken bones from saloon fights, and injuries from being dragged by livestock or gored by cattle. Gunfighters used morphine and laudanum to relieve the pain of gunshot and knife wounds. Railroad workers were subject to a variety of accidents. In 1900, more than 50,000 railroad men were injured in derailments, train crashes, by being burned, by exploding boilers, and from careless operation of equipment that cost workers hands, fingers, and even whole limbs. Miners were frequently blown up or injured in accidents in the mines.

Another source of pain was surgery. Before general anesthetics such as chloroform and ether were developed in the 1840s to put a patient to sleep, surgeons loaded their patients up on whiskey, laudanum, or opium to render the patient semiconscious before surgery. This induced muscular relaxation and provided at least some measure of relief from pain.[27] The most important skill of a surgeon was speed, essential in order to spare the patient from protracted pain during an operation. Besides, assistants could hold a patient still for only a few minutes during the agony of being cut open. A skilled surgeon could perform an amputation to treat a gunshot wound in an arm or leg in two or three minutes. After the introduction of general anesthetics, speed was no longer such a concern and doctors were able to take more time to operate.

Surgery was not always able to effect a cure. One of the worst injuries in the Old West was a gunshot wound to the abdomen, which was a not uncommon outcome of a gunfight. Wounds such as this were not always immediately fatal but frequently became infected, causing the victim to linger in agony for several days. As well as damaging the intestines and releasing the intestinal contents into the abdominal cavity, the heavy bullet from a .44 or .45 caliber revolver carried deep into the wound dust, dirt, fragments of clothing, grease from the bullet, and other debris. The result was that wounds that punctured the stomach or small intestine were nearly always eventually fatal. Wounds that hit the large intestine did not have a much better outcome and were fatal about 90 percent of the time. With this knowledge, the only course of action for a doctor was to try to stop any obvious bleeding and to dose the unfortunate victim heavily with laudanum to try to stem the anguish until his eventual demise.

During the famous gunfight that took place at the O.K. Corral in Tombstone, Arizona, on October 26, 1881, Billy Clanton was shot in the belly close to his navel. When a doctor arrived, there was nothing he could do but inject morphine next to the wound to try to relieve Clanton's agony. Billy died about ten minutes later.[28]

THE CIVIL WAR AND THE ARMY

Though popular legends of the American Civil War call up images of men dying bravely after being blown to bits on the battlefield, the reality was somewhat more sobering. Of the 359,528 Union soldiers who died during the war, only 110,070 died as a result of the fighting. More than twice as many, or a horrific 224,586, died directly as a result of various diseases such as dysentery. Accidents and miscellaneous causes claimed the lives of the remaining 24,872. The Confederate army suffered similar numbers of casualties. Fighting claimed the lives of 94,000 men, as opposed to 164,000 who died as a result of disease.[29] Army records show that men became ill due to such diseases as malaria, pneumonia, scurvy, tuberculosis, typhoid, typhus, scarlet fever, and yellow fever. Records further show that 5,825,480 soldiers reported for sick call in the Union army during the Civil War. Diarrhea or dysentery accounted for 1,585,236 cases with 37,794 deaths. Malaria accounted for 49,871 cases with 4,059 deaths attributed directly to the disease. Typhoid accounted for 73,368 cases with 27,050 deaths caused by the disease.[30]

Injury and illness during the Civil War resulted in two common conditions that required the extensive use of opium. One was the control of pain. Opium and morphine were used to treat pain in the wounded and for relief of pain during surgical operations to treat battle injuries. If extensive wounds included fractures of the legs or arms, or the associated nerves, blood vessels, or soft tissue, amputation was typically required. The soft lead of the recently developed Minié bullet created tremendous damage by ripping flesh and shattering and splintering bones when it hit. Chloroform was used for surgery about 75 percent of the time, followed by opium for pain control, given either as a pill or dusted into wounds, even though dusting was not particularly effective. Morphine was also used to calm patients and suppress their pain in field hospitals.

The Civil War was the first time that opiates received widespread use in treating pain, dysentery, and fatigue, as well as such diverse illnesses as the typhus and typhoid that often broke out due to overcrowding and poor sanitary conditions. The wounded were usually given an opium pill (containing ⅛ to ¼ grain of morphine) because they came to expect it. Pills were the most convenient form in which to store, transport, and administer opium. During the Civil War, over 10,000,000 pills of opium were dispensed to troops in the Union army, along with 2,000,000 ounces of powder and tincture of opium. Morphine was administered as a powder or a pill or by hypodermic injection.[31]

As a result of this extensive use of opium and morphine, many of the veterans who had been wounded during the fighting and discharged after the Civil War were addicted to opium. Narcotic addiction was so widespread that it became known as "old soldier's disease" or "army disease." This abuse also led to an increase in the general consumption of opium after the Civil War as these men tried to cope with their addiction. Opium had another, grimmer use during the Civil War. In an early form of triage, many of the soldiers who were mortally wounded were left to die on the battlefield if nothing could be done to save them. They were given opium and water to ease their pain and suffering, then simply abandoned to die.[32]

The other major condition that required the use of opium during the Civil War was the constant diarrhea and dysentery (bloody flux) that plagued both armies. Dysentery and malaria were the most common fatal diseases among soldiers, and opium and ipecac were the most common medicines used to treat the condition. Curiously, diarrhea and dysentery may have prevented the killing of some soldiers on both sides. Dysentery was so prevalent and so debilitating that there was an unwritten gentlemen's agreement among the soldiers of both armies that they would not fire on any man who was squatting in the bushes.[33]

One Confederate surgeon remembered how he carried a ball of blue mass in one pocket of his trousers and a ball of opium in the other at sick call. "Blue mass" was the name for the large blue-colored lumps of calomel (mercurous chloride) that was administered for a variety of bowel complaints and acted as a purgative of heroic proportions. The physician recalled that "all complainants were asked the same question, 'How are your bowels?' If they were open, I administered opium; if they were shut I gave a plug of blue mass."[34]

Later, during the Indian wars in the West that lasted from 1865 to 1890, chronic diarrhea and its treatment with opium continued to be a problem due to inadequate sanitation and poor nutrition at army posts across the West. Typical expeditions into the field against the Indians took with them bandages, splints, whiskey, opium, morphine, Dover's powder, quinine, and cathartic pills.

A related problem was that not much was known about camp sanitation. Purification of water was not practiced and hand washing was minimal. Men would relieve themselves wherever and whenever they felt the need. Disease was further spread by flies, mosquitoes, lice, and rats. Often the water supply was located too close to pit toilets and contaminated water contributed to typhoid and other diseases. Typhoid was also known by the grandiose name of "malignant bilious fever."[35]

Poor cooking and eating habits, such as the constant diet of food fried in grease and a lack of green vegetables, contributed to extensive scurvy and constant diarrhea. One military surgeon claimed, perhaps not too inaccurately, that "beans killed more than bullets."[36]

DENTAL CARE

Dental care was minimal in the Old West. Dentistry was primitive and consisted mostly of tooth extractions by a dentist — if one was available — or by a doctor. If neither of these was available, a blacksmith might be pressed into service because he had pliers and pincers that could be used for extractions. Typically, little attention was paid to the teeth in the way of preventive care until something started to be painful; then the offending tooth was pulled. Because of the pain involved, a visit to the dentist was often delayed until too late and extraction became essential. Cowboys commonly used this as an excuse to drink copious amounts of whiskey before and after visiting a dentist.

Extraction consisted of holding the patient down with one knee while yanking, prying, and twisting the bad tooth out of its socket. The better dentists put opium into the cavity of a decayed tooth to dull the nerve before pulling it out or gave their patients some opium to quiet them down. Patients might be ambivalent about its use. The small amount of opium used to treat a toothache produced relief from pain but also resulted in constipation and a deeper than usual sleep.

In the Western motion picture *Bite the Bullet* (1975), "Mexican" (Mario Arteaga) follows the recommendation of a bartender and uses a mixture of heroin pills and whiskey to dull his severe toothache. That combination should certainly have made him oblivious to pain.

Alcohol as Medicine

Alcohol is a drug, though many people do not realize that it fits this definition. It has been used as a medicine as far back as recorded history. In fact, old-timers in the West would have appreciated a quote from one older translation of *The Arabian Nights* which said wine "disperseth stone and gravel from the kidneys and strengtheneth the viscera and banisheth care, and moveth to generosity and preserveth health and digestion; it conserveth the body, expelleth disease from the joints, purifieth the frame of corrupt humors, engendereth cheerfulness, gladdeneth the heart of man and keepeth up the natural heat; it contracteth the bladder, enforceth the liver and removeth obstructions, reddeneth the cheeks, cleareth away maggots from the brain and deferreth gray hairs."[37]

In medieval Europe, distilled spirits were widespread and called by the

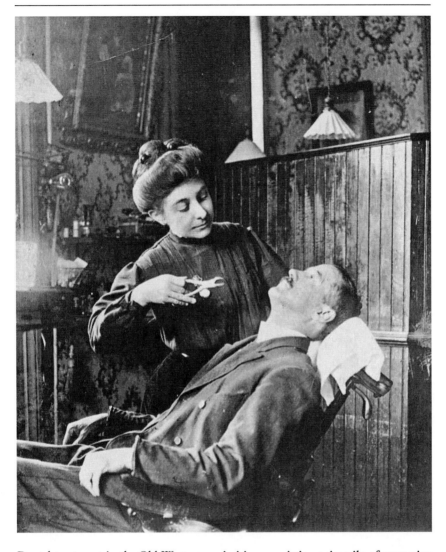

Dental treatment in the Old West was primitive, consisting primarily of extracting teeth when the pain became unbearable. Before the use of anesthetics, the better dentists put opium into a cavity to dull the nerve before extraction, or gave the patient opium or laudanum to temporarily dull his wits. Cowboys used visits to the dentist as an excuse to drink copious quantities of whiskey before and after the experience (author's collection).

Latin name of *aqua vitae*, or "the water of life." They were dispensed as a valuable medicine for "curing" various diseases. As far back as the 1400s the use of alcoholic spirits was well known as a pain killer and primitive anesthetic during and after surgery. In the Old West of the nineteenth century, alcohol in the form of whiskey was popularly prescribed to treat many diseases. Medicinal whiskey was known by the grand Latin name of *Spiritus frumenti* (spirits of corn). Medicinal brandy was known by the similar magnificent title of *Spiritus vini gallici* (spirits of French wine). Strong spirits were used to treat ailments such as influenza, malaria, childbirth fever, typhoid, typhus, cholera, dog bites, snakebites, and diabetes. Whiskey was also used as an anesthetic and an antiseptic to clean wounds due to its high alcohol content.

It was considered to be the standard cure for those with wasting diseases to build up their strength. Conversely, if children grew too fast, alcohol was often given in medicinal doses in the belief that it would slow down their excessive growth.[38] In a strange quirk of logic, the medicinal administration of whiskey was sometimes used as a cure for alcoholism. A typical prescription was for *Spiritus frumenti* to be administered as a tablespoon of medicine daily. Whiskey might also be administered via the other common method of the time as a enema, so that the alcohol could be rapidly absorbed into the bloodstream via the mucus membranes of the rectum. Whiskey was also administered by hypodermic injection, which would ensure an immediate rise in blood-alcohol level and rapid sedation.

Typical were the treatments given in the case of a nineteen-year-old youth named Rufus who had crushed his left leg in an accident on November 21, 1889. The attending physician ordered *Spiritus frumenti* every hour. By November 24, Rufus was well enough for surgery and had most of his leg amputated. After the surgery, the patient's pulse was up to 150, so the doctor gave an enema of whiskey. By November 25, the prescription was upped to drinking half a glass of whiskey. Apparently this treatment was successful, as Rufus was up and walking around the house on crutches by December 25.[39]

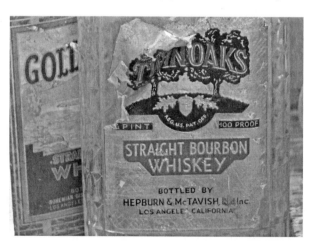

Bourbon whiskey was the beverage of choice among the hard drinkers of the Old West. A large variety of whiskeys was available, either as a legitimate product shipped from the East or the West Coast, or home-made booze concocted in the back room of a saloon and poured into bottles with fancy labels to fool inexperienced drinkers (author's collection).

As well as being used by itself, alcohol was a favorite mixing additive for medicines.

Whiskey and wine were commonly used as a base for opium-containing medicines. Whiskey was used on both sides of the fence. As well as being a treatment for patients, doctors themselves used it. With the long hours, fatigue, and hardship involved in treating patients in widely scattered rural areas, many frontier doctors drank for relaxation. Some reportedly had a glass of whiskey to relax and steady their nerves before starting an operation.

One of the odder uses for alcohol as a medical cure turned out to be a circular type of treatment. In 1780, a physician from Edinburgh named John Brown developed what he called the Brunonian system. According to this theory, Brown proposed that all diseases could be treated as one of two types: under-excitement or over-excitement of the system. If the system was under-excited, Brown prescribed alcohol in the form of wine or brandy, which he felt were stimulants. If the attending physician felt that the patient was over-excited, Brown recommended bleeding, purging, and emetics. Naturally, after this type of vigorous treatment for over-excitement, the patient was usually exhausted and so his behavior was considered to be under-excited. Alcohol was then prescribed to act as a stimulant, which tended to put the patient back into the over-excited category, thus starting the entire cycle all over again. Ironically, Brown died in 1788 as a result of his own self-treatment with an overdose of opium, which he believed to be a stimulant.[40]

CHAPTER FIVE

"Those Heathen Chinee"

Opium for medicinal purposes accompanied the pioneers and settlers who decided to journey to the West to seek a new life. As discussed in the last chapter, the drug was employed widely for the control of pain and to relieve the symptoms of dysentery. Opium as a medicine was primarily ingested by mouth as a powder or pill, or drunk as laudanum.

In the Old West, smoking opium for recreational purposes was nonexistent in the 1840s. The story of how smoking opium emerged as a popular recreational pastime and opium dens subsequently appeared in most towns across the Old West is inextricably linked to the history of how Chinese immigrants came to the West Coast of the United States.[1]

Smoking opium in the Old West started among the Chinese population in California. From about 1850 to about 1870, it remained primarily a Chinese habit. Then as Chinese workers left the worked-out placer mines of California for the gold fields of Nevada during the 1870s, smoking opium spread eastwards from California, and Chinatowns appeared in the new bonanza mining towns, such as Virginia City and Carson City. Though still considered to be a Chinese vice, opium smoking spread to the denizens of the white underworld such as pimps, prostitutes, gamblers, and criminals. The first white man recorded to have smoked opium was reportedly a gambler in San Francisco named Clendenyn, who hit the pipe in 1868.[2]

The anti-opium attitudes that developed during the late 1880s and the 1890s were partially inspired by the anti–Chinese attitudes that proliferated during the intervening years. Opium, which was also called "yellow booze" at the time, was used as an excuse for persecuting the Chinese. The widespread, but unreasonable, propaganda that created a morbid fear of opium dens among Americans was used to further the impression that the Chinese were "undesirables."

In all fairness, not all Chinese were addicted to opium and the majority of those who smoked it were probably only social users. Estimates are that between 15 and 30 percent of the Chinese in California were addicted to opium.[3] Smoking it was limited to some degree because it was relatively expensive. The opium habit cost a Chinese addict about 50¢ a day. To put this in perspective, a Chinese laborer typically only made about $1 a day.

The Lure of Gum Shan

Smoking opium in the Old West started with the mass immigration of Chinese laborers into the American West during the second half of the nineteenth century. The primary reason they left China was to escape the overwhelming conditions of famine and political unrest that had become widespread during the 1840s after the First Opium War.

In spite of the Treaty of Nanking of 1842, tensions continued to increase in China. Crop failures, high taxes, economic dislocation, and antigovernment sentiment stirred up urban riots and resulted in continued social discontent that caused many workers to emigrate from China. Thousands tried to escape famine and economic hardships. Though the Chinese were not allowed to emigrate, the Treaty of Nanking allowed foreigners to recruit Chinese laborers to work overseas. Most of those coming to the United States came from the coastal areas of China, particularly around the poverty-wracked province of Guangdong and its port city of Canton. Conditions were so bad in the villages of the Pearl River Delta in Guangdong Province that most of the young men left to find better working conditions overseas.

Most of the Chinese who initially came to America worked as low-cost laborers in the gold diggings during the California gold rush of 1849. Many more came later as construction workers for the building of the transcontinental railroad during the 1860s. Chinese workers were also important in California fishing and agriculture industries, working in wineries, dairies, vegetable fields, fruit orchards, and canneries. Other Chinese immigrants who could not find work in the mines or on various railroads often found employment as laundrymen, cooks, gardeners, or woodcutters.

Previously established trade ties caused widespread emigration of the Chinese to the United States. America, however, was not the only destination for Chinese men seeking a better life. Many Chinese workers went as contract laborers to plantations owned by the British in countries such as Jamaica, Trinidad, and Borneo to replace black slaves. Emigration also took place at the same time from China to South Africa, Australia, South America, and Canada. New Zealand, for example, had a sudden gold-mining boom that was similar to that in California. Mining communities such as Arrowtown, near present-day Queenstown on the South Island, had a short-lived community of eager Chinese laborers in the 1860s trying to scratch a living out of the dirt and gravel.

Many Chinese in the late 1840s and early 1850s were attracted in particular to America by news of the 1849 California gold rush and stories that all a man had to do was pick up the gold nuggets that were lying around on the ground. As a result of this erroneous vision of easy wealth in the American West, the Chinese called America *Gum Shan* (also sometimes written in English as *Gam Saan*), which translated as "Gold Mountain." For poverty-stricken workers in China, this image represented a dream of a better life and the riches to be made in the California mining camps. In 1852 alone 30,000 Chinese left Hong Kong for San Francisco to work as laborers in the placer claims. Many were young men who were sent originally to augment the family income by working in the United States. They were expected to return the money they earned to their family in China. The men were loosely categorized as "coolies," which was a generic Oriental name that was applied to a native worker who performed unskilled labor for very little pay.

These Chinese immigrants generally stayed in the American West rather than migrating eastwards because manufacturers and other employers in the East had already found plenty of cheap labor among the immigrants flooding the East Coast from Europe. The 1870 census showed that of the Chinese who lived in the continental United States, 99.4 percent of them lived in the Western states and territories with 78 percent in California. Most of these men did not plan to stay in the United States. They assumed that they would make their fortunes by collecting the gold lying around in the land of opportunity and then would soon return home to their families and China with plenty of money. The common dream was to purchase a small farm or other business in their homeland and live out the rest of their days in relative financial comfort. The reality was that most of them ended up as indentured servants in America. Their passage to California was paid for in advance by Chinese merchants who acted as intermediaries and moneylenders. The catch was that the money advanced to cover the journey had to be repaid with a high rate of interest attached, which has been reported to have been anywhere from 4 to 8 percent per month.

Most of the men were simple farmers who had become deeply in debt to the merchants who had financed their passage. These men were easily persuaded to sign contracts of employment that bound them to servitude for a number of years. If the men couldn't be persuaded or tricked into signing labor contracts, they might be simply abducted and unwillingly put onboard a ship bound for California. Perversely, at the same time, sailors were being

Opposite: A large number of Chinese immigrants flooded the West Coast between 1850 and 1890 to escape severe economic conditions in China. Many of the men were employed in the gold mines of California, on the Central Pacific section of the transcontinental railroad, and in the agricultural and fishing industries of California (Library of Congress).

VOL. XXI.—No. 1049.] NEW YORK, SATURDAY, FEBRUARY 3, 1877. [WITH A SUPPLEMENT. PRICE TEN CENTS.

Entered according to Act of Congress, in the Year 1877, by Harper & Brothers, in the Office of the Librarian of Congress, at Washington.

CHINESE IMMIGRANTS AT THE SAN FRANCISCO CUSTOM-HOUSE.—[See Page 91.]

kidnapped in San Francisco to crew ships headed for the Orient in a process known as "shanghaiing" because of their destination, which was often the port city of Shanghai in China.

In China, farmers and other unskilled workers formed the basis of a brisk export business conducted by Chinese agents and American ship captains. Because kidnapped Chinese men were often imprisoned during the journey by ship in quarters that resembled pens used for pigs, this international trafficking in people became known as the "pig trade." Kidnapped Chinese women were sometimes part of the "pig trade" cargo. Opium smuggling, on the other hand, was known as the "poison trade."

During the sea voyage, the poorer immigrants were treated like cattle. Chinese men leaving Hong Kong by ship were frequently painted with the letter P, C, or S to designate their destination. These initials stood for Peru, California, or the Sandwich Islands (now Hawaii).

The food and living conditions on many of the ships during the passage to San Francisco were appalling, usually with as many coolies jammed onboard as the captain could possibly manage. Sometimes as many as 500 were crammed into the hold of a single ship and the men had hardly enough room to move around or lie down. Perhaps with little exaggeration the *San Francisco Examiner* of August 28, 1888, commented: "The space assigned to each Chinaman is about as much as is usually occupied by one of the flat boxes in a milliner's store. It would be a strange sight to one not accustomed to it to see a framework of shelves, not eighteen inches apart, filled with Chinese." On some ships, as many as 40 percent of the Chinese passengers died during the sea voyage as a result of poor food, overcrowded conditions, the spread of diseases, and a general lack of sanitation.[4]

Once the coolies reached California's supposed golden shores, they usually did not find the idyllic working conditions that they had anticipated. They were paid poorly and treated badly. As a result, many of these men ended up working as virtual slaves until they were able to pay back the loan for their passage — if they ever could. At the same time, many of the men tried to save money to send home to their families or to eventually return to China. But saving money was not as easy as it sounded, as a large part of the workers' wages went to pay off the exorbitant finance fees for their travel from China. The typical cost for the passage by ship to San Francisco was between $40 and $60, paid in advance by the lender as a loan. Though this does not sound like a large amount of money today, the typical coolie was paid only minimal wages and often had living expenses that exceeded his income. Though a few of the Chinese immigrants were convicts being expelled from the country and a few had been kidnapped by unscrupulous ship captains, roughly 95 percent of the men ended up as voluntary indentured workers trying to repay their loans. In spite of the poor working conditions, though,

Chinese men were in high demand as cooks and servants. It was theoretically possible for most of them to eventually work off their debt, though it might take as long as five or ten years.

More than any other immigrant group to the United States, the Chinese in California retained their own customs and their own national identity. They lived together, worked together, and followed their own forms of recreation in tightly knit Chinese communities that became known across the country as "Chinatowns." To supply their specialized needs, the coolies were soon followed by Chinese traders, who provided them with traditional Chinese food, opium, and, later, Chinese women. Most Chinatowns became well-known for their opium, gambling, and prostitution. (An early slang name for opium was "hop." This name came from the colloquial Cantonese *nga pin* [pronounced "ha peen"], which literally means "bird droppings."[5] As a result, Chinatowns, or at least the area of them that had the opium dens, had related names. The Chinese section of Denver was nicknamed Hop Alley. In Tombstone, it was called Hoptown.)

When the first Chinese arrived in California they preferred to live in close proximity to other Chinese because of their mutual customs and language. Later arrivals preferred to band together in Chinatowns because of violence against the Chinese, thus creating mutual aid and protection. In some cities, for example San Francisco, segregation was later forced upon them and Chinese were not allowed to live outside local Chinatowns. Even though most Chinatowns were crowded slums, this seclusion into an ethnic community may have provided some unrealized benefits for the Chinese inhabitants because, in general, they stayed healthier than the whites. Part of the reason for this may have been that by living in concentrated Chinese communities they were not exposed to the many deadly diseases such as tuberculosis, smallpox, cholera, typhoid, and dysentery that were rampant among the predominantly white population of the mining camps.

Another factor in the better health of the Chinese may have been that their typical diet of rice, seafood, and green vegetables was much healthier than the constant inevitable potatoes and beans and greasy pork and salt beef that the whites ate. The Chinese diet of vegetables, such as gourds, pumpkins, and squash, was alien to the California miners but contained plenty of vitamin C. As a result of this diet, the Chinese seldom suffered from scurvy. By contrast, it has been estimated that perhaps 10,000 white men died from scurvy during the California gold rush, half of them in 1848 and 1849.[6] A third factor was that the Chinese drank hot tea, which was made with water that had been boiled first, thus killing off most of the bacteria that were in the streams and lakes that the American miners drank from.

Among the customs and habits that the Chinese considered to be commonplace and brought with them was smoking opium, which provided them with an escape from the drudgery of their daily lives. Opium was an integral part of the lifestyle of the coolies and formed one of their few forms of relaxation. Smoking opium relieved the muscular aches and pains of the hard labor required in the mines or working on the railroad. It also served to produce forgetfulness and temporary relief from the homesickness and mental stress of being in a strange land. As the Chinese were stuck in a foreign country with very few Chinese women, opium also served to lower the level of sexual desire of the predominantly male immigrant population. As a result of these somewhat dubious benefits, many of the men who did not previously smoke opium took it up after they arrived in California.

Smoking opium gradually spread to the white population in areas where the Chinese had settled, then eventually moved eastwards with them into the rest of the West. As the immigrants moved, the opium followed. As the Chinese continued toward the East, they congregated with members of their own race, particularly in large cities. By 1876, a Chinatown had even been established in New York.

The First Arrivals in the Old West

A San Francisco newspaper noted that the first Chinese to arrive on the West Coast were two men and a woman who arrived from Canton on the brig *American Eagle* in February of 1848.[7] They immediately left for the gold fields. By the end of 1848, seven Chinese were known to be living in California.[8] Then the numbers started to grow. In 1849, a total of 323 Chinese arrived in California, and 450 landed in 1850.

During the first two years of the gold rush, most of the immigrants traveled straight on to the gold diggings after they arrived in California. By 1851, however, some of the immigrants started to settle in San Francisco after they arrived, rather than going directly to the gold fields. In addition, San Francisco's Chinese population started to grow with those who had little success in the gold fields or who had been treated as racial outcasts and had returned to where they could become part of a familiar Chinese community. Some of the other Chinese men who had come as miners or railroad workers, but couldn't find employment in these occupations, ended up working at menial tasks in San Francisco — cooks, errand boys, gardeners. Other, more entrepreneurial, Chinese businessmen set up small businesses and shops, such as laundries, restaurants, bakeries, and tailor shops.

As the major port on the West Coast, San Francisco was the entry point for most of the Chinese immigrants. In 1852, a wave of probably 20,000 more Chinese arrived in San Francisco. By then the Chinese population of California was estimated to be approximately 22,000, most of whom were scattered across the gold country of the Sierra Nevadas. By 1870, the U.S. census showed that the Chinese population of California was 71,328, with approximately half of them living in San Francisco.

During the 1880s, approximately 25,000 Chinese (10 percent of the city's population) lived in San Francisco's Chinatown, which covered more than twelve city blocks in the area of Nob Hill. In 1889 an official count showed the number of Chinese in San Francisco to be 45,000, of whom approximately one-third were women and children.

San Francisco was not the only city in California that attracted Chinese residents. Permanent Chinese communities were founded near Sacramento in the 1860s with agricultural field workers from China, and, in the 1870s, Chinese workers were widely employed in the citrus groves and packing houses of southern California.

Chinese Women, Slavery, and Prostitution

As more and more Chinese men came to the West to work in the gold fields and on the railroads, the ratio of Chinese men to Chinese women became highly disproportionate. In the early California gold camps there might be 2,000 Chinese men for every Chinese woman. The few Chinese women who were in the early gold camps were nearly all prostitutes and, as a result, the white miners assumed that all Chinese women were prostitutes. Of the Chinese women in San Francisco, a few were merchants' wives and some were servants. By 1880, Chinese men still outnumbered women in the Chinese community of Denver by thirty-to-one. A further factor in the gender imbalance was that Chinese women were forbidden by Chinese law to emigrate.[9] Besides this, they were unwilling to leave their homeland because China was a male-dominated society and traditional Chinese beliefs kept women at home. As a result, male workers left their women and families in China to seek better jobs and then sent part of their wages home to support them.

Because of the shortage of Chinese females in California, a large traffic in women arose. Single Chinese men wanted women of their own race. The owners of plantations in the South and the Caribbean who employed Chinese men as field hands under conditions of virtual slave labor wanted women so that the Chinese men would stay and have children and would thereby decrease the need to import more workers. To serve these demands, women were "procured" in China — which essentially means kidnapped — and shipped to the West Coast to serve as prostitutes. Most ended up in San Francisco, or were taken to the mining supply centers of Sacramento or Stockton and then shipped into the gold diggings in the mountains. The 1860 census showed that there were almost 450 Chinese women living in the camps around the southern mines of the Sierra Nevada mountains. Little is known about these women as there are no firsthand accounts that accurately document their experiences.

Chinese women were obtained by a variety of methods. Some were lured with the promise of marriage. Many were told that they were going to marry a rich Chinese man or a wealthy respectable Chinese merchant when they arrived in America. Others were sold by their families and brought to California with the understanding that they would be able to live their own lives freely when they arrived. Some were young girls who were purchased to be "servants" or "concubines-in-training," careers which were considered acceptable to the parents. In reality, when they arrived in America, women sold into bondage by their families had to redeem their selling price by working as prostitutes.

Young Chinese women were easy to obtain. When southern China erupted with famine and fighting as a result of the Taiping Rebellion of 1850, conditions became so bad that many families were willing to sell their daughters to slave traders. Daughters were perceived to be a disadvantage because they were less productive as workers than sons and, by tradition, they couldn't carry on the family line and name. Poor families with several young daughters and who were considering infanticide or abandonment of one of them often sold a daughter instead.[10] Selling young Chinese girls was seen as a way to help their families financially. Selling them to procurers brought in money and, at the same time, eliminated another mouth that had to be fed at home.

Chinese men working abroad provided a ready market for women, so the illicit trade was elaborate and lucrative, and some of these women were sold as wives to rich Chinese merchants in California. A good-looking young Chinese woman might bring $1,800 in gold when sold in San Francisco in the 1880s.[11] These women were typically sold on the streets of Virginia City, Montana, for $400 to $600.[12] According to the *Montana Post* of April 20, 1867, "[these women] are bought and sold like hogs, the religion of their country pronouncing them to be without souls, and created only for the use of man."

If the attractive women were not sold as brides to rich Chinese merchants, they might be sold to high-class brothels. Here they were dressed in elaborate and expensive clothes, and they worked in exotic Chinese surroundings of teak, bamboo, and silk. The unlucky ones ended up as crib girls, forced to sell themselves to anyone for 25¢.

Chinese women were needed for the Chinese men in the gold camps. White prostitutes would not accept Chinese men as customers for fear their white customers would boycott them.[13] The reverse was not true, however, and white men visited Chinese prostitutes. Chinese women turned out to be a novelty for whites, as few had ever even seen a Chinese woman before and many were interested in the unfounded rumor that Chinese women were anatomically different from white women. Accepting white customers, however, turned out to be a problem for the women because Chinese men believed that the ultimate degradation for a Chinese woman was to have sex with a Caucasian man. As a result, the best Chinese brothels in San Francisco catered only to Chinese men. Chinese prostitutes who catered to whites were considered to be the lowest of the low and could usually be had for as little as 25¢. These women were called *baak haak chai* in Chinese, which means "one hundred men's wives."[14] Another, more vulgar, name was *loungei*, which literally means "woman always holding her legs up."

The close ties of different types of vice led to opium dens locating in the red light district of a town and opium being supplied in houses of prostitution, in particular the high-class Chinese brothels of the West Coast. In addition, many of the women were deliberately addicted to opium in order to tie them to the house and their pimps.

Most historians attribute the first Chinese prostitution in San Francisco to a Chinese prostitute named Ah-choi (variously spelled as Ah Toy or Achoy), who has been credited with importing female slaves from China to the American West. She arrived in San Francisco in 1849 at age 20. By 1850 she had seven other Chinese women working for her. By 1852 she was involved in the immigration of several hundred Chinese prostitutes. By 1859, she had disappeared into obscurity and she died in 1928 in San Jose, California.[15]

In gold-rush San Francisco the estimated prostitute population was three hundred, of which ninety were Caucasian, seventy-five were Chinese and the remainder were of various ethnic descents.[16] Some of the other mining towns had different ratios. In 1880, twenty-eight of the fifty-six prostitutes in Helena, Montana, were Chinese. Despite an influx of prostitutes by 1877, they were still mostly Chinese.[17] By contrast, the largest Asian brothel in Virginia City, Nevada, in 1875, had only six women.[18] In Denver, there were probably no more than four or five Chinese women in the cribs at any one time.[19]

The Chinese Exclusion Act of 1882 caused Chinese men further problems, as no Chinese women who were not married to a man already in America or who had not been born to domiciled merchants were allowed to enter the United States. Families of Chinese men outside these definitions were denied entry and single men were not allowed to send for Chinese wives.

The Railroads

One of the largest importers and employers of Chinese labor was the Central Pacific Railroad. The Central Pacific was organized as the western half of the transcontinental railroad that was authorized in 1862 by President Lincoln to connect the East to the West Coast. The Central Pacific was authorized to build eastwards from San Francisco and meet the Union Pacific, which was simultaneously building west from Omaha, Nebraska.

As the lengthening tracks of the Central Pacific left the central valley of California and penetrated the Sierra Nevadas, the task of construction became difficult and hazardous due to rockslides, avalanches, and bitterly cold temperatures. The common laborers, who were mostly Irish, became reluctant to expose themselves to risk in these harsh working conditions. These men also tended to be somewhat unreliable, as they had a tendency to drink too much after payday and disappear from the job without warning.

Furthermore, railroad officials soon realized that many of the men they hired for construction jobs in cities such as San Francisco had no intention of working for the railroad. The men signed up simply as a way to obtain free transportation to the end of the railroad line, then immediately hustled off in the direction of the gold camps. Typically, out of every 2,000 men who signed up to work for the railroad, only a couple of hundred were still there after a week. The final straw for the Central Pacific occurred in 1865 when a group of Irish workers threatened to go on strike over more pay and what they perceived to be dangerous working conditions.

One of the partners in the railroad, Charles Crocker, considered hiring Mexican laborers or freed slaves from the South, but couldn't find an adequate

Chinese immigrants were capable and hard-working on the transcontinental railroad. They excelled at blasting out tunnels with black powder, and later with nitroglycerine. Much of the heavy labor of pushing the railroad over and through the Sierra Nevada mountains was performed using only shovels and handcarts. This photograph, taken at Tunnel No. 8 on the Central Pacific side in 1867 shows a young Chinese man taking tea to other workers in kegs carried on each end of a yoke. The kegs were originally used for storing black powder, then were washed clean before transporting the hot tea (Library of Congress).

number of willing men to replace the strikers. Finally, Crocker told the construction foreman for the railroad, James Strobridge, to hire a group of fifty unskilled Chinese laborers from the nearby mining town of Auburn, California. Strobridge was skeptical, but to his surprise, the little Chinese men turned out to be excellent workers. Much of what they had to do was completed with only picks, shovels, handcarts, and mules. The small Chinamen dug and packed the railbed essentially by hand and carried away the surplus dirt in baskets and wheelbarrows.

The Chinese quickly became skilled in work that required black powder explosives (also known as "blasting powder" or "giant powder"), such as blasting tunnels through solid rock and blowing down overhanging cliff faces.[20] Dynamite wasn't used on the Central Pacific. When black powder proved to be inadequate to complete the tunnels, Strobridge turned to the newly developed explosive nitroglycerine. Workers were lowered over the face of a cliff in baskets to the work area, where they drilled holes in the rock, set the charges, and lit the fuses. Unfortunately, not all of them were hauled back up quickly enough and a number of them were killed in the resulting explosions.

Overall, though, the novel experiment of using Chinese workers was so successful that Strobridge hired as many Chinese as he could recruit until he had basically emptied the Chinatowns of Sacramento and San Francisco. When Strobridge couldn't find enough Chinese workers in California, the railroad sent agents to recruit laborers directly from China. By the spring of 1866, the Central Pacific had 8,000 Chinese working on the railroad. This comprised about 80 percent of the entire workforce.[21]

It turned out that the use of Chinese workers had other merits. Though the men spent their free time gambling at Chinese games, such as fan-tan and other games of chance, they did not go to whorehouses and generally drank only tea. These habits contrasted sharply with the workers of the Union Pacific Railroad, on the east side of the Rocky Mountains, who spent their leisure time in saloons and brothels in the company of gamblers, saloonkeepers, conmen, thieves, pimps, and prostitutes. These tough Union Pacific railroad construction workers were noted for brawling, gambling, boozing, consorting with wild women, and being involved in frequent fights and killings.

One custom that the Chinese workers on the Central Pacific brought with them was smoking opium for relaxation. Opium smoking was acceptable because it was generally restricted to Sunday, which was the laborers' day off. Strobridge reluctantly tolerated the smoking because it helped to keep the men quiet and relatively content. On the other hand, he once caught forty of his Chinese workers smoking in a makeshift opium den for relaxation and was not pleased. He destroyed all the pipes and opium and beat up the organizers. (Because of the contemporary racial prejudice against the Chinese, existing photographs of the joining of the Union Pacific and the Central Pacific at Promontory, Utah, do not show any of the Chinese laborers who made the completion of the transcontinental railroad possible. They were deliberately excluded.)

When the placer gold mines of California played out and construction was completed on the Central Pacific Railroad, many of the Chinese laborers were left without a job and most of them did not have enough money to return to China. As a result, many of them stayed on and worked in the mining towns of Nevada, Utah, and Wyoming. Other unemployed Chinese construction workers and laborers drifted back to the West Coast to cities such as San Francisco, Portland, Seattle, and Tacoma, all of which developed large Chinatowns. As the men spread to these cities, the habit of smoking opium followed them.

The Chinese men took whatever menial jobs they could find, becoming servants, cooks, restaurant proprietors, and laundrymen. They did not necessarily enter the laundry and restaurant businesses by choice, but discriminatory labor practices that kept Chinese workers out of the mines meant that occupations for them were limited. Before Chinese laundries opened in San Francisco, many of California's rich sent their shirts to Hawaii (then called the Sandwich Islands) or to Hong Kong to be laundered. The price was as much as $20 for a dozen shirts and the voyage there and back took about four months. Prices dropped dramatically to about $5 a dozen when enterprising Chinese opened local laundries.

Chinese laborers also worked on other Western railroads. One was the Virginia and Truckee Railroad in Nevada. Coolies had been present in Nevada since 1851 when John Reese hired Chinese labor to build a water ditch for irrigation and mining.[22] In 1869 the Virginia and Truckee was built from Virginia City to Carson City. The route was twenty-one miles long with an elevation change of 1,600 feet that could be achieved only by laying out a meandering, curved railbed. Much of the railbed was blasted through solid rock. The railroad took three years to complete to Reno with a crew of 1,200, most of whom were Chinese.

In Arizona, the Southern Pacific Railroad, which reached Tucson on March 20, 1880, employed over 3,000 Chinese laborers. The railroad was thus responsible for creating a large settlement of Chinese laborers in Arizona, including 1,100 individuals in Pima County.[23] After the railroad was completed, some of the workers went back to China, but many stayed. Several hundred went on to work in Tombstone in the silver mines.

The Rise of the Tongs

The power behind Chinese businesses in San Francisco was soon concentrated in the hands of associations called "tongs" that were created to resolve disputes, to protect their members, and to watch out for the welfare of the Chinese community. Virtually all the Chinese business enterprises in San Francisco were controlled by a consortium of these associations named the Chinese Consolidated Benevolent Associations, better known as the Chinese Six Companies. These societies served to support the Chinese who wanted to come to America. They lent money for the sea passage to the West Coast to potential immigrants, arranged for them to get jobs and lodging after they arrived in the United States, and made sure that their loans — along with a hefty rate of interest — were repaid.

The Chinese tongs eventually became clannish secret societies made up mostly of outcasts and criminals. The tongs posed as social clubs, but in reality they controlled vast business empires that dealt in opium smuggling, gambling, prostitution, and the importation of Chinese women as slaves. Many of these women were deliberately made to be addicted to the smuggled opium in order to keep them docile. In the 1860s, the entire underworld of San Francisco was controlled by twenty or so tongs. Business competition naturally led to rivalry and war between the different associations. These wars included feuds, assassinations, and even open battles. One of the favorite weapons of tong enforcers was a hatchet with the blade sharpened to a razor's edge; thus these assassins were nicknamed "hatchet men." With this lethal weapon they could literally chop a man to pieces. Tongs ruled the underworld in Chinatowns in other cities also, where they controlled the opium supply and opium dens whose services often included prostitution.

One of the odder incidents in tong warfare occurred in the northern California gold camp of Weaverville in July of 1854. Two rival groups from the Chinese section of town, the Red Caps (the Cantons) and the Hong Kongs, armed themselves with swords, spears, iron helmets, and tin shields, and tried to intimidate each other in a mock battle.[24] The white population of miners looked on with amused interest as the two groups postured, strutted, and menaced each other. Finally, a Dutch miner who was impatient for the action to start fired his pistol into the crowd of participants. That was the impetus for a bout of frenzied fighting. After probably not more than ten minutes of enthusiastic brawling by the 260 participants, eight men lay dead and six had been wounded. The bodies of the dead included the Dutchman who had provoked the fight. With perhaps a dash of poetic justice, someone (who was never identified) had shot him in the head. Neither group ever said what caused — or settled — the dispute. Apparently the brief encounter between the two tongs had satisfied whatever breach of honor had occurred and the two groups never fought again.[25]

A more typical fight among rival tongs occurred on September 26, 1856, among the 5,000 Chinese living in the aptly named Chinese Camp, California. The fight started after a minor incident when a stone rolled from where one group of miners was working to where another group was digging. Each group was connected to a tong and both groups sent to their headquarters in San Francisco for reinforcements. After the inevitable fight, the casualties were listed as four killed and twelve injured. Like the earlier Weaverville incident, honor was satisfied by a brief battle and the two groups went peaceably back to work.

A type of arrangement different from the tongs, but one that achieved essentially the same results, controlled the Chinese power in the silver-mining town of Tombstone, Arizona. Like most mining towns, Tombstone had sizeable groups of Irish, German, Mexicans, and Chinese. The size of the Chinese community was estimated to be between 400 and 500 people.

The virtual dictator of Tombstone's Chinatown, which was known locally as "Hoptown," was a woman named China Mary. Mary arrived in Tombstone in late 1879 or early 1880 and married a man named Ah Lum (or Chum). The two ran a store that dealt in Oriental goods. She and her husband also ran a profitable gambling operation, a bordello, and an opium den. She supplied most of opium in town, much of it going to the local white prostitutes.[26]

As part of her business interests, Mary helped the Chinese population with employment, typically arranging for the men to have jobs as servants and the women as prostitutes.[27] The Chinese workers that Mary placed did most of the laundry, cooking, and housekeeping in town. As an added incentive to the employer, she guaranteed that the servants she supplied would not steal. In the unlikely event that they did, she guaranteed that she would provide restitution. On a more philanthropic note, Mary also helped Chinese unfortunates who were sick or injured and acted as a negotiator between the residents of Chinatown and the town's leaders.

Discrimination and Racial Prejudice

Though the Chinese were a success as laborers on the railroads and in the gold diggings and mines, they were probably the subject of more prejudice and hate than any other immigrant group to the American West in the second half of the nineteenth century. In the beginning of the mining rush, gold was plentiful and the Chinese were tolerated, but their very success as laborers and small businessmen was their undoing. The white racial prejudice that had formerly targeted Mexicans and American Indians was also quickly extended to the Chinese.

Though most Chinese were continually looked down upon by the whites, many Chinese doctors were well-liked. They were particularly popular among white women, who often felt that American doctors of the time were not par-

This cartoon from the satiric *Puck* magazine in 1886 illustrates the general feeling of Americans towards Chinese immigrants. They could either stay or leave, both of which are illustrated here as not much of a choice. Sentiment against the Chinese ran high and smoking opium was used as an excuse for persecution as the use of opium was considered to be a dreadful Oriental habit (Library of Congress).

ticularly sympathetic to medical complaints that involved the female reproductive system.

The attitude of discrimination that was prevalent at the time against anyone who was not white and of Anglo-Saxon descent was typified by comments from artist Frederic Remington, who once said, "Jews, Injuns, Chinamen, Italians, Huns — the rubbish of the earth I hate — I've got some Winchesters and when the massacring begins, I can get my share of 'em, and what's more, I will."[28]

The Chinese culture, eating habits, language, unusual clothing, religion, and generally different way of life made the Chinese repellent to the American miners. The Chinese ate food, such as dried fish, bamboo shoots, mushrooms, and seaweed, that was strange and undesirable to the whites. The preferences of Chinese men for opium over alcohol and of gambling for only low stakes were viewed as suspicious activities by the white miners, who drank heavily and gambled hard for high stakes. The Chinese clannish tendency to work, live, and socialize together also aroused suspicion among the whites. Some believed that the Chinese symbolized vice in the form of opium and opium dens and barbaric customs, such as smoking opium. Because of these characteristics, the Chinese were almost always subjected to persecution, and were commonly racially abused.

Chinese music sounded unfamiliar and dissonant to western ears. The music at one gambling resort in San Francisco was described as "an orchestra of five or six native musicians, who produce such extraordinary sounds from their curiously shaped instruments as severely torture the white man to listen to. Occasionally a songster adds his howl or shriek to the excruciating harmony."[29]

In a description of life in Virginia City, Montana, in the 1860s, author Larry Barsness summed up the prevailing attitude of the white miners towards the local Chinese: "They couldn't see him, because he was a heathen and a slave. To them his food was revolting, his music god-awful, his women all whores, his scent of musk and opium sinful. Furthermore, they couldn't hear him because his language was an offense to the ears, even names being abominable."[30] This prejudice was amplified by whispered lurid tales and rumors, such as the one that Chinamen "ate mice fried in axle grease."[31]

Public attacks on the Chinese were continued and scathing. In 1882, the editor of the *Tombstone Epitaph* wrote, "The Chinese are the least desired immigrants who have ever sought the United States. The most we can do is to insist that he is a heathen, a soup made of the fragrant juice of the rat, filthy, disagreeable, and undesirable generally, an encumbrance that we do not know how to get rid of, but whose tribe we have determined shall not increase in this part of the world."[32] The *Seattle Call* called them names such as "scurvy opium fiends," "treacherous almond-eyed sons of Confucius," and "rat-eating Chinamen."[33] These suspicions were "confirmed" by "authorities" on the subject, who cited such things as a pest-control product called "Rough on Rats," which showed a caricature of a Chinaman holding a rat in the air, just ready to pop it into his mouth.[34]

The Chinese were given derisive collective names such as "Celestials," "heathen Chinee," "dirty Chinese," or "filthy heathens," as the miners thought was appropriate to an undesirable group.[35] Because the Chinese all looked the same to Westerners, they were all called "John" or "John Chinaman." Chinese women were typically called "Mary," but sometimes were also generically called "John Chinawoman." In the mining town of Silverton, Colorado, the Chinese operated laundries and restaurants for many years in the late 1800s. For the most part they were industrious, hard-working people, but still the local newspapers called them such derogatory names as "pig-tailed, almond-eyed celestials."[36]

Not everyone, however, had this same attitude. Mark Twain (Samuel Clemens), who lived in the booming mining town of Virginia City, Nevada, from 1863 to 1864, offered a few relevant comments on the Chinese population that he encountered. In his book *Roughing It*, the description of his travels in the Old West, he stated quite matter-of-factly, "Of course there was a large Chinese population in Virginia [City] — it is the case with every town and city on the Pacific coast." He added, "They are quiet, peaceable, tractable, free from drunkenness, and they are as industrious as the day is long. A disorderly Chinaman is rare, and a lazy one does not exist. So long as a Chinaman has strength to use his hands he needs no support from anybody; white men often complain of want of work, but a Chinaman offers no such complaint; he always manages to find something to do."[37] And this last was what basically underlay much of the prejudice.

The Chinese were at the bottom of the labor scale and were willing to work for very low wages, which created white resentment of cheap Chinese labor. All over the West white miners were angry that the Chinese were willing to toil harder for less pay, mostly reworking abandoned mines, tailings, and diggings, and extracting only minute specks of gold. Unusual for a mining camp, Leadville, Colorado, in 1879 had no Chinese. The town had specifically banned them, citing these very reasons.[38] The 1890 census, on the other hand, showed 602 Chinese living in the mining town of Helena, Montana, and 400 more in nearby Anaconda.

The Chinese also tended towards running cheap restaurants. They were often able to make money from such businesses due to hard work and a willingness to make a smaller profit, whereas white owners could not or would not. In 1898 the mining town of Deadwood, South Dakota, had eleven restaurants, seven of them run by Chinese proprietors.[39] Of course some of the economies were gained at a cost to the customer. At one Chinese restaurant

in Deadwood the owner was noted for saying, "What kind pie you want —
we got apple."[40]

Prejudice and the fear of losing jobs was voiced as a fear of economic
competition among the whites. A common cry in the 1880s was "the Chinese
must go," but their cheap laundries, restaurants, and willingness to work in
jobs for wages that were lower than the whites made them an essential part
of the economy. Labor unions complained about the Chinese working long
and hard for only minimum wages. These competitive economic fears were
actually groundless. The Chinese weren't hired by mine owners, they merely
sifted through old worked-out mine dumps that the whites had abandoned
as worthless. The Chinese operated stores, but sold mainly Chinese goods
that whites didn't want. When the Chinese worked as cooks or in laundries,
they worked for much lower wages than the whites would accept.

A series of peculiar laws discriminated against the Chinese. The Natu-
ralization Act of 1790 was interpreted to mean that Chinese immigrants could
not become naturalized citizens because they were not "white persons" according to immigration regulations. Though immigrant Chinese parents were
denied citizenship, their children who were born in America became citizens
by birth. Nevertheless, this did not grant them equality with the whites. They
were restricted to living in Chinatown ghettos, were still denied the right to
vote, and were not allowed to own land.

In a very convoluted ruling in 1878, Hugh Murray, the chief justice of
California, decided that the Chinese were actually Indians, which opened the
door for further discrimination by the white miners.[41] Many states passed discriminatory laws, such as a Montana Supreme Court decision in 1883 that said
that the Chinese were not allowed to own claims or mines. The Chinese also
found out that there were other inequalities in applying the law. Chinese women,
for example, made up a small percentage of the overall prostitute population
of the Old West. In spite of their low numbers, however, local police in many
communities tended to arrest and fine them more frequently than their white
counterparts. White women plying the same trade were often overlooked.

In 1881, forty thousand Chinese entered the country. As the numbers
continued to grow, this became too much for the anti–Chinese agitators.
Western politicians and labor unions persuaded Congress to pass legislation
that ended the recruitment of more laborers from China and banned Chinese
from becoming a naturalized citizens. In 1882, President Chester Arthur signed
the Chinese Exclusion Act, which banned for the next ten years the importation of Chinese laborers for the purposes of mining. This legislation essentially halted any further Chinese immigration. As a result, the number of
Chinese allowed into the country in 1884 was only 279, and in 1885 this
number dropped to twenty-two. Only ten entered in 1887. In 1888, the Scott
Act expanded on the 1882 Chinese Exclusion Act and essentially prohibited

Chinese laborers who returned to China to visit their families, or for other reasons, from reentering the United States.

The Chinese population in the Western states reached a peak of 8 percent in 1880. In 1882, when Congress passed the Chinese Exclusion Act, there were 100,000 Chinese living in the West. By the turn of the century, the number was down to 2 percent.[42] In 1890, one thousand lived in Denver, but the number dropped to 306 by 1900 as many of the Chinese left for the West Coast or went back to China.[43] The total number of Chinese in the United States in 1890 was 103,620, but in 1900 this total had dropped to 85,341 as many left to avoid persecution and massacre.

Violence

Some anti–Chinese agitators went a step further and translated their attitudes of racial prejudice into violence. The Chinese were frequently cheated, beaten, and robbed. They were often run out of town and were sometimes even murdered. Retribution for these events was slow — or mostly nonexistent.

On July 4, 1868, for example, a Chinese prospector was hanged at the camp of Rocker in Montana by an American miner named Don Faffie, who thought that by this act he might improve his luck.[44] In 1878, when businessman Hing Lee was murdered in German Gulch in Montana, the attacker stole $7,000 in gold dust and thirty cases of opium. The culprit was never found.[45] In 1891 three Chinese were beaten to death in Butte, Montana, by unknown assailants who were never tracked down.[46]

On February 17, 1893, the *Anaconda Standard* reported that a Chinese corpse with a bullet hole in it had been found hanging by the neck from a tree. This exposé by the newspaper stimulated the authorities to initiate an investigation — at least they did several weeks later. A bottle of brandy and a bottle of poison had been found in the man's pocket. The newspaper's conclusion was that the dead man climbed the tree, placed a noose around his neck, drank the brandy and the poison, then shot himself in the heart. This led him to hang himself when he fell.

The Chinese were arbitrarily lynched and persecuted all over the West. In 1871, an unruly mob killed twenty Chinese in Los Angeles. In 1885, twenty-eight Chinese were killed in Rock Springs, Wyoming, in a race riot, and hundreds more were driven out of town before federal troops were called in.

THE WEST COAST

Violence was turned not only against individuals, but mob violence also targeted the entire Chinese race. The Chinese realized that they were unpro-

Racial prejudice against the Chinese was extreme across much of the Old West and
violence broke out in many communities. Anti-Chinese riots broke out at various
times in Los Angeles, San Francisco, Seattle, Denver and other large cities that had
extensive populations of Chinese residents. This was the 1885 riot at Rock Springs,
Wyoming, in which twenty-eight Chinese railroad workers were killed before federal
troops were called in to quell the disturbance (Library of Congress).

tected in the mining camps, and this was one reason they tended to congregate
in Chinatowns in cities such as San Francisco or Seattle, as they thought the
police would protect them. Unfortunately, the local police often turned a
blind eye to mob violence. One of the ludicrous high points of anti–Chinese
sentiment had to be when the governor of California dedicated March 4,
1880, as a legal holiday for anti–Chinese demonstrators.[47]

Various race riots took place in San Francisco throughout the 1860s and
1870s. One riot in July of 1877 continued with robberies, looting, and killings
(four dead, fourteen wounded) for three days before the police could finally
stop it. Race riots in 1877 in San Francisco were so bad that the California
National Guard was called out to patrol the streets.

At the same time that the Central Pacific was importing Chinese by the
thousands to build the railroad, its president, Leland Stanford, was denouncing
the "yellow menace."[48] The Chinese were blamed for many of the ills of the
day. While Stanford, the founder of Stanford University, was campaigning
for governor of California (1861 to 1863), he spoke out vehemently against
Chinese immigration, calling the Chinese the "dregs of Asia."[49] This attitude

came back later to haunt him. Stanford had a large vineyard and employed over three hundred Chinese workers. During the height of the anti–Chinese sentiment in the 1890s, white workers rioted and caused extensive damage to the vineyard.[50]

In Tacoma in 1885, the rallying cry of the mob was "the Chinese must go" and many Chinese were run out of town. During racial agitation in Seattle in 1886, several groups of Chinese were forcefully deported in ships bound for San Francisco. Rioting was stopped only when President Grover Cleveland declared martial law.

THE DENVER RIOTS

The first Chinese to arrive in Denver were brought to the area in 1869 to work on the Denver Pacific Railway between Denver and Cheyenne, Wyoming, to the north. Work was finished on June 22, 1870. On August 18, 1870, the Kansas Pacific Railway arrived in Denver from the east. With the completion of these two railroads, thousands of Chinese laborers were suddenly out of work. Not knowing where else to go, some of them stayed in Denver. As they were cast loose in a strange town in a strange land, many clustered together in Denver's first Chinatown, along with the first Chinese women in the area, who came from San Francisco with the completion of the railroad.

In the 1870s, most of the Chinese population of Denver lived along the 1600 block of Wazee Street, near Union Station. In time, Denver's Chinatown grew to an area from about Sixteenth to Twentieth streets, between Blake and Wazee. The white population later called the area Hop Alley, after the slang Chinese name for opium. The 1880 census listed 238 Chinese residents in Denver out of a total population of 35,000. A second Chinese neighborhood was established in the 1880s around Blake and Thirteenth Street. A third grew up, starting in 1889, on Holladay Street (later renamed Market Street) between Twentieth and Twenty-first streets.

Hop Alley was situated behind Holladay Street, the main red light district, in the alley running parallel to it. This was the location of the opium dens, Chinese laundries, Chinese gambling, and small stores catering to Chinese residents. Typical was the shop of Lily Chin, who ran a store on Holladay Street that sold Chinese clothing, jewelry, and specialty foods, such as pickled bamboo shoots and bird's nests. Like other Chinatowns, the air around Hop Alley was said to be permanently perfumed with the faint sweet smell of opium smoke. By 1880 Denver had seventeen opium dens and Chinese gambling establishments. Most had entrances on Holladay Street for the convenience of the patrons of the bordellos. Favorite gambling games were fan-tan, pi-gow, and Chinese lottery. Except for a weakness for gambling and opium, most of the residents of Hop Alley were peaceful and law-abiding.

The Denver anti–Chinese riot took place on October 31, 1880. Prior to this, the *Rocky Mountain News* had been carrying on an anti-opium crusade. The paper had been editorializing strongly against the Chinese and stirring up local sentiment by calling them names such as "wily heathens."[51] The flames of hate were further fanned and focused into action after an incident of October 8, 1880, in which an eighteen year-old young man died. The city coroner ruled that the death was from typhoid and a perforated intestine, but added that the death *could* have been hastened by being treated with opium, which masked the pain of the perforation. The coroner's jury, going one step further, ruled that the young man's death was due to the perforated intestine and opium use.[52] The local papers, of course, immediately jumped on the lurid aspect of opium involvement. The *Denver Tribune* headline of October 12, 1880, was "The Deadly Drug: A Young Man of Denver Falls Victim to the Prevailing Chinese Vice." The same day, the *Rocky Mountain News* trumpeted on their front page, "Deadly Opium — Kills a Lad Eighteen Years of Age." The public fumed and fretted.

The immediate cause of the riot was a fight between a Chinese man and an ugly drunk ironically known as "Happy Jack." Two Chinese men and a white man had been playing pool at John Asmussen's saloon at Sixteenth Street and Wazee when three or four white drunks, inflamed by all the anti–Chinese hysteria, came in and started taunting them. The verbal abuse escalated into fighting. The anti–Chinese element joined in and wide-scale fighting broke out all over the city. Many of the 2,000 Chinese who eventually became involved were innocent bystanders, but many were seized and beaten by the white crowd. A mob stormed through the streets, wrecking Chinese businesses and dragging the Chinese outside. The mob violence inevitably led to looting, vandalism, and the burning of Chinese houses and businesses. Most of Chinatown was destroyed. During the rioting a Chinese man named Sing Lee was beaten and kicked to death, but those indicted for his murder were later acquitted. The mayor ordered out the police and fire departments to try to control the rowdy crowd, but they were ineffective and weren't able to make much progress. The rioting continued from noon until midnight before the violence was finally suppressed when the militia was called out.

The gambling dens and opium joints of Denver's Hop Alley were closed permanently by the sheriff in 1915.

CHAPTER SIX

Boozers, Users and Abusers

By 1860, the nonmedical use of opium in America had become a major social issue. Heavy drinking, however, was an accepted and visible part of the way of life for many men in the latter half of the nineteenth century. This practice went back to the early colonists, who also drank heavily. Many men started the day with a drink, had another with breakfast, dinner, and supper, and then again after supper at the local tavern. A drink of whiskey was considered to be good for the stomach to prepare it for an upcoming meal and was popular after the meal to help settle the digestion.

Whiskey, beer, and wine were consumed in large quantities in the Old West and provided a method of relaxation and temporary escape from the harsh realities of life on the Western frontier. Drinking made life more endurable for many of the population of young single men, who typically worked at grueling physical tasks and were often not happy with their bachelor lives. The consumption of whiskey and other forms of alcohol was a common pastime for miners, loggers, cowboys, railroad construction workers, and other young men who worked hard in the Old West. A newspaperman from the mining town of Central City, Colorado, said, "We have never lived in any country where the use of intoxicating drinks was so prevalent. We do not know of over a dozen men in the Territory who abstain from their use altogether."[1]

Alcohol

Most towns in the Old West had a section that was devoted to the bawdier types of male recreation, which usually consisted of the proverbial wine, women, and song. In this case it was drink, women, and gambling. Myers Avenue, for example, the red light district of the booming mining town of Cripple Creek, Colorado, was lined in the 1890s with a variety of theaters, opium dens, and saloons, and brothels which provided all three. All of these establishments could usually provide opium for those desiring it.

Drunkenness had been variously characterized as consisting of too much talking, too little talking, excessive bad humor, excessive good humor, swearing, being brutally honest about everyone else's faults, singing, roaring, making animal noises, dancing naked, and throwing things. The excessive use of whiskey was equated by reformers to be associated with idleness, lying, and fraud. It was also associated with quarreling, fighting, obscenity, and problems of loose morals. Even in moderate quantities, whiskey lowered a drinker's mental capability and, at the same time, lowered his sense of good judgment, concentration, and insight. It also made many drinkers excitable, impulsive, and argumentative. As a result, drinking to excess was the cause of many gunfights in the Old West.

The incidence of alcoholism among men in the Old West was high. Heavy drinkers might put away a quart of whiskey a day. Bulbous noses red with broken blood vessels and bloodshot eyeballs were a common sight. The more severe cases of alcoholism produced hallucinations, delusions, and the visible tremors of delirium tremens ("the DTs"). Although they were not visible, the major elements of the medical side of alcoholism were internal damage caused by cirrhosis of the liver, kidney deterioration, and the dulling of mental capacity. Nonetheless, heavy drinking was usually overlooked and might only be noticed if the drinker was exhibiting symptoms of the DTs.

For women, more common than the use of alcohol was the use of opium. Heavy drinking by women was not a practice accepted by contemporary society, so women tended to seek their pleasure in private through drugs such as opium. Drug usage was not uncommon for many Victorian women, and recreational smoking of opium was a popular pastime across the West. The *Denver Medical Times* reported in 1903 that women outnumbered men as opium users by a factor of ten to one.[2] Though often thought of as a drug of prostitutes and the criminal class of women, opium was commonly used by middle-class women, some of whom were as young as thirteen or fourteen. A quick swig from a bottle of laudanum could be used to calm the nerves and settle the disposition. Estimates are that 60 to 70 percent of women childbearing age (approximately between the ages of twenty-five and fifty-five) used opium, morphine, or laudanum for relief from menstrual pain or menopausal symptoms. Many women kept a bottle of whiskey discreetly hidden among the kitchen supplies and could secretly take a small drink or two if they felt the need for pain relief at "that time of the month."

DRINKING IN EVERYDAY LIFE

When reflecting on his years in Kansas City in the 1870s, Wyatt Earp recalled "there was steady drinking. Kansas City offered a change from the raw liquor of the camps. Saloons were as well stocked with beers, wines, cordials, and fine whiskeys as the choosiest drinker could require, and the best in the land was none too good for the frontiersman who could pay. Some men went on sprees which lasted for days and weeks, but for the majority one protracted session immediately after hitting town was enough; then they'd be satisfied with an occasional drink in the daytime, and a reasonable amount of sociable drinking at night."[3]

One odd nondrinking use for whiskey was as the stakes in a bet. Reportedly one teamster bet a pint of whiskey that he could cut the seat of another one's pants without marking the skin underneath. The other man unwisely agreed to the bet and bent over. The first man cracked his whip, but wasn't as good as he thought — and lost the bet.[4]

GUNMEN AND DRINKING

Many of the gunfighters of the Old West were drinkers who became violent after too much whiskey and their drinking resulted in much of the gunplay that permeated the Old West. Gunfighter Clay Allison was a good example. Author Dale Schoenberger summarized Allison's behavior well when he said, "While not in his cups (which wasn't often) Allison was mild-mannered, sober-minded, and congenial, but when drinking he became surly and destructive, his bloodlust reaching a fever pitch."[5] On December 21, 1876, Allison killed deputy sheriff Charles Faber in a violent shoot-out when Faber tried to stop a drunken spree of Allison's in Las Animas, Colorado.[6]

Gunfighter Ben Thompson was another hard-drinking man-killer. Among other incidents, Thompson was involved in a drunken shoot-out in Ellsworth, Kansas, on August 15, 1873. He, gambler John Sterling, John "Happy Jack" Morco, and Thompson's brother Billy were all in various stages of inebriation when an argument broke out. The participants went to get their guns and returned to stage an all-around shoot-out that resulted in the death of unarmed sheriff Chauncey Whitney.[7] In another incident of violence, on a train leaving San Antonio, Texas, Thompson was already drunk when he grabbed a whiskey bottle from another passenger. When one of the train's porters didn't immediately jump to carry out one of Thompson's requests, Thompson hit the man on the head with the bottle.[8]

One of the few gunmen who was not a heavy drinker was Wyatt Earp. He claimed that he did not take a drink of liquor until he was well past the age of forty. Fellow lawman Bill Tilghman said, "In all the years during which I was intimately associated with Wyatt, as a buffalo hunter and as a peace officer, I never knew him to take a drink of liquor. He never questioned another man's right to drink as he pleased, and I have been with him in more than one all-night session where whiskey was consumed as rapidly as drinks could be drawn from the barrel, but Wyatt did his tanking-up on coffee."[9]

DRINKING IN THE MILITARY

Heavy drinking has been common among soldiers throughout history. The Old West was no exception. John Billings, who enlisted during the Civil War, made the following comment in his memoirs: "The opinion was very prevalent, and undoubtedly correct, that the liquor was quite liberally sampled by the various headquarters, or the agents through whom it was transmitted to the rank and file. While there was considerable whiskey drank by the men 'unofficially,' that is, which was obtained otherwise than on the order of the medical department, yet, man for man, the private soldiers were as abstemious as the officers. The officers who did not drink more or less were too scarce in the service."[10]

Ironically, one of the requirements for enlisting in the army was that the candidate not be a drunkard and part of the initial examination of recruits was to eliminate known drunks. If a man was found to be a drunkard, he would be rejected for service. In another stroke of irony, one of the responsibilities of troops on the Western frontier was to prevent the manufacture and importation of whiskey to the Indians. However, instead of suppressing the trade, the soldiers were some of the most energetic consumers of what was called "vile liquor." The medical director of the army concluded that stationing the troops to suppress the whiskey trade was a mistake. The parallel would be the old saying of using the fox to guard the chicken coop.

The number of soldiers, suffering from various diseases, who reported for sick call in the Union army during the Civil War was 5,825,480 cases. Of this number, the delirium tremens associated with alcoholism accounted for 3,744 cases, with 450 deaths attributed directly to the disease. Drinking was not exclusive to enlisted men and soldiers. The carnage that occurred during the Civil War drove many army physicians to drink. Hospital wards were sometimes unattended because the physician on duty was drunk.[11]

Few enlisted men wanted to be nurses because this involved obvious unpleasant duties. It was for good reason that they were nicknamed "bed-pan pushers." Because nobody would volunteer — despite extra-duty pay — some of the more shiftless privates were simply assigned to these duties. This was not always successful. In one case, "a soldier-nurse drank all the liquor he was supposed to be administering to a dangerously sick sergeant. The next morning the surgeon found the nurse in a drunken stupor and the sergeant dead."[12]

During the Indian Wars on the Western frontier that lasted from after the Civil War until 1890, the army had a particularly difficult problem with alcohol. At some posts one of the few off-duty pastimes for soldiers was drinking and, fueled by boredom, many of the soldiers became alcoholics. While at Fort Dodge, Kansas, General George Armstrong Custer wrote to his wife Libbie: "You would be horrified [if you knew] the vast quantity of liquor drunk by the officers. Even some of the temperate ones dispose of one canteen full each day."[13]

Except for officers' wives and the wives of a few enlisted men, there was no family or female companionship for soldiers on post. Army wives on the Western frontier suffered similar effects of boredom, isolated on remote posts with nowhere to go and only a few other women for companionship. Many posts were so small that everyone's business quickly became common knowledge, such as which officers were drunks or who was having an affair with another officer's wife. Duane Green, a former lieutenant who left the army after a scandal involving the post doctor's wife at Camp Bowie in Arizona in 1877, stated that whiskey and wives were the most corrupting influences at western posts.

Military life was often harsh, isolated as it was in some remote area of the frontier. Captain F. Van Vliet, stationed with the Third Cavalry at Fort Fetterman in Wyoming in 1874, wrote that there was "no opportunity for procuring fresh vegetables, and gardens are a failure. There is no female society for enlisted men. [T]he enlisted men of the company are leaving very much dissatisfied, as they look upon being held so long at this post as an unmerited

Excessive drinking was a problem for the army, in spite of various attempts to limit it. However, some post commandants viewed drinking as one of the few forms of relaxation for lonely soldiers stuck at a remote post on the Western frontier. Here a group of soldiers enjoy a social drink in the post canteen at Fort Keogh in Montana in the early 1890s (National Archives).

punishment.... [W]henever men get to the railroad there are some desertions caused by dread of returning to the post."[14]

To relieve boredom, liquor, beer, and wine could be obtained from the post sutler or from nearby towns with saloons.[15] Sutlers and post traders sold whiskey by the bottle or glass, typically charging 10¢ a drink. Though certainly some enlisted soldiers didn't drink liquor or smoke tobacco, the majority did. Whiskey sales at the sutler's store increased after payday. Many men were heavy drinkers and spent most of their meager $13-a-month pay on whiskey and beer. Other soldiers who were alcoholics were known to steal army supplies and trade them to civilian dealers for cash or liquor, even though that was an offence that merited a court-martial.

Alcohol was the most persistent problem for the army. One reason was that intoxicated soldiers might become rebellious and less inclined to follow orders than when sober. An example of this took place in Kelley and Beatty's saloon in Dodge City, Kansas, in July of 1874: "[T]he Officer of the Day came in and ordered the men to camp. One of the men, full of liquor and beer, grabbed the Officer of the Day, took his belt off and threw him under the billiard table."[16]

Soldiers might also become so drunk or hung over that they were unable to perform their duties adequately. At Fort Dodge, Kansas, in 1872, men forming the escort accompanying the mail to Fort Supply in Oklahoma were so drunk that they could not even stay on their horses.[17] Another significant problem for the army was that fighting among soldiers who had been drinking frequently resulted in injuries and occasionally in killings. In 1868, a patrol sent out from Fort Dodge to destroy an illegal whiskey shipment decided to sample the goods themselves and became so drunk that several of them died in the resulting brawl.

Drunken fights commonly broke out in saloons after payday and visits to the post surgeon to patch up cuts, bruises, and knife wounds increased dramatically. One soldier reported from Fort Ellis in Montana in 1871 that he observed "a perfect pandemonium in the saloon, it was crowded all the time, everybody drunk and trying to outtalk everybody else. Every few minutes somebody would get knocked down, and occasionally a free fight shook the whole house."[18] Hangovers were common after these payday binges and the guardhouse was regularly full of recuperating enlisted men. One of the unpleasant ways the post surgeon might treat men with hangovers was to give them a large laxative dose of castor oil.

It was not uncommon for enlisted men and officers to be drunk on duty. For an enlisted man this might result in fines or in punishments that ranged from a reduction in rank to physical punishment, depending on the severity of the offense. Punishments in the army could be severe, ranging from carrying around a heavy weight, such as a log or a rock, all day to being tied to stakes in the ground in a spread-eagle position until the drunken soldier sobered up. A common punishment for a drunken soldier was to have him march around carrying a barrel suspended by straps over his shoulders. As an extreme punishment, consistently drunken soldiers might have their heads shaved, be branded, and then be drummed out of the fort with a dishonorable discharge.

An officer found drunk on duty might face a court-martial or a suspension of rank. If this was a serious or repeat pattern of behavior, he might even be discharged from the army. John Billings wrote in delicate terms in his memoirs "there was nothing but his sense of honor, his self-respect, or his fear of exposure and punishment, to restrain a captain, a colonel, or a general, of whatever command, from being intoxicated at a moment when he should have been in the full possession of his senses leading his command on to battle; and I regret to relate that these motives, strong as they are to impel to right and restrain from wrong-doing, were no barrier to many an officer whose appetite in a crisis thus imperiled the cause and disgraced himself."[19]

In her memoirs, Libbie Custer, General George Armstrong Custer's wife, mentioned one newly transferred officer who came to present himself to her as she was the commanding officer's wife. He had apparently been drinking heavily before observing this military protocol and, rather than walking into the house, he literally fell through the door when he arrived. After he unsteadily regained his feet, he proceeded to tangle his sword between his legs and fell over a chair. After an investigation into this disgraceful breach of protocol he was forced to resign his commission.[20]

Army officer Charles Veil recalled the post commandant at Fort Crittenden in Arizona in this way in his memoirs: "When not under the influence of liquor, he was a very elegant gentleman, but as he was subject to very frequent intoxication, he was a very unpleasant officer to serve under." During one dress parade the men were all assembled in front of a crowd of onlookers, waiting for the commander to appear and put them through the manual of arms. As Veil remembered, "Unfortunately ... the colonel was on the drunk that day. After waiting some time, he finally appeared, but in such a sad state of intoxication as to be almost unable to stand on his feet." After some embarrassing moments when the colonel was drunkenly unable to issue the correct commands, Veil, as second-in-command, took over and dismissed the troops while the colonel staggered unsteadily back to his quarters. As a result of his performance, the colonel was relieved of his duty and ordered to report to the departmental headquarters. The officer was so mortified at the incident that he eventually committed suicide.[21]

Some soldiers deserted to avoid punishment. Albert Barnitz, an officer in the Seventh Cavalry under General Custer, wrote in his journal on March 24, 1868: "My 1st Sergeant Francis S. Gordon was reduced to the ranks for absence without leave, and drunkenness, on the e'vg of 22d of March, and confined in the guard house." The next day, however, "Serg't Gordon was released from the Guard House this morning, and at once absconded."[22]

The combination of boredom and hard work that soldiers experienced in the army often resulted in a high rate of desertion — as well as a high rate of alcoholism for those who stuck it out. Soldiers who deserted were said to have taken "French leave" or "the grand bounce." In 1872, the desertion rate was about one-third of the total number of enlisted men. Army wives did not have the option of deserting. Instead, they used whiskey, laudanum, and opium for a temporary escape.

Attempts were made by the army to reduce liquor consumption and drunkenness among soldiers. One method was to require drinks to only be sold with lunch, theoretically to lower the chances of a soldier drinking on an empty stomach. Another method that was tried was to have post sutlers limit the number of drinks that they could serve to a soldier at one drinking session. This policy was usually not popular with either the men, who wanted to drink, or the sutler, who wanted to sell drinks. It was also seen by the men as a poor example of leadership when they had to limit their drinking yet the officers did not.

The local policy towards drinking was often decided by the post commandant and many commanders looked upon even heavy drinking with tolerance. Many of them realized that liquor was an escape from the dull, lonely life at a remote army post. As a result, the methods to lower drinking were either only marginally successful or were often not enforced by the local commandant. Indeed, drinking was sometimes encouraged. Soldiers building Fort Cottonwood on the Platte River were regularly issued a ration of whiskey by their commander during construction. By the time the fort was completed, eight barrels of whiskey (comprising 250 gallons) had been consumed.[23]

In the 1880s, approximately 4 percent of the army's soldiers were hospitalized for alcoholism. This may not seem like a very large number, but it occurred at a time when heavy drinking in the army was an accepted practice and alcoholism had to be extremely advanced for treatment to be even considered. Military records for Fort Larned, Kansas, showed that 34 percent of the six officers and 110 enlisted men were alcoholics.[24] The use of liquor among the African-American regiments — the so-called buffalo soldiers — was much less, at only about half-a-percent.[25] As well as less alcoholism, these troops had a very low incidence of desertion.[26]

Alcoholism became such a problem for the army that the sale of whiskey on military reservations was finally banned by President Rutherford Hayes in March of 1881. Curiously, the War Department immediately responded by ruling that beer and wine were not intoxicating substances.[27] So even with Hayes' proclamation the level of drinking was not reduced as anticipated, but merely moved to nearby "hog ranches" and other low-class drinking establishments that grew up just outside the limits of military posts to provide the soldiers with whiskey, gambling, and women. Unfortunately for many soldiers stuck on the lonely frontier of the West, some posts were so isolated that there were no nearby towns in which to find a drink.

Temperance societies tried to influence drinking in the military, but with only limited success. A Good Templars lodge, for example, was organized in 1874 at Fort Randall in Montana to try to combat excessive drinking. An incentive for the soldiers was that if a soldier became drunk the commandant would suspend his sentence if he joined the Good Templars and took the pledge of abstinence.

Though drinking among soldiers was common at the post sutler's or trader's store, or at a nearby hog ranch, it was not common for soldiers to drink in saloons in neighboring towns. One reason was that local townspeople were often suspicious and unappreciative of soldiers because the military was often the only police force in the early West. Even though the army was charged with protecting settlers, the attitude of civilians towards soldiers

Some "saloons" in early Western settlements were quite primitive, consisting of unfinished pine boards on the walls, a few tables and chairs for drinking and gambling, and a few dim and smoky oil lamps for illumination (author's collection).

tended to vary according to the current state of hostilities. When the threat of Indian confrontation was high or actual fighting broke out, the civilian population was usually enthusiastic about the soldiers and the job they were doing. At other times, when the Indians were confined on their reservations and firmly controlled, the tolerance of soldiers by civilians tended to fall.

Another reason for the dislike was that soldiers were blamed for spreading venereal diseases among the prostitutes who frequented local saloons. Local cowboys, miners, or loggers, and the town's other residents who also visited them did not want to catch diseases themselves. A third reason was that many local inhabitants had come west to escape the trappings of rigid Eastern society and, to them, the military represented the authority that they had come to the West to escape.

WOMEN AND DRINKING IN THE WEST

Though heavy drinking by men was an acceptable form of recreation and was commonly overlooked, heavy drinking among women was not considered to be acceptable and carried a social stigma. Mrs. Annie Doran of Lake City, Colorado, asserted that "'respectable' women did not drink intoxicating beverages in public or in private. At public events men who had been drinking were asked to leave. If they tried to force their attentions on a lady or become obnoxious, they were jailed. A lady who danced with an intoxicated person became the subject of unfavorable comments for weeks."[28]

Dr. Mary Wood-Allen, national superintendent of the Purity Department of the Woman's Christian Temperance Union, stated in 1898, "It is a sad fact that many women, even of good social standing, are fond of alcoholic beverages. I saw a very bright, pretty young woman, not long since, at a reception, refuse to take ice-cream or cake, but drink four glasses of punch, with many jests as to her fondness of the same, apparently without any glimmering of the thought that she was drinking to excess, although her flushed face and loudness of manner were proof of this to those who were witnesses."[29]

Though not as common as for men, alcoholism was a problem for some women. Records for the Nevada State Hospital in the early mining era indicate that a large number of women, both prostitutes and respectable women, were institutionalized for drug and alcohol abuse. Sallie Herndon, a young schoolmistress in Virginia City, Montana, wrote with apparent horror in her diary: "I have just witnessed a most shocking sight — a woman so intoxicated that she couldn't walk without assistance. She was taken into a house just opposite and as she stepped in the door she fell sprawling to the floor beastly drunk."[30] Women who appeared in public in a drunken state like this were considered to be immoral. This did not necessarily imply sexual transgressions, as the Victorian perception of "moral" was somewhat different than today's definition. As an example, a woman who did not keep her house in a clean and tidy fashion was considered to be immoral.

Women who drank were suspect and unfairly targeted by a male population that was obsessed with the morals of others. A tract from the National Temperance Society stated that moderate drinking "is a mighty strengthener of lawless desire in man, and a great weakener of the resisting power of women."[31] This thought is still prevalent today. As MacAndrew and Edgerton slyly put it in 1968, "While a woman's resistance to a man's amorous advances may undergo erosion by gifts and kindnesses of one sort or another, this same effect can often be brought to pass far more rapidly with the aid, say, of a few martinis."[32] Humorist Ogden Nash said it more succinctly when he commented that "candy is dandy, but liquor is quicker."

On a more serious note, Orson S. Fowler, one of the Fowler family that promoted phrenology, said, "A man or woman, be they ever so moral or virtuous, when under the influence of intoxicating drinks, *is of easy virtue*. Before the *first* advantage can be taken of a virtuous woman, she must be partially *intoxicated*, and the advantage can be taken of almost any woman thus stimulated."[33] A widespread Victorian concept was that men were constant infernos of lust and that women had to be protected by self-appointed moral authorities from these beastly desires. This begs the obvious question of who was supposed to be doing the protecting and who would guard against the protectors.

Opium

While Western men drank in the local saloons, wives dosed themselves in the privacy of their homes with patent or prescription medicines that contained large amounts of opium and morphine. Opium was effective, available, and cheap, and those who couldn't afford medical care or didn't trust doctors dosed themselves with opium or one of many patent medicines. Opium did indeed relieve many symptoms of disease even if it didn't cure the disease itself. In the 1830s, when opium was used primarily to relieve pain, the concept of people taking drugs for recreational use was an unknown one, though probably some opium users enjoyed this aspect anyway. This changed over time. By the 1870s authorities estimated that only 20 percent of imported opium was going to legitimate medical channels.[34] Due to widespread epidemics, taking opium was common by 1840. Increased supplies of opium drove down the price so that even common factory workers had access to it. Enough morphine for an injection could be purchased at any local drug store in San Francisco in the late 1850s for 10¢ to 15¢. For an extra jolt, chloral hydrate, chloroform, or ether might be added to the morphine solution.

Annual importation of opium rose from 24,000 pounds in 1840 to

110,470 pounds in 1865 and to 416,864 pounds in 1872.[35] Opium was produced primarily in India, Turkey (which supplied most of the domestic needs
of the United States), and Egypt. By the 1880s narcotic importation into the
United States was still gradually increasing. From 1880 to 1896 opium imports
were fairly level at about 400,000 to 500,000 pounds per year, then peaked
in 1897 at 1,072,914 pounds.[36]

The general, unwarranted, image of opium use in America in the late
1800s was one of the lower classes of men and women in Eastern cities trapped
in a dark, downward spiral of drug use. The adverse nineteenth-century
stereotype that emerged was that of the "drug fiend." In reality, the typical
opium addict of the late nineteenth century was a middle-aged Caucasian
woman who was married, had children, and was financially stable. She had
been introduced to opiates either by a physician through a legitimate medical
prescription or through self-dosing with patent medicines for ailments such
as the periodic pains of menstruation. This medical addiction to opium among
middle- and upper-class women had no stigma attached. When interviewed,
one druggist from Ayer, Massachusetts, said, "Those addicted to opium are
all females; and most of them contracted the habit from the use of physicians'
prescriptions during sickness."[37] Many of the worst addicts were society ladies
who had become addicted through years of use of these medicines.

One of the common Victorian diagnoses for women was "hysteria,"
which was an imprecise diagnosis (derived from the Greek name for the womb)
that was used to describe a series of nebulous symptoms that could be related
to almost every type of disease in women. The "disease" was supposedly
accompanied by a variety of symptoms, such as laughing and crying for no
reason, amnesia, tremors, vomiting, sleepwalking, limb paralysis, and psychotic episodes. Exhibition of these symptoms is now diagnosed as "hysterical
neurosis" or "hypochondriasis," where misinterpretation of physical symptoms
by the patient leads to the belief that serious disease is present, even though
medical evaluation can prove no physical basis. The corresponding nebulous
mental "disease" of men, with symptoms supposedly similar to hysteria in
women, was neurasthenia. The patient showed symptoms of various diseases
without any organic cause, reportedly accompanied by fatigue, weakness, irritability, an inability to concentrate, and various aches and pains. Both of
these supposed diseases were treated with opium and morphine.

In 1880, physician Charles W. Earle presented a paper on opium use to
the West Chicago Medical Society. Some of his statistics are revealing. Out
of a total of 235 habitual users of opiates, 66 were male and 169 were female.
Forty-five of the 169 were housewives and the rest had various careers. Their
jobs covered a spectrum of classes and occupations, from physicians and attor-
neys at the upper end to washerwomen and common laborers at the lower.
Fifty-six of the 169 females were prostitutes. Of the 235, the number of opium

addicts was 115 and the morphine addicts 120. Of the morphine addicts, seventy-two reported using less than twenty grains of morphine each day.[38]

Of this total in the survey, 160 were Americans, thus refuting the popular perception of the time that most drug users were evil Orientals. The commonest age group was thirty to forty, consisting of nineteen men and thirty-nine women, with the largest percentage from the affluent middle class. Most of the men were businessmen and the women were housewives. These statistics were eye-opening but generally ignored. The fact that these were respectable men and women was considered contrary to the traditional American work ethic and the concept that all drug users were of poor moral character.

A similar study by the Massachusetts State Board of Health concluded that the largest proportion of opium addicts were women.[39] Women were addicted more than men by a factor of three-to-two, which showed the same trend as Earle's figures.[40]

THE PARTICULAR PROBLEMS OF WOMEN

Women in particular used large amounts of opium. They had to face two issues that were specific to their gender. One was that drinking to the point of drunkenness was an accepted practice for men, but Victorian women who appeared intoxicated in public were considered to be immoral. Therefore, the social stigma that was applied to women who consumed alcohol led many to use opium in the guise of medicine, often home remedies taken for "female complaints." Many of the women who became temperance supporters and denounced the drinking habits of men were habitual opium users. While vehemently denouncing alcoholic drinks, they nevertheless believed in the healthy use of patent medicines. They proudly claimed that they were teetotalers while at the same time dosing themselves with tonics that contained large amounts of alcohol, morphine, and opium. It was not just society women who held these beliefs. Mary Parker, who was known as a habitual drunkard, pleaded not guilty to charges of singing at the top of her lungs and disturbing the peace in Virginia City, Nevada, in 1872. Her defense was that she had reformed and now took only opium.[41]

The second issue specific to women was that a large proportion of adult middle-class American women legitimately used opium or morphine for the relief of menstrual symptoms. Drugs that were promoted as being effective for periodic pain were obviously very appealing to women. As contemporary physician Norman Kerr delicately put it, "Though much less in vogue with women than with men, those of the former sex who have been enslaved by it have taken an opiate narcotic to calm the perturbation of a delicate organization, or for the relief of natural pain."[42] Some women consumed a quart or more of laudanum or paregoric a week either to treat "disease" or, eventually, to feed their addiction. One young woman who habitually drank large amounts of laudanum confessed that "it got me into such a state of indifference that I no longer took the least interest in anything, and did nothing all day but loll on the sofa reading novels, falling asleep every now and then, and drinking tea."[43]

Another source of medical problems and associated pain specific to women was caused by the tight corsets that were used to produce the fashionable tiny waists of Victorian women. The inward and downward pressure created by these garments on the lower abdomen caused a high incidence of prolapse of the uterus and resulting pelvic pain. Opium or morphine or the same opiates prepared in various proprietary "tonics" were used for relief of the pain. A typical recommendation for pelvic pain was to take a large dose of castor oil and follow it with hot poultices on the belly and a good dose of opium.[44] The bitter taste of a dose of opium could be easily improved by sweet substances such as sugar.

Morphine was often used by women instead of opium because it didn't taste as bad or have as many unpleasant side effects on the stomach as opium. Morphine was also smaller in bulk than the equivalent amount of opium. One way to take the drug was by mouth. Another method used by some addicts was to dissolve a teaspoon or so of morphine in warm water, then inject it with a hypodermic syringe into an arm or leg. Others injected the morphine solution into the rectum with an enema syringe or used the drug in suppository form in order to avoid the constant tell-tale bruising and disfiguring puncture marks of the hypodermic needle on their legs and arms.[45] Those wanting a fast result drank laudanum, thereby knowingly or unknowingly also using it as a substitute for alcohol.

The addiction that existed in some women is shown in the motion picture *Tombstone* (1993), where Wyatt Earp's (Kurt Russell) common-law wife, Mattie Blaylock (Dana Wheeler-Nicholson), is seen periodically swigging from a bottle of laudanum. The real Blaylock eventually died of an overdose of laudanum in Pinal, Arizona, in 1888.

LADIES OF THE NIGHT

Virtually all prostitutes used drugs and alcohol and some spent their working days in a total haze of addictive substances. The use of opium and laudanum, for example, was common on "The Row" in Denver's red light district as early as the 1860s, only a few years after the founding of the city. Many prostitutes suffered from alcoholism or drug addiction, and it was an accepted part of their lives. Out of 2,000 prostitutes interviewed by physician William Sanger, 181 (9.1 percent) claimed that they became a prostitute because of "drink and the desire to drink."[46] Further insight into the drinking problem from Sanger's research is shown in Illustration 6–1.

ILLUSTRATION 6–1

Data Adapted from Sanger in Response to a Question About the Use of Alcohol by Prostitutes

Use of Alcohol	Number	Percent of Total		
Do not drink	359	18		
Drink moderately	647	32	}	} 82 percent
Intemperate drinker	754	38 }		} 82 percent
		} 50 percent }		
Habitual drunkard	240	12 }		}
TOTAL	**2,000**	**100**		

(William W. *The History of Prostitution*. New York: Harper and Bros., 1858, pp. 540–541.)

Court records and local newspapers regularly noted the drunken condition of prostitutes. Drunk and disorderly charges were common, often combined with charges of assault and offensive language. Even though many prostitutes drank tea disguised as whiskey with customers in order to keep a clear head, alcohol was drunk with customers in saloons, dance halls, brothels, and cribs as a profitable part of their work. The women commonly added opiates from a nearby pharmacy or local Chinese opium den.

A quick swig of laudanum made a woman appear bright and happy, even after a tiring evening of entertaining multiple customers. Opium and other narcotic drugs helped these women with the chronic and often painful muscular and pelvic discomforts that accompanied continued sexual activity over long periods of time. Drugs were also used to relieve boredom between customers and often made it easier for a prostitute to handle a busy night of men. Some prostitutes used opium to relieve the symptoms of the venereal diseases that were epidemic among these working women.

The use of opium is part of the background of the motion picture *McCabe and Mrs. Miller* (1971). One scene shows madam Constance Miller (Julie Christie) preparing her opium pipe and spirit lamp for her opium smoking ritual. At the end of the movie, as McCabe (Warren Beatty), fatally wounded by the hired killers, crawls through the storm and dies in a snowbank, his partner, Mrs. Miller, is seen in a Chinese opium den ready to fall into an uncaring opium-induced trance.

Drugs allowed prostitutes to keep working regularly and sustained them in their often dreary daily routines. Many prostitutes smoked opium to trade the squalor of their jobs for a brief period of euphoria and frequented opium dens as a temporary escape from their working world and a chance to join in a social atmosphere away from their usual environment. A woman might go to an opium den during the morning, when she was off work, in order to relax with a pipe. Many of the women on Blair Street, for example, the red light district of Silverton, Colorado, smoked opium to relieve their dreary existence. In Virginia City, Nevada, it was well known that two prostitutes named Frankie Norton and Big Mouthed Annie frequented the local opium dens.

The incidence of mental depression was high among prostitutes, so many of them turned to drugs and alcohol to relieve the loneliness and unhappiness of being far from family and friends. Most prostitutes went through periods of severe depression at one time or another, and suicides were common. In a book based on the letters of a prostitute named Rosa May, who lived in Virginia City, Nevada, during the late 1870s, author George Williams said, "She may start to drink hard, snuff 'snow' (cocaine) or take laudanum ... to ease the pain of her loneliness. If she goes low enough, she may kill herself, which is not uncommon."[47] Christmas in particular was depressing in the cribs and parlor houses, and was one of the few days of the year when there were almost no customers. As a result, there were more suicides among prostitutes at Christmas than at any other period of the year.

Pimps and madams often created or encouraged drug addiction among prostitutes, as addicts were easier to manipulate through controlling their supply. Though some pimps and unscrupulous madams helped to create drug addiction in their women in order to bind a woman closer to them, most madams were alert to the excessive use of recreational drugs. Madams in high-class parlor houses were generally strict and would not keep a woman if alcohol or a serious drug addiction interfered with her ability to work. One of the unfortunate unintended problems of drug addiction among prostitutes was that if one was arrested and held in jail, she might become violently ill if she did not receive her regular dose and suddenly go into unexpected withdrawal.

WANTON WOMEN AND CRIME

Alcohol and opium were often used by prostitutes for more nefarious purposes than to give their customer pleasure, but to drug customers to rob them. The straightforward method was to encourage the client to drink, so that he became so drunk that he could not tell what was happening. Large amounts of liquor could be used, or a drug such as laudanum could be slipped into his drink to make him pass out. This technique also had the benefit for the woman that if the customer were drunk enough she might not have to have sex with him because he might pass out or be unable to function. The *Black Hills Daily Times* of Deadwood, South Dakota, reported on March 20, 1882, that a local cattleman out for a good time at the Gem Theater had been drugged and robbed of a large sum of money. The report said that when he was found, he was nearly dead from the effects of the drugging.

Prostitutes commonly used the drug chloral hydrate to drug customers. First synthesized in the 1860s, this was a mild sedative that was used to induce sleep. Chloral hydrate was also known as "knock-out drops" (K.O. drops) or "Mickey Finn." Chloral hydrate could be readily dissolved in whiskey, which enhanced the sedative effects. This practice was the origin of the expression "to slip someone a Mickey." Chloral hydrate was readily soluble in alcohol or water, acted within ten or fifteen minutes, and produced a sleep resembling natural sleep that lasted five hours or more. After a shot or two of drugged whiskey, unconscious drunks might be dragged into an unoccupied corner of the room or outside behind the building and left there. Robbers could then take wallets, valuables, and gold dust at their leisure. When the unfortunate customer woke up, he found himself on the sidewalk or somewhere in a back alley with his pockets picked clean of gold, money, valuables, and other belongings. More serious was that a man who had passed out and been dumped outside could freeze to death in winter or in the night cold of the high-altitude mining camps.

The case of William Joos illustrates what could happen. Joos, who worked at a brewery in Golden, Colorado, went to visit a woman at a bordello in Denver's Market Street red light district on May 27, 1891. While he was there he drank some beer into which madam Blanche Morgan had previously mixed some morphine. After Joos passed out, the two women robbed him of $55 and tossed him out into the alley behind the brothel. He called for police help, but when they arrived they found him already dead.[48]

LOVE AND LUST

Rightly or wrongly, opium and alcohol have long been mentally associated with an increased desire for sex. Alcohol did indeed induce this desire, but through a lowering of inhibitions rather than inciting lust itself. Individuals who used opium said that the desire for sex increased at first, then with continued use the interest and the ability to perform soon decreased. This usually corrected itself, however, when the drug usage was stopped.

Due to the mental association with illicit activity and sexual prowess, opium was reputed to be an aphrodisiac, though reports of its effectiveness in practice varied. One of the Victorian treatments for impotence was for a man to take a dose of opium, musk, and ambergris (a waxy substance secreted by sperm whales) every day. This combination was supposed to incite male desire. To keep this in perspective, however, around the same time, eating ants was being recommended in France and Germany for curing impotence.[49]

One of the seemingly odder cures for impotence involving drink was practiced in Chinese medicine and required soaking a live rattlesnake in a jar of alcohol. The resulting "tonic" was said to produce a painful, but very effective, "tightening of flaccid tissue."[50] The usefulness of opium as an aphrodisiac was refuted by physician George Wood, who stated that the mechanism of opium use differed from that of alcohol in that opium did not stimulate "erotic excitement, and that incapacity of combined muscular movement for a given purpose, which are so strongly characteristic of alcoholic stimulation."[51] Quite the opposite in fact. The prolonged use of opium resulted in a decrease in the level of sex hormones and a heavy user of the drug usually experienced a reduction in the desire for both food and sex.

The Victorian notion still persisted, however, that women who took opium would be consumed with lust and pleasurable sensations. Self-appointed guardians of public morals were convinced in their own minds that opium incited immoral behavior. As a result, drug abuse, and particularly the use of opium, was equated with sexual license. Typical was this dark and knowing quote from author H.H. Kane: "Female [opium] smokers, if not already lost in point of virtue, soon become so."[52] Similar was F.E. Oliver, who said, somewhat unfairly, "The fact generally remarked that women constitute so large a proportion of opium takers, is due, perhaps, more to moral than to physical causes."[53] Even as late as 1956 one nursing text contained the following comment: "The habitual use of opium *in any form* [italics in original] not only affects the body but also causes moral degeneration."[54]

In reality, the regular and sustained use of opium, morphine, and laudanum, as was frequently common among prostitutes, disrupted ovulation or caused menstruation to cease altogether. This tended to reduce the birth rate among prostitutes and other heavy users of opiates. This may have acted (either deliberately or coincidentally) as a crude form of contraception and may partly explain why prostitutes of the time were not surrounded by children in an era of uncertain birth control.

Some Victorians were envious of any rumors of sexual activities they were not participating in, and they envied anybody else's allegedly licentious lifestyle. As a result, whispered rumors made the rounds that opium-smokers were using drugs to seduce innocent women. Also supposedly associated with opium were rape, seduction, and other criminal acts. This negative public image was reinforced by the fact that prostitutes commonly used opium, even though the evidence was that in real life opiates reduced sexual desire and performance.

In similar fashion, rumors of sexual misdeeds were widespread when chloroform was first discovered to be an anesthetic. Chloroform supposedly affected the pelvic regions and its use was alleged to excite women, some of whom shouted wild obscenities while going under anesthesia. There were also wild unfounded rumors of the seduction of women patients while they were under anesthesia.

Secret Remedies and Patent Medicines

The use of opiates in the late 1800s was more widespread than most people realized. Some distilleries, for example, added opiates to their alcoholic beverages to increase the feeling of intoxication and to stimulate repurchase of the product. Cocaine and morphine were sometimes added to soda-fountain beverages and cigarettes for the same reason. Women who swore that a drop of liquor would never cross their lips dosed themselves with a tablespoon or two a day of one of the many alcoholic patent medicines that were available, never realizing that they were drinking the equivalent of up to 80 proof liquor. Author Frederick Powell, commenting on patent medicines in *Bacchus Dethroned* said, "It is our conviction, founded on extensive observation, that the injury done to the nervous system of children by the administration of these nostrums, leads, in after years, to the development of the drunkard's appetite, and the misery of the drunkard's career."[55]

ILLUSTRATION 6–2

Powerhouse Patent Medicines

The following are percentages of alcohol found in some over-the-counter patent medicines. They contained an amazing 17 to 44 percent of alcohol by volume (34 to 88 proof).

Ayer's Sarsaparilla	26%	Hostetter's Stomach Bitters	44%
Boker's Stomach Bitters	43%	Luther's Temperance Bitters	17%
Burdock Blood Bitters	25%	Lydia Pinkham's Vegetable	21%
Drakes' Plantation Bitters	33%	Compound	
Faith Whitcomb's Nerve Bitters	20%	Paine's Celery Tonic	21%
Flint's Quaker Bitters	23%	Peruna	28%
Golden Liquid Beef Tonic	27%	Psychine	10%
Hooflander's German Bitters	25%	Warner's Safe True Bitters	36%
Hooker's Wigwam Tonic	21%		

There were no legal limits to prescribing opium in its various forms. Narcotic drugs such as opium, cocaine, and morphine were not controlled substances in the late 1800s and could be easily purchased over the counter at a local drugstore or even purchased legally without prescription by mail order.

Another common unregulated source of patent medicines was peddlers at traveling medicine shows, which consisted mostly of entertainment to draw in potential customers so that the pitchman could then sell them the "medicine." Most of these nostrums were touted as secret tonics, often supposedly obtained from American Indians. Genuine Indians might even perform at the shows.

The problem of addiction to patent medicines was recognized late in the 1880s. One physician wrote in 1898: "Another cause of inebriety in women is found in the patent medicines advertised as a panacea for all pain, which chemical analysis shows to be largely alcoholic. Many temperance women would be horrified to know that they are taking alcohol in varying quantity, from 6 to 47 percent, in the bitters, tonics and restorative medicines they are using."[56]

When physicians protested against the misuse and overdosing by the general public that was associated with patent medicines, they were seen as opposing "the competition." Druggists, fearing a loss of revenue, continued to sell narcotic drugs, correctly assuming that if they didn't someone else would. One pharmacist in the late nineteenth century who derived a large part of his income from sales of opium claimed that "if it were not for this stuff and my soda-water I might as well shut up shop."[57]

The per capita consump-

The patent medicine Psychine claimed to cure pneumonia, consumption, indigestion, dyspepsia, catarrh of the stomach (whatever that was), malaria, night sweats, and "speaker's sore throat." One advertisement for this tonic claimed that it would restore the "vigor of girlhood." At least the 10 percent alcohol that the "medicine" contained may have made the user feel that way (author's collection).

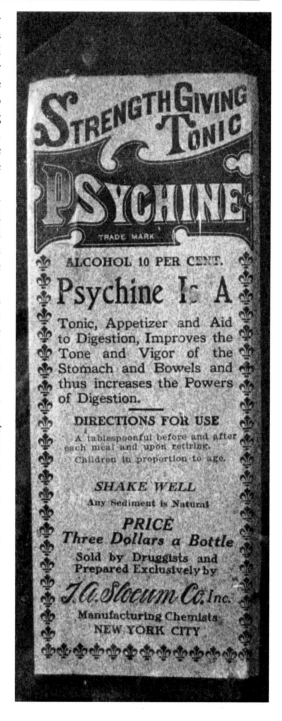

tion of opium gradually rose during the nineteenth century, reaching a peak in the 1890s. Between 1898 and 1902 the importation of opium into the United States increased by five times and morphine by six times, primarily for compounding in patent medicines. Narcotic importation then declined until about 1915 when federal laws regulated legal imports.

LYDIA PINKHAM

One of the most popular patent medicines was Lydia Pinkham's Vegetable Compound, which was advertised as the "only positive cure and legitimate remedy for the peculiar weaknesses and ailments of women." It was developed by Mrs. Lydia Estes Pinkham of Lynn, Massachusetts, who claimed that it contained only vegetable ingredients. It was said to be derived from various roots that were soaked in alcohol. According to the company's advertising, the alcohol was used "solely as a solvent and preservative"[58] The tonic, however, was at various times composed of from 12 to 21 percent alcohol. The 1920 formulation contained 15 percent alcohol. Pinkham's tonic was also specifically recommended for pneumonia, tuberculosis, and appendicitis, but particularly for "the recurrent problems of women."

Like many other housewives of the time, Pinkham had started brewing her own remedies at home. One of her formulas in particular was popular among friends she gave her concoctions to. As a result, in 1875, she started to manufacture the brew for sale as a patent medicine. She developed a very effective marketing campaign that turned it into one of the most successful of its kind. In 1883 her company grossed nearly $300,000.[59] Though the ingredients were not stated on the label, an analysis of Lydia Pinkham's herb medicine showed that it contained unicorn root (*Aletris farinos*), life root (*Senecio viscosus*), black cohosh (*Cimicifuga racemosa*), pleurisy root (*Asclepias tuberose*), fenugreek seed (*Trigonella foenum-gracecum*), and alcohol.[60] These herbs had all previously been used in herbal medicine as natural remedies to treat various menstrual and menopausal symptoms. Unlike many other patent medicines, Pinkham's did not contain opium.

AND SOME OF THE OTHERS

Hostetter's Celebrated Stomach Bitters was touted as being good for the treatment of dyspepsia, ague, dysentery, colic, and nervous prostration. It contained as much as 44 percent alcohol. A clue to its contents, however, should have been obvious, because the term "bitters" was sometimes used as a generic name for alcohol. Limerick's Liniment consisted primarily of alcohol with a few token additives; it was also claimed to be good for diseases of horses. Ayer's sarsaparilla, which was a carbonated drink made from various roots and herbs, originally contained 26 percent alcohol.[61]

Some of the tonics packed a punch that was due to more than alcohol. Hamlin's Cough Syrup contained ipecac, antimony, syrup of wild cherry, and twelve grains of acetate of morphia (an older name for morphine). Kendall's Balsam contained 61 percent alcohol and was fortified with five grains of opium per ounce. Old Sachem Bitters contained opium and alcohol. Piso's Consumption Cure contained morphine, alcohol, and *Cannabis indica* (*Cannabis sativa* is more commonly known as hemp, hashish, or marijuana). A similar tonic was Dr. J. Collis Browne's Chlorodyne, which contained morphine, chloroform, and Cannabis. Godfrey's Cordial and Mrs. Winslow's Soothing Syrup both contained morphine. Jayne's Carminative contained 23 percent alcohol and over half a grain of opium to the ounce.

And there were those that were a little misleading. Kaufman's Sulfur Bitters, which contained 21 percent alcohol by volume, baldly stated that it "contains no alcohol."[62] Howe's Arabian Tonic contained 13 percent alcohol, but was advertised as "not a rum drink." Parker's Tonic, which contained a whopping 43 percent alcohol (86 proof!), was advertised as "purely vegetable."

CHAPTER SEVEN

Saloons and Other
Parlors of Iniquity

Though colonial Americans, regardless of gender, age, class, or geographical region, drank large amounts of beer, wine, brandy, gin, and corn whiskey,
their favorite distilled spirit was rum. They also drank several variations of
rum, such as the popular "bumbo," which consisted of rum, sugar, water,
and nutmeg. Mixed drinks also took the form of slings, flips, toddys, and
juleps.

ILLUSTRATION 7–1

A Guide to Colonial Drinks

Flip: a hot drink that was a combination of rum and beer with sugar, and sometimes
    milk, an egg, or spices added.
Julep: a cold drink made with whiskey or brandy with sugar and fresh mint added.
Sling: an iced drink made with gin or brandy, with sugar and lemon juice.
Toddy: a hot drink made with brandy, whiskey, or gin with water, sugar, and spices,
    such as cinnamon and cloves.

In addition, alcohol was an important part of the colonial economy in
the trade triangle of rum, slaves, and molasses that cycled between America,
Africa, and the Caribbean. In the 1700s, ships from New England carried
rum to the coast of West Africa, where it was traded for black slaves. The
slaves were transported to the West Indies to work in the sugar-cane fields
and traded for molasses. The ships then carried the molasses back to New
England for use in the rum distilleries and repeated the triangle all over again.
When the slave trade was outlawed in 1808, one result was a large dent in
profits from the rum-slave-molasses trade.

The per person consumption of alcohol in America appears to have been
at its highest during the fifty or so years before the Civil War. Part of this tradition arrived with the flood of people emigrating from Europe. French and
German immigrants, for example, came from cultures where drinking large
amounts of alcoholic beverages was routine. As pioneers moved westward,

123

corn whiskey took the place of rum, but drinking in the Old West continued to be widespread. This practice led naturally to an increased growth in the number of places to drink. These were the saloons of the Old West, which have been described in many Western novels and nonfiction books and used as the setting for countless plots in Western movies. Saloons were important centers of social, cultural, and political life for adult males in the Old West from about 1870 to the closing of most saloons in 1920 at the start of Prohibition.

The saloon of the movies is a popular part of the myth of the Wild West. It is one of the mandatory locations for action involving the hero, the villain, various dance-hall girls, and frequent shoot-outs. In reality, saloons were rarely that wild and woolly. They were instead places where men could enjoy a social drink, eat, catch up on the latest gossip, and conduct their business over beer or a whiskey. Most Victorian men did not like to drink at home or alone, but preferred to drink in the social atmosphere of the saloon in the companionship of other customers. As one observer aptly summed it up, "Like taverns throughout history, the primary function of the saloon was to offer the basic amenities of the home in a public place."[1] Similar to most homes, the Western saloon offered drink, food, shelter, and congenial companionship. In addition, those who wanted the company of willing women could find it there.

The lifestyle of the young single male population of the West drove many men to the saloons, as they often lived in small uncomfortable rooms in boardinghouses. Young males in a booming mining town with mines and mills that ran around the clock might have to share accommodations due to a shortage of rooms, with different men sleeping in the same bed at different times, depending on their particular work shift. If it was not their turn to sleep, they needed a place to go.

In addition to filling the obvious roles of a drinking and gambling establishment and as a contact point for prostitution, saloons often served other functions in a newly founded town. They were used as meeting halls, churches for itinerant preachers, trading posts, employment agencies, impromptu operating theaters after saloon fights, temporary mortuaries, post offices, and hotels. Some saloons offered mailboxes where customers could receive letters. Saloons and their bartenders were gossip centers for the latest news or the most recent joke making the rounds. A traveler or a newcomer to town could usually get a drink, a bath, a cigar, a meal, and perhaps a room for the night. There might be a bulletin board where "help wanted" or "for sale" notices could be posted. One story, in particular, emphasizes the perceived importance of the saloon by the residents of a developing town. When the first saloon was constructed near Placerville, Colorado, it was built a half-mile from the existing cabins of the small community. The horrified settlers decided that they couldn't be that far away from their local drinking establishment, so they abandoned the existing town site and rebuilt their cabins around the new saloon.[2]

In rural areas of colonial America, drinking places started as taverns, or establishments where a traveler could get a drink, along with food and lodging. In the larger cities, separate businesses gradually became available to provide food and lodging, so taverns eventually evolved into places to relax and drink while discussing the latest news and gossip in a congenial atmosphere. Taverns thus evolved into saloons.

The word "saloon" was derived from the French word *salon*, which was the name used to describe a large public meeting hall that was intended for receptions or entertainment. The word was eventually corrupted into "saloon." The name had a somewhat more elegant ring to it than "tavern" and the designation "saloon" entered the popular vocabulary by at least 1840. The general meaning came to include any establishment where drinks were sold to be consumed on the premises. Thus the saloon became a drinking place independent of the functions of the earlier tavern and inn. Further adaptations of the name were used to describe specific types of saloons, such as "billiard saloon" or "beer saloon."

By the end of the century, as the functions and activities in saloons changed over the next sixty years or so, the name "saloon" became associated with vice and drunkenness, and the institution of the saloon became the target of reformers and temperance crusaders.

A Home Away from Home

A saloon-keeper was often one of the earliest residents to arrive at a new mining strike or logging camp in the West. For a businessman who could afford it, a saloon was a good investment and provided a good source of income for the owner. His saloon often served as the social hub of an infant town. As the early towns matured, saloons and other drinking establishments quickly added gambling in order to provide entertainment for patrons between drinks. Some games of cards were friendly; others were more serious and could invoke hard feelings and fights. Gambling was always a popular activity and it substantially increased the profits for the saloon.

Another clever innovation to bring in customers and generate more sales was the "saloon lunch." This consisted of free food provided to patrons who continued to drink. Drinking alcohol stimulated the digestive juices, thus producing hunger. The patrons then nibbled on something from the saloon lunch table. Most of the food was intentionally salty in order to stimulate thirst and have the patrons buy more drinks, thus leading to a circular round of drink, food, drink, food, and so forth. Salty foods that rated high on the menu were sardines, smoked herring, pickled fish, spicy sausage, salt crackers, soup or stew, salted nuts, pickled eggs, and pretzels. In Telluride, Colorado, the Corner Saloon offered possum for those with Southern tastes. Even when the saloon's cost of the "free" lunch was factored in, the negligible cost of the food stimulated far more than its worth in sales of additional drinks.

Judging by old Western movies, the saloon was where men just sat and drank and passed the time of day. Though not common, this sort of behavior was not totally unknown. One historian commented that at Dowell's Saloon in El Paso, Texas, "the 'white men' in the community did practically nothing for the very simple reason that there was nothing to do, and the very natural result of this pleasing state of affairs was that Uncle Ben Dowell's saloon sheltered the entire American male population of the town for the greater part of every day and for nearly all of every night."[3]

In the mining town of Bodie, California, the snows of winter frequently piled deep on the buildings and the temperatures regularly dropped to well below freezing. The frigid weather virtually shut down mining in the winter, and, as one old miner complained, there was nothing to do but hang around the saloons. One young man in Ouray, in the mountains of Colorado, told a temperance worker that the saloon was the only place that he could find a warm place to sit.[4] This was not unusual in the mountain mining camps where the temperatures might drop well below zero in the wintertime. In 1906, the town of Creede, Colorado, passed an ordinance closing saloons on Sundays. The ordinance was soon repealed when the local newspaper pointed out that many of the miners did not have a warm place to go during cold winter evenings.[5]

The saloon was usually the largest building in a new town, so it often doubled as a meeting hall and might be the focus for other community activities. Before permanent churches were established in the Old West, for example, the religious needs of early frontier communities were served by itinerant preachers who rode from camp to camp by stagecoach or on horseback, stopping to preach at each new settlement. If a newly founded town had no church building, a saloon might be temporarily used to hold services. A saloon almost always had a built-in audience for church meetings, and saloon-owners knew that after listening to a fiery preacher for a couple of hours the audience would be ready for a drink or two or three. When a preacher passed through town, drinking and gambling were temporarily suspended and the paintings on the walls were discreetly covered up while the parson was busy saving the men's souls from the evils of drink. After the preacher left, the gaming tables and paintings were uncovered again and saloon activities went back into full swing.

Saloons were the places to go for the latest local gossip and news events. Even newspaper reporters used saloon patrons with tongues loosened by alcohol to uncover information on events that were newsworthy. Sometimes they assisted in loosening them. When Wells Drury was hired as a reporter in 1874 on the *Gold Hill Daily News* in Gold Hill, which was near Virginia City, Nevada, he was paid $7.50 a day, plus a $2.50 a day allowance for saloon expenses. The latter was an expense account to be used while interviewing the local citizenry, who tended to gather in the saloons.[6]

Saloon patrons were almost exclusively male, men who were seeking the social companionship of other men of similar age, marital status, and economic standing. Many of them, such as miners, loggers, railroad workers, and cowboys, often shared the same working conditions, ethnic background, and were of roughly the same age. Many men started to drink because drinking provided their primary day-to-day social contact. Though most Western men drank to some degree or another, saloons were typically patronized by single men. Married men who had families to support did not have extra money for drink, as the cost of living in a frontier town where everything had to be shipped in was high. Aside from this, most wives did not want their husbands wasting money on liquor and gambling. One sociable alternative for married men who did not drink was to join one of the local lodges of a fraternal organization, such as the Elks.

Single men, on the other hand, had no immediate family to answer to and often lived in a small rented room in a boardinghouse or rooming house. For them, the saloon was a type of social club where they met fellow bachelors after work and passed the time in what they considered to be friendly pursuits such as drinking or gambling. In addition to liquor and male socializing, womanizing with the female companionship in a saloon was considered to be a healthy pursuit and method of relaxation for an active young male. As well as drinking, gambling, and women, an enterprising saloon owner might provide other masculine types of entertainment. Cock fights, dog fights, wrestling matches, and bare-knuckled boxing bouts were all used to try to attract patrons and increase business.

Because of the importance of the social aspect of saloons in the early settlements, the Temperance Movement did not make much progress in the West until near the end of the nineteenth century when settlement of the West was shifting from a population of predominantly young single men to older men with families.

Evolution of the Basic Saloon

Early saloons in a newly founded town or mining camp were often only a canvas tent brought in on a wagon. This was the cheapest and easiest way to start a saloon and was the smartest way for a saloon-keeper to protect his investment. If a fledgling settlement prospered and grew into a permanent town, the saloon could be easily moved from a tent into a more substantial wooden building. If the camp did not prosper and last, the saloon-keeper could pack the tent back into his wagon and move on to the next new town. On rare occasions, though, the process worked in reverse. The town of Arland, Wyoming, was built specifically to supply local cowboys with whiskey and women. The entire town consisted of a dancehall, a brothel, a store, and the local post office.[7]

Many early mining camps had saloons constructed with a wooden floor and partial wooden walls, with canvas stretched over the top like a tent. Most of these structures were not very substantial and strong winds or heavy snows could cause them to collapse. The bar in a saloon in an early mining camp might consist of only a rough board balanced across two whiskey barrels. Some enterprising saloon-keepers served drinks off the tail-boards of their wagons until they could erect more permanent structures.

Bars in early saloons in the Old West often consisted of only a simple wooden counter made of rough boards with a barrel of whiskey and a selection of bottles without labels on a shelf behind. The "whiskey" in these unmarked bottles might be watered down or might be concocted in the back room in order to increase profits for the saloon-owner (author's collection).

Improvements in saloons typically came later in the development of a town. Businessmen wanted to find out if the town was going to survive before they invested substantial amounts of money to build a permanent saloon with elaborate furnishings. Towns built on gold and silver mining strikes, in particular, tended to boom like a flash in the pan and then fade away just as rapidly if the gold played out, which it eventually and inevitably did. The modern West is still scattered with historic mining towns from the last half of the nineteenth century that were all heralded as the next Eldorado but that fizzled away within a year or two.

Early saloon construction depended on the building materials that were on hand locally. In a mining camp in the mountains where trees were readily available, saloons were typically low-roofed, log-walled buildings. On the plains to the east, such as in early Kansas and Nebraska where trees and wood were scarce, the saloon might consist of an earthen dug-out with sod walls and a sod roof supported by poles laid crosswise. In towns of the desert Southwest, the walls of a saloon might be made of adobe or brick.[8]

A typical early saloon in a mining town in the Rocky Mountains or a Sierra Nevada mining camp was a narrow, deep, log building with a long wooden bar that stretched from front to back along one of the longer walls. The interior of the building typically consisted of a large, open, low-roofed room that ranged in size from fifteen feet wide by thirty feet deep to perhaps thirty feet wide and eighty feet deep. The first saloon in Deadwood, South Dakota, was a fourteen-foot by twenty-foot log building located on Main Street.

The floor of an early saloon might be only hard-packed dirt and the walls unfinished logs. The swinging batwing doors popularized by the movies were not in general use in most saloons, particularly in the cold climate of the mountains of the West where there was a need to keep the heat inside. Standard doors were more common, though sometimes they were never closed, such as in some Kansas towns during the cattle-shipping season.

Windows were usually few and small in the early log saloons, so the interior of the saloon was dark and gloomy. Dim light was provided by candles or oil lamps hung from the ceiling. Often the smaller saloons were poorly ventilated. The patron entering one of these establishments was greeted with a characteristic aroma that was a combination of body odor from unwashed customers, the sickly smell of stale beer, greasy black smoke and coal oil fumes from the lamps, and the strong smell of tobacco. One visitor described the typical atmosphere of gamy aromas as "a strong sickening smell, while the worst steamed with odors from empty beer kegs around [the] entrance and obnoxious receptacles [urinals] just to the rear."[9]

Men at the bar drank standing up. There were no bar stools, though most saloons featured a brass rail that ran along the front of the counter for patrons to rest a foot on while drinking. Towels were usually hung every few feet along the front of the bar counter so that patrons with moustaches could wipe off any foam from beer. Needless to say, this practice contributed to the spread of many of the lung diseases, such as tuberculosis and pneumonia, that were rife in the high-altitude mining camps.

Brass cuspidors were placed at various locations around the saloon, including in front of the bar, for the convenience those who chewed tobacco. Contemporary photographs, however, show that the aim of most customers was not particularly accurate. Presumably as the tobacco-chewer drank more and more, the accuracy of his aim deteriorated. Saloon-owners were somewhat philosophical about it. A sign in one saloon read, "If you spit on the floor at home, spit on the floor here. We want you to feel at home."[10]

To compensate for missed aim and other debris dropped by messy patrons, the floor was often covered with sawdust to soak up spills from beer and whiskey glasses, as well as food and anything else that might end up on the floor. Even when early dirt floors were replaced by wooden planks, sawdust was still spread on the boards to soak up beer, tobacco juice, and other falling detritus. Some saloons featured a mesh mat along the front of the bar to serve the same purpose. The mat also provided better traction on the floor for unsteady patrons who might slip and slide on floors that were slick with spilled beer, liquor, and unmentionable debris.

During the early development of a town, this sawdust on the floor might be used for bedding. Because there was typically a shortage of housing as a new mining town boomed, saloon tables and floors might be rented out after closing hours for 25¢ a night to new arrivals in town or to travelers. Unfortunately, this sawdust might become contaminated by germs, and was one reason for the rapid spread of lung diseases, due to infected saloon patrons spitting and missing the spittoon.

Some saloons incorporated a barber or bathing facilities in the back of the building. This brought in additional trade, as customers who stopped in for a shave, a haircut, or a bath had to pass the bar on the way to the back and often succumbed to the temptation of a quick beer on the way past. It was also convenient for customers who publicly denied drinking. They could go into a saloon, ostensibly for a haircut, and sample a drink or two at the same time. Another hypocritical aspect was that some accommodating bartenders would sell small bottles full of whiskey labeled "medicine" to those who did not want it publicly known that they drank.

Owning a saloon was generally the most profitable business in a Western town. The profit that a businessman could make in a saloon depended on a combination of the local freight rates, the wholesale cost of whiskey, and the going price for drinks on the retail market. Whiskey sold to the saloon for between $2 and $10 a gallon (128 ounces). Assume for this example that it was $8 a gallon. Drinks were from 1 to 1½ ounces, thus providing 80 to 120 drinks per gallon, giving a bar-cost of about 8¢ per drink. The expense of freight would also have to be added to the costs. Freight rates were typically between 8¢ and 12¢ per pound. Ten gallons of whiskey in a small barrel weighed about 100 pounds, giving a freight cost of about 1¢ per drink. The selling price was typically 25¢ a shot. Thus the profit per drink would be around 16¢ per drink, or $16 per gallon. If the original whiskey could be purchased for only $2, then the profit would increase to around $22 per gallon. In the 1870s, the cost of a gallon of whiskey freighted to Deadwood, South Dakota, was $1.65. Sold by the drink at 50¢ each, the resulting profit was about $62 per gallon. Also deducted from the profit would be rent if the saloon-keeper did not own the building and the expense of wages for barmen and other employees. Rent for a large saloon in a booming mining town could be as much as $500 a month.

In the 1880s at the Bird Cage Theater in Tombstone, beer sold for 50¢ a glass on the main floor. The price went up to $1 if it was served by a "waiter girl" in one of the upstairs curtained boxes that lined the theater. Bottles of Sonoma wines sold in Tombstone for 50¢. In 1867, champagne sold for $5 a bottle in Hays City, Kansas. In Leadville, a large glass of beer sold for 10¢ and a small one for 5¢.

The price of drinks was proportional to the relative remoteness of the saloon. In Dawson, Yukon Territory, during the Klondike gold rush of 1898, so-called whiskey sold for 50¢ a shot. By comparison, a shot of whiskey in Cripple Creek, Colorado, at the same time typically cost about half that amount. Nonetheless, saloons in turn-of-the-century Dawson might take in $15,000 on a good night. Overall profits are hard to calculate but, as an example, George Hoover's Saloon in Dodge City, Kansas, did $6,228.67 in business in October of 1883, which was during the height of that year's cattle season. During 1883 and 1885, he averaged about $33,000 of liquor and saloon supplies per year.[11] Incidentally, Hoover's Saloon was the first commercial structure (albeit in a tent) in Dodge City, showing the speed with which whiskey sellers moved into a booming town and the importance of their presence.

Liquor distributors also made handsome profits. John Herrman and John Trebor started a wholesale and retail liquor dealership in Deadwood in 1877. By 1884 the business was doing $100,000 a year.[12] Unfortunately for them, this flood of money coming in did not last due to a series of anti-liquor laws passed in South Dakota in the 1890s. Another Deadwood businessman who profited handsomely while the liquor boom lasted was Harris Franklin, who was bringing in $125,000 a year by 1884.

As temporary mining camps matured into established, permanent towns, the early tent saloons made from wood-frame and canvas evolved with the rest of the buildings, and the saloons became permanent structures made from logs or rough lumber. If a town lasted long enough and business was good enough, the saloon evolved into a more ornate building with finished boards on the outside. Saloons in two-story wooden buildings were common, and often had false fronts to give them a substantial and imposing air.

As saloons became more permanent, the bars became fancier. Early bars made of rough boards evolved into elaborate wooden counters with ornately carved fittings. Cherry, walnut, oak, and mahogany were popular for bars. Elaborate back-bars were carved to match the counter, with inset mirrors behind the counter to store and show off elegant bottles, glasses, and perhaps a few ornaments. The ultimate expression of ornate bars was reached in the late 1800s and building them became a significant industry that employed many skilled craftsmen. These elaborate bars were very expensive. Back-bars made by the Brunswick Company of Chicago sold for around $500, with the counter in front of it costing almost as much.

The Western saloon of the movies, with a huge ornate bar, plate-glass mirrors, crystal chandeliers, and rows of pretty girls dancing the can-can in a stage show, were more common in larger cities, such as Leadville, Tombstone, Portland, Seattle, or San Francisco, where gold dust flowed like water and there were enough customers with gold or silver to support such extravagances. Such saloons would include plush furniture, fancy glassware, and diamond-dust mirrors. Bartenders in these fancy places might be hired from as far away as Chicago or St. Louis.

The following quote applies specifically to the Alamo Saloon in Dodge City, but is representative of fancy saloons across the West: "The Alamo was the most elaborate of the saloons, and a description of it will give an idea of the plan of them all. It was housed in a long room with a forty-foot frontage on Cedar street, facing west.... Inside and along the front of the south side was the bar with its array of carefully polished brass fixtures and rails. From the back bar arose a large mirror, which reflected the brightly sealed bottles of liquor. At various places over the walls were huge paintings in cheaply done imitations of the nude masterpieces of the Renaissance painters."[13]

The following description was penned in 1876 to similarly describe a typical saloon in San Francisco: "In the bar-rooms there are large plate glass mirrors, alternating with fine paintings in the panels of the walls. There are exquisitely chiseled vases, always containing brilliant and fragrant bouquets of flowers.... [T]he floors are formed of marble tiles, the ceilings finely frescoed, and the windows are of heavy plate glass, ornamented with graceful designs."[14] The larger saloons usually provided music from an orchestra to attract and entertain patrons. The "orchestra" might range in size from only an accordion and banjo to a larger group, which might include a cornet, drums, fiddle, and piano.

As towns and mining camps matured, saloons featured a fancy wooden counter with an ornate back-bar with mirrors and shelves behind. In this typical example, a brass rail ran along the front on which to rest a weary leg, the spittoon was hopefully the target for projectiles of chewing tobacco, and the towel hung on the counter was used to wipe beer foam from moustaches. Note the saloon lunch on the near end of the bar with a selection of cheese, pickles, and salty meats (author's collection).

Saloon Art

The interior walls of saloons were usually decorated with a variety of objects and pictures that were intended to appeal to male tastes and make the men feel at home while they drank. Typical male-oriented ornaments on the walls were animal heads with trophy horns or antlers, stuffed birds, and mounted fish.

Popular pictures included famous contemporary sports figures, seafaring scenes, horse racing, boxing matches, and portraits of American presidents. One picture consistently found in saloons was one of the several variations of General Custer's defeat with the Seventh Cavalry at the battle of the Little Bighorn. One very popular version was a huge lithograph by F. Otto Becker, based on Cassily Adam's painting of *Custer's Last Fight*. The lithograph was commissioned in 1896 by the Anheuser-Busch Brewing Association of St.

Louis, Missouri, which distributed 150,000 copies to saloons around the country.

Aside from these symbols of male bravado, the most widespread and popular type of saloon art was the barroom nude. Typically these were large paintings in elaborate gold frames of a standing or reclining nude woman gazing dreamily off into space. The contemporary Victorian male's taste ran to classical nudes, which were plump feminine figures with large bosoms, tiny waists, and full hips and thighs. To lend a veneer of respectability and taste, most of the paintings were of women from the literary or art classics, such as Diana, Venus, Psyche, or Cleopatra. These reflected the Victorian fascination with the Greek and Roman classical period. Many of the pictures showed a well-endowed, semi-clad or nude young woman ready to take a bath, preparing for a nap, undressing for bed, or reclining on a couch, bed, or similar type of furniture. To meet the ideals of Victorian propriety, the subjects were usually discreetly draped in the appropriate places with veils of filmy cloth.

Critics of saloons claimed that these prominent displays of naked women inflamed the desires of men already aroused by the "demon rum." Though these pictures certainly depicted mostly nude women, they were not lewd or obscene, but were in general very artistic. The pictures were hung on the walls behind or near the bar so that a customer could look at them discreetly while tipping up his glass.

One rather clever way of combining this type of saloon art with increased profit for the saloon-owner was the use of saloon tokens as change for a drink. If, for example, the price of a beer was a bit (12½¢), a drinker paying with a quarter might receive a saloon token as change. The use of tokens was profitable for the saloon owner because the patron either used them for more drinks or did not redeem them at all, which was even more profitable. To encourage the patron not to redeem them, some saloons used tokens that had on them a small image of a nude woman like the saloon paintings. The drinker was often only too happy to keep it instead of redeem it.

Saloons and Women

Men looking for women knew that places that sold liquor and many of those that provided entertainment could also provide willing partners. Brothels, parlor houses, and cribs were the primary establishments for men seeking women in the Old West. Other frontier businesses, however, such as saloons and dance halls, found that having prostitutes available increased their income by having women drink with their customers. Therefore, loose women frequently plied their trade in saloons, dance halls, and gambling halls, which were often the same establishment.

The women found in saloons were not necessarily all prostitutes. Some were merely barmaids who served drinks. However, prostitutes were certainly found in saloons and the chances were good that most of the women who were not fallen women would negotiate if the price was right. The men knew that respectable Victorian women did not frequent saloons. The city physician of Denver, Frederick Bancroft, felt that "the evils caused by houses of ill fame scarcely are inferior to those resulting from the intemperate use of ardent spirits."[15]

The women were present primarily to sell drinks. In a saloon, whether they sold themselves or not was a separate business transaction. These women flirted and cajoled the men to buy them the most expensive liquor. For this they typically received 25 percent of the price of whatever their customer drank and what he bought for them. In order to keep a steady head during a full evening of drinking, the bartender usually served the woman cold tea that looked like whiskey instead of the real thing but charged the man the full price for a drink of whiskey. Sometimes the women drank watered-down whiskey but managed to dispose of most of it in the nearest spittoon.

In Denver a popular watering hole was Hi Dingwall's combination saloon and dance hall, which had two bars, one in the front of the dance hall and the other at the back, so that patrons had to buy a drink at whichever door they entered. The patrons paid $1 for a dance, with 75¢ going to the house and 25¢ to the female partner. The music was intentionally fast-paced and lasted for only a few minutes. At the end of each vigorous trot around the dance-floor, the thirsty man was expected to buy a drink for himself and one for his partner at $1 a round.

In most brothels a customer was also expected to buy a drink for his choice of the women. In her case it was usually a glass full of cold tea, but his was real whiskey. Serving drinks added additional profit for the house and usually stimulated the man to spend more money and often to unknowingly treat all the girls to cold tea at whiskey prices.

The sale of liquor was an integral part of bordello profits, and, as part of the operation, the consumption of large amounts of wine and champagne was encouraged. Liquor was sold at a markup that might be five or six times cost, and was an extremely profitable part of the house business. A bottle of wine that sold in a saloon for $1 might cost the brothel customer $15 and a quart bottle of champagne that was worth $5 could cost him up to $30 (at a time when a common miner made $3 a day and a cowboy made $30 a month). Because of these large potential profits, parlor houses were occasionally backed by liquor merchants, or a merchant would put up the initial cost of operating the house with the understanding that the madam would supply only his particular brand or brands of liquor.

The *Rocky Mountain News* of July 23, 1889, claimed that beer halls were the most common source of prostitution. And, indeed, many saloons featured waitresses, dancers, bar girls, and prostitutes to attract customers. Dancing with such women was often the only way that a lonely bachelor could put his arms around a woman. In some saloons the owner or bartender might be married to a prostitute. In such cases, it was not unusual for him to act as her pimp, not only tolerating her activities but actually expecting her to solicit customers. These were often marriages of convenience or were a business arrangement, rather than being the more conventional emotional attachment.

Except for prostitutes and occasional "barmaids," patrons of saloons were essentially male. Respectable Victorian women were typically barred from entering saloons, either by local custom or in extreme cases by local law. A few saloons did cater to women customers by providing a "Ladies' Entrance," but these establishments were in the minority. Even if women were not technically excluded from saloons in many towns, male patrons often found ways to discourage them and make them feel unwelcome. On the other side of the

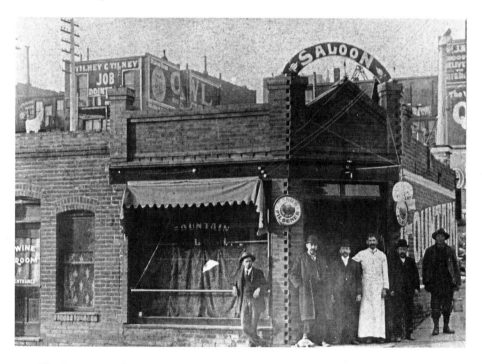

The Fountain Saloon in Cripple Creek, Colorado, sported a fancy brick exterior. Note the separate wine room entrance for women on the left. "Wine rooms" may or may not have been used solely for drinking, but they were also used for quiet assignations by couples and to stage bawdy entertainment for male customers (Glenn Kinnaman Colorado and Western History Collection).

coin, a respectable Victorian woman did not want to frequent saloons as this would have compromised her reputation.

If a saloon did try to attract women customers, it would typically have a separate entrance and facilities for ladies, often labeled a wine room and intended just for women. On the other hand, the name "wine room" could be deceiving. Some wine rooms purposely provided a secluded entrance and quiet back rooms away from main bar of the saloon that were intended for use by couples seeking a discreet rendezvous. Wine rooms were also used to put on male-oriented shows of a somewhat vulgar nature.

Not even trying to be discreet, some saloons served as quasi-brothels and a convenient meeting place for women. The distinction between the two types of establishments was often blurred, as saloons provided women and most brothels served liquor to their customers to make additional profit.

The Saloon as an Economic Force

On the Western frontier, one measure of a town's success was the number of saloons it contained. The faster saloons were established the more successful a town was considered to be. Most early towns were proud of their saloons. Contemporary guidebooks often listed the number of saloons in a town next to information about churches, hotels, and banks as an indicator of the community's success.

As immigrants surged westward to populate the prairies, deserts, and mountains, drinking, the number of drinkers, and the number of saloons proliferated. By 1867, the rowdy town of Hays City, Kansas, had twenty-two saloons and three dance halls — along with one grocery store and one clothing store.[16] Bodie, California, founded as a gold-mining town in 1860, had 15,000 residents by 1870, thirsty miners who were served by three breweries and thirty-five saloons that were open around the clock. A year after its founding, Sawtooth, Idaho, had forty-one retail stores, of which twenty were barrooms.[17]

One single block on West Second Street in Leadville, which was known to the locals as "Whiskey Row," had twenty-four buildings on one side. Fourteen of them were saloons. Lake City, Colorado, founded in 1875, had twenty-nine establishments selling liquor by July of 1877.[18] In 1876, Dodge City, Kansas, had nineteen establishments selling liquor. In all fairness, though, this many were needed during the summer and fall months when the ranks of the town's 1,200 permanent inhabitants were swelled by hundreds of cowboys and cattle buyers, along with the professional gamblers and prostitutes who flocked in to grab their share of all the money floating around. In 1853, the young town of San Francisco had 537 saloons. By 1890, this had increased to a staggering (so to speak) 3,117 licensed establishments selling beer and whiskey.[19] In 1883, a year after its founding, Livingston, Montana, had a population of 3,000 and thirty-three saloons.[20]

By 1860, a year after Denver's formal founding, the infant town had thirty saloons, dance halls, and gambling houses serving a population of 5,000. By 1890, it had 478 saloons, which implied a bar on almost every downtown corner. One of them was Mundy's Sample Room, which offered choice wines and liquors, the finest cigars, and "delectable female companionship." A saloon by any other name was still a saloon, and "sample room" was sometimes used as an alternate name for a saloon. In Tombstone, Arizona, James Earp (Wyatt's older brother) ran a "sampling room" saloon.

Hardcore drinking started in Denver before it was even a town. To help the future Denverites celebrate Christmas Day of 1858 mountain man and trader Richens Lacy "Uncle Dick" Wootton arrived from Taos, New Mexico, with a wagon laden with ten barrels of Taos Lightning. In doing so, Wootten brought the first commercial load of whiskey to Denver. He and his wife arrived on Christmas morning and opened a saloon in a tent. He started the festivities by taking a barrel outside and announcing free drinks in honor of Christmas. With the celebration rolling, drinkers then started on the barrels inside. The original bar consisted of a plank laid across a row of barrels. Wootton did so well that within a few weeks he was able to erect a wooden building thirty feet deep and twenty feet wide called the Western Saloon. At about the same time, two enterprising businessmen named Reed and Hiffner opened their own saloon in the competing town of Auraria, just across Cherry Creek from Denver.

Minot, South Dakota, had twelve saloons by the time it was only a few weeks old. In 1879, Leadville, Colorado, which soon gained (and probably deserved) its reputation as the most wide-open boom town on the Rocky Mountain mining frontier, proudly boasted 120 saloons, 19 beer halls, and 118 gambling halls. At the end of 1880, Leadville had 249 saloons, which comprised the third largest type of business after mining and banking. In 1881, the rowdy silver-mining town of Kokomo, Colorado, had a hundred saloons along its main street. Though some of these numbers seem high, these figures may have included other establishments that sold alcohol, such as brothels, restaurants, and drug stores. Be that as it may, saloons often outnumbered churches in many early Western towns. By 1870, Denver boasted forty-eight saloons, but only six churches and four schools.[21] The local newspaper in the early mining town of Georgetown, Colorado, complained vocally that the town had dozens of saloons and bawdy houses and yet not a single school.

A district judge who visited Miles City, Montana, in 1881 said, "[It is a] lively little town of 1,000 inhabitants, but utterly demoralized and lawless. It is not safe to be out on the street at night. It has forty-two saloons and there are on an average about a half-dozen fights every night. Almost every morning drunken men can be seen lying loose about the city."[22]

"Fees" and "licenses" for all these drinking places were important in the economy of the Old West as they raised municipal revenue to pay for city services. This practice had tradition associated with it. During the Civil War, the federal government imposed taxes on liquor to help pay for the war. Surprisingly, anti-liquor supporters objected to this because they felt that to tax liquor was to condone it. The government continued to collect the tax even after the war was over. Similarly, saloons were looked upon by city fathers in the West as convenient generators of revenue, and a welcome byproduct of the number of saloons in a successful town was a boost to the money taken in. Typical saloon license "fees" were anywhere from $25 to $250.

Saloons made up a dependable source of public income. People in towns that were based on mining, logging, and cattle came and went as the fortunes of the town rose and fell, or the mines the town was founded around boomed and went bust. Houses and property changed hands frequently and it was difficult for towns to keep track of the current owner to collect property tax. Besides, frontier settlers typically balked at paying taxes. Saloons, on the other hand, tended to be more stable and provided steady sources of income.

A good example is what happened in Denver. In 1862, a few years after the city's founding, Denver saloonkeepers paid $50 to $100 a year for a saloon license, depending on whether they sold beer and wine or hard liquor. In 1866, the fee for selling hard liquor was raised to $200. By 1875, the city was taking in $35,000 a year in liquor license fees. By 1889, saloon fees had increased to $600 to $1,000 a year. By 1900, Denver was collecting $215,538 in license revenue, or about one-fourth of the expense of running the city.[23]

Like most frontier towns, Denver wasn't the most lawless town, but wasn't the most law-abiding either. But the urge to drink was just as great as anywhere else. On August 5, 1875, Charley Ward, owner of the Mint saloon, had his license revoked and was fined $25 for keeping a "disorderly saloon." He was fined an extra $15 for knowingly having women on his premises to attract customers. On August 7, Ward was at it again and was arrested for selling drinks without a license. The case was dismissed two weeks later, however, because the Mint was considered to be such a popular and profitable institution in Denver.[24]

Between August of 1879 and April of 1880 saloon fees provided two-thirds of Leadville's public income. Tombstone, Arizona, in 1881 received half of its municipal income from saloon fees. In Silverton, Colorado, this figure was closer to 90 percent.[25] In Dodge City, the *Ford County Globe* of April 15, 1879, reported, "The City Council did a wise thing in endeavoring to wipe out the city indebtedness by raising the dram shop license from one hundred to three hundred dollars. The city has a debt of nearly $3,000 hanging over it."

As well as raising revenue, fines and fees were used to control prostitution in saloons by charging a very high amount for liquor licenses. This was achieved in Fort Collins, Colorado, in 1883, when the town had thirteen saloons and five brothels that also sold liquor. To try to eliminate what the city saw as an escalating stream of vice, the license fee for selling liquor was raised from $300 to $1,000. This severe penalty worked. The number of saloons shrank to six, and many of the prostitutes left town.

Deadwood, South Dakota, found itself in a curious situation after it was founded. It was technically on an Indian reservation, thus the sale of liquor was illegal according to federal law. With great understanding, the city government kept the fees for liquor licenses low to offset the risk of arrest by the federal government. This must have been an acceptable incentive, because by July 1877, there were seventy-five saloons in town.

In Cripple Creek, Colorado, in 1893, a somewhat contradictory law was passed that prohibited dancing in a dance hall where liquor was sold. It should be noted that the same lawmakers also prohibited Cripple Creek residents from appearing in a state of nudity in a public place and barred the immoderate riding of a horse within the city limits, at faster than six miles per hour. A perhaps more sensible law that they passed was one that made it illegal to maintain any premises for the preparation or smoking of opium — not that any of these laws was particularly effective.

As the number of saloons in a town grew, the potential for drunkenness, fights, crime, and other rowdy behavior increased. The saloon district in Denver was located along Larimer Street, which had once been the city's main street. The red light district on adjacent Holladay Street was rated third in the nation for raucous activity, close behind San Francisco's Barbary Coast and New Orleans' Storyville. Notable saloons were the Arcade, the Chicken Coop, the Mammoth Pavilion, and the Little Casino. A tough place called Murphy's Exchange was also known as the "Slaughterhouse," because of the many killings that had occurred there. Violent-sounding names like this were commonplace to add a little spice to the image of the drinking place. San Francisco in the early 1880s also had a saloon known as "The Slaughterhouse." It was renamed the "Morgue" in 1885 when the owner smashed a drunken customer on the head with a beer bottle.[26] Havre, Montana, boasted a saloon called the Bucket of Blood. So did Albuquerque and Gallup in New Mexico, Virginia City in Nevada, and Everett in Washington.

In 1890, the saloon district of Colorado City, Colorado, which was appropriately known as "Saloon Row," stretched for four blocks along the south side of West Colorado Avenue, with a total of twenty saloons. Many of these were housed in two-story buildings that had saloons on the ground floor with dance halls and gambling tables on the upper floor. The rear exits of the buildings conveniently connected via a short walk across an alley to the back entrances of the brothels on the next street, Washington Avenue (later renamed Cucharras Street), which was the red light district.

As towns matured, saloons concentrated on drinking and gambling and lessened their other activities. Noise and confusion reigned on a busy night in a big mining town, such as Leadville or Tombstone, or a cattle town such as Dodge City. Shouts, cries, laughter, and curses from drunken revelers blended together and filled the air. Estelline Bennett, an early Deadwood pioneer, recalled the raucous sounds that drifted out of a local theater: "The Gem Theater for nearly a quarter of a century was a clangorous, tangling, insidious part of Deadwood's nightly life. The raucous tones of its ballyhooing brass-band in the street outside threaded through the pealing church bells like an obligato. They shrieked in blatant brass the interdependence of the good and bad in Deadwood Gulch."[27] At the Theatre Comique on Chestnut Street in the booming mining town of Leadville, the activities were so frenzied that patrons on the main floor often found themselves being pelted by food and liquor bottles thrown by lively drunks in the balcony.

Saloon Reform

Not all saloons were dens of vice, but as they were generally all located in the part of town that contained the brothels, dance halls, billiard parlors, gambling halls, opium dens, and other drinking places, all saloons were lumped together in the eyes of reformers. Victorian moralists were determined to close the saloons in order to protect the inherent values of home and church and maintain a civilized town. This attitude put many city fathers on the horns of a dilemma. The towns wanted the taxes that came in from the saloons, saloon-owners wanted the profits to be made from drinks, and town boosters wanted a vigorous local economy.

Many saloons were raunchy places and were proud of it. One saloon in Amarillo, Texas, had a sign outside that proudly proclaimed, "Whiskey, the road to ruin. Come in."[28] Another in Buena Vista, Colorado, was named the "Road to Hell." Taking a reverse tactic in advertising, the Wells Fargo Saloon in Junction City, Kansas, boldly stated that it had the worst liquor and the poorest cigars on the frontier.

As a town matured, however, and tried to shake off its often disreputable beginnings, the early open attitudes towards saloons changed. Liquor and the easy women that accompanied it were popular with most men but were not always accepted by wives and other respectable women. The same saloons that had served an important social function in the early days of a town's development were despised by reformers, who tried to close all saloons, gambling halls, and brothels.

Reformers tried first of all to remove women from the saloons. One way was to pass local laws that barred them as waitresses and bartenders. An example was Section 5 of the 1879 ordinances of the mining town of Silverton, Colorado, which stated, "Any keeper of a draw shop, beer house, ale house, saloon, hotel or other place of public resort who shall employ a lewd women or any woman having the reputation of a prostitute as a carrier of beer or any other article or to sing or dance in a lewd or indecent manner or permit any such lewd woman to act as bartender in any such house or place shall be guilty of a misdemeanor and upon conviction be fined not less than $70 nor more than $100."

Critics claimed that saloons were associated with disorder, violence, assaults, homicides, gambling, prostitution, and other crimes. Other, more minor, disruptions were shooting at the ceiling, loud singing, and generally disturbing the peace. This was pretty much true throughout the West. In 1867, for example, Butte City, with only 500 residents, became known as the most lawless town in Montana. By 1905, Butte's red light district was reported to be the second largest in the United States, just behind New Orleans' Storyville. In May of 1905, the Rev. William Biederwolf proclaimed Butte to be the "lowest sinkhole of vice in the West."[29] In 1908, Butte still had saloons that were open for business twenty-four hours a day.

These aspects of the saloon were seen as threatening the family and contrary to the Victorian values of self discipline, upright behavior, sexual restraint, community stability, and stable homes. On the contrary, the saloon was seen as a symbol of permissiveness, self-indulgence, and loose women who served to tempt young men, husbands, and fathers into immoral ways. The reformers' obvious solution was to eliminate the saloon and restore the old values. Anti-liquor crusaders — typically women — soon banded together to try to convert their men from drinking. One such group was the Sons and Daughters of Temperance, which was organized in Virginia City, Nevada, in 1863 and met every Monday evening. Liquor and drinking were felt to be an evil fate from which men must be saved.

Due to the association of saloons with loose women, the temperance movement considered alcohol and prostitution to be two related evils. And, admittedly, reformers rightly felt that a lack of family and atmosphere of community led to a lack of restraint in these matters in a working population that was dominated by young single males. Temperance crusaders held meetings in which they listened to anti-liquor speeches. Then, worked up to an almost religious frenzy by fiery speakers and anti-liquor songs, they marched to the nearest saloon carrying temperance banners and singing temperance hymns. When they reached the saloon, they sang more hymns and knelt on the boardwalk outside the saloon to pray.

This type of behavior has been shown with humor in Western movies. One example occurs in *Dodge City* (1939). Algernon "Rusty" Hart (Alan Hale) has signed "The Pledge" and refuses to go into a saloon with his friends to drink. So he ends up drinking tea next door with the ladies of the Pure-Prairie

Temperance supporters often sang hymns outside saloons and prayed to try to shame patrons into signing the pledge of abstinence. Drinkers were not always amused and might flood the sidewalk outside with beer to prevent the women from kneeling and fill the air with invective to embarrass them. Neither side usually achieved any agreement from the other (Library of Congress).

League of Dodge City. As he is standing in front of the ladies explaining his reformed situation, a sprawling, wild fight breaks out in the saloon, a connecting door crashes down, and drunken, brawling participants are hurled into the middle of the tea party. Rusty joins in the fight with great delight. Another aspect of the temperance movement is shown as blatant comedy in the rabble-rousing antics of crusader Cora Templeton Massengale (Lee Remick) in *Hallelujah Trail* (1965), as she tries to enlist the inhabitants of Fort Russell into her cause.

In reality, all this singing and praying didn't seem to have much effect on the habits of the hard-drinking males of the West and they treated it mostly as a game. As one form of retaliation, some men in saloons acted as lookouts. When they saw a band of temperance women approaching, the men inside would shout all of the obscenities and profanities they could think of at the tops of their voices. This usually resulted in some red-faced ladies running back down the street with their hands over their ears.

As another tactic, the men might pour beer on the boardwalk outside the door of the saloon in an attempt to prevent the ladies from kneeling and praying. If these tactics didn't work, the men might invite the ladies to come in and join them for a drink. In retaliation, women temperance volunteers stood watch outside saloons to try to shame men away from saloons by recording who went in and how long they stayed. Among the few exceptions to male retaliation tactics were when the women of the Salvation Army or the Volunteers of America came around collecting for the poor. Then the men generally behaved and were willing to contribute to the cause.[30]

An example of how temperance work did not always go as planned was Albrecht's Saloon, which catered to a working-class clientele in Manitou Springs, Colorado, in the late 1800s. At one point, the Manitou Springs town government made the decision that saloons should remain closed on Sundays. Unfortunately — or perhaps with great foresight on the part of the city fathers — Sunday was the only day off for many of the working-class clientele. Albrecht, however, continued to sell liquor quietly in the back room but posted a lookout to give the alert so that drinkers could run out of the back door if the town marshal was spotted.

A second example of laws gone wrong was what happened in the mining town of Pinos Altos, New Mexico, when a law was passed to prohibit women from entering saloons. The local newspaper reported that, instead, the "disreputable" women simply stood outside on the street and had their drinks brought out to them.[31]

Another target for vice reformers was gambling. Many women considered gambling to be the work of the devil and believed that gambling should be outlawed. In a weak attempt to pacify them, some saloon owners covered up or moved out the gambling tables on Sunday. It was back to business, however, on the following Monday.

CHAPTER EIGHT

Opium Dens

Just as drinkers had saloons as places in which to socialize and drink, those who smoked opium had opium dens in which to congregate and social-ize. Opium dens were common in almost every large city of the Old West. Popular features were the accessibility of opium, the social atmosphere of the surroundings, the camaraderie of fellow smokers, and the temporary refuge from worldly pressures. The opium den was a colorful secret place to smoke and a safe haven to sleep off the effects of the drug.

Morphine injected directly with a hypodermic syringe provided fast results. It was, however, typically a solitary habit pursued by those who wanted a rapid jolt of euphoria then forgetfulness. Smoking opium, on the other hand, was part of a social interaction pursued by those who wanted congenial company, a place to tell stories and jokes, and the opportunity to discuss events of mutual interest. For this reason it was not as common for a man or woman to smoke opium alone or at home, because the ritual and social aspects were missing.

On a more practical level, raw opium taken by mouth had a bitter taste and absorption into the body through the digestive tract was slow. Both of these problems were avoided if the opium was smoked instead of taken by mouth. The smoke reached the bloodstream through the lungs and resulted in a quick narcotic effect. Hypodermic injection of drugs produced a stronger reaction, was less expensive, and took less time, but it was never as popular as opium smoking for recreational use in places such as the Comstock mining district of Nevada around Virginia City.

Though opium smoking was not as widespread as morphine injection, it was the subject of widespread horror. This was created not so much out of a fear of addiction as it was from the racial hatred associated with the Chinese and their reputation as the "Yellow Peril." There were associated whispered rumors of debauchery and respectable women smoking opium and then engag-ing in wild orgies with Chinese men afterwards. In reality, the effect of smok-ing opium would be to depress any such urges of lust and was more likely to put the smoker into a deep sleep before anything improper could take place.

As we have seen, smoking opium started with Chinese immigrants who arrived to work in the California mines and after the Civil War to work on railroad construction. By the 1880s, opium dens had spread eastwards and were established in New York, Chicago, Boston, and other places that had a substantial Chinese population. Even though Americans participated, smoking opium in sordid surroundings in the Old West was considered to be a dreadful Chinese wickedness. Taking opium for medicinal use was considered to be acceptable, but smoking it was considered to be a vice. As a result, the recreational use of opium and smoking it in a social atmosphere in an opium house was limited to the part of town that included the other major establishments of vice, such as low-class saloons, gambling houses, brothels, and dance halls.

The Art of Smoking

Smoking opium, also called "hitting the pipe" or "sucking the bamboo," followed a well-defined ritual procedure.

A typical opium pipe consisted of a hollow tube about twenty inches long and two inches in diameter, sealed at one end and open at the other. About two-thirds to three-quarters of the way down the shaft was a small cup-shaped bowl. The bowl did not use the traditional design of a tobacco pipe, as the bowl of an opium pipe was designed to vaporize the drug rather than to burn it like tobacco. Most pipes were made from wood, with the type of wood corresponding to the wealth of the smoker. The cheaper pipes were made of bamboo, hence "sucking the bamboo." Wealthy smokers had pipes that were made from ivory, jade, or fine porcelain. The bowl of the pipe was typically made from metal, porcelain, or clay. An ordinary pipe cost around $5, with a good one costing up to $50.[1]

The smoker rolled some raw opium into a small ball, or "pill," and placed the ball on the end of a needle or piece of wire. Alternately, the smoker dipped the needle or wire into the gummy opium to pick up a few drops of the extract. The ball of opium was then dried by holding the needle over the flame of a lamp and cooking the opium until it swelled and turned from its original dark-brown to a golden color. This bead of flame-dried cooked opium was put into the tiny bowl of the opium pipe. The smoker reclined on his side, leaned over and held the bowl of the pipe at an angle over the flame of the lamp. The flame vaporized the pill and the smoker took a deep breath to inhale the smoke into the lungs and hold it there. As described by physician H.H. Kane, who personally investigated opium dens in the 1880s, "inhaling strongly and steadily, the smoke passes into the lungs of the operator, and is returned through the mouth and nose."[2]

The opium vaporized quickly, so ideally inhalation was done in a single

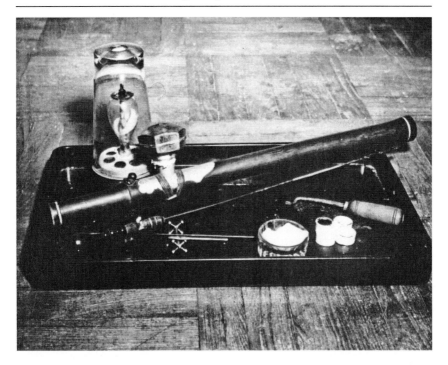

An opium pipe consisted of a hollow tube with a bowl for vaporizing the opium bead about three-quarters of the way down the length. This pipe is shown next to the other paraphernalia required for smoking, such as cleaning tools and an open-topped spirit lamp used to heat and vaporize the opium in the pipe. The cost of a pipe was between $5 and $50, depending on the quality of materials and the workmanship (courtesy of the World Health Organization and the National Library of Medicine).

large breath. The ability to inhale an entire opium pill with one breath was called the "long draw." In the "short draw," the smoker used several small breaths to inhale the smoke. The smoking habit was also known as "yen," from a Chinese word meaning "to smoke." Hence, the later expression "to have a yen for something" came to mean to want something very badly.

A "pipe" of opium lasted for only about fifteen to thirty seconds. The fumes were held for as long as the smoker could hold his breath, then exhaled slowly through the nose to try to absorb the most opium possible. After observing smokers in Deadwood, South Dakota, the *Black Hills Daily Times* commented on July 16, 1878: "A vent is made by means of the wire passed through the opium into the tube. The pipe is then placed over the lamp. The smoker sucks or inhales all that can be taken in one breath and then exhales the smoke or fumes from the nose or mouth as the smoker prefers. Two whiffs were all that the pipe contained." The smoker became drowsy almost immediately and lay down to sleep. First-time smokers usually experienced nausea, but after two or three pipes, the effect diminished. Experienced smokers inhaled three or four pipes in quick succession, each consisting of one pill. Each pill typically cost between 50¢ and 75¢.[3]

The effect was almost immediate. Users described a state of relaxation and complacency where their cares seemed to float away. They described an initial enhancement of mental activity, then a calmness that gave way to serene euphoria. After a few minutes they fell into a deep sleep that lasted from fifteen minutes (for one pill) to several hours (for several). Smoking opium did not result in aftereffects (at least until addiction occurred), such as a hangover when the sleeper awoke, but in a calm state of lethargy. As the smoker was already lying down, he fell quickly asleep.

The Perceived Road to Degeneration

Nineteenth century Americans were fascinated with any kind of vice and they expected opium dens to meet their expectations. Men toured Chinatowns hoping to see ladies in fancy silk dresses — skirts raised to their knees revealing their calves and striped stockings — sprawled out helplessly in an opium trance. This type of image was commonly depicted in the pages of the popular magazine *Police Gazette*, which specialized in that type of lurid reporting.[4] If there was a narcotic-related sudden or scandalous death, particularly one involving a respectable woman or an "innocent victim," the police would crack down on opium dens for a while, then the fuss would die down and be forgotten, and it was business as usual again.

When opium smoking was first introduced among the Chinese on the West Coast in the 1850s, it was generally tolerated as long as it remained a Chinese habit. However, as opium smoking became more widespread in the mid–1870s and the practice spread to whites, anti-opium sentiment became rampant. The opposition was fueled by articles such as one from April 1877 in the *Territorial Enterprise* of Virginia City, Nevada, which reported on a raid on an opium den. Police netted four young men and a girl, all of whom were American.

The anti-opium flames were intentionally fanned by the news media, such as those generated by the lurid confessions of a former addict that appeared as a twelve-part serial that ran in the *Denver Post* in 1926 and 1927, titled "My Thrills and Horrors as a Drug Slave." "Decadent" and "socially-polluting" were some of the terms used in the article to describe the vice of smoking opium. Readers came away with the idea that drug use, sexual shenanigans, and the opium den were all integrally linked together.

Opium dens were automatically assumed to be perverters of morals. With the increasing fear of the Chinese came the rumors of respectable women

The *National Police Gazette*, founded in 1845, achieved great popularity, particularly among male readers, in the late 1800s. It was an illustrated tabloid-type of publication that specialized in lurid coverage of murders, events in the Wild West, and particularly scandalous events that involved women (author's collection).

being seduced in opium dens. Self-appointed experts claimed that a woman's morals were liable to be compromised, even if they smoked opium with friends. Contemporary author Mary Mathews claimed, "Not only men and women visit the opium dens but I am informed, by good authority, that girls and boys visit them and often have to be helped home by their companions. Girls and boys, from twelve to twenty, are daily being ruined by this opium smoking." In the typical fashion of many of the nineteenth century women who crusaded against vice, she added, "I never visited one of these dens, but have had them described to me."[5]

Opium Dens

Smoking opium created a market for opium dens. Typically located in Chinatowns, they were a place to find opium and to smoke in the company of fellow drug users. These dens gave a sense of identity and protection for minor criminals. An opium den was also known as a "dive," a nickname derived from the word "divan," to describe the cot or bed on which the smoker lay or reclined.

The lavishness of opium dens was often exaggerated. They were commonly described as outlandishly decorated suites with comfortable divans, intricate exotic tapestries, and beautiful Chinese women gliding around with opium pipes. While some of this extravagance did exist in large cities such as San Francisco, the reality was more often a crowded, smoky, run-down small room behind a saloon or brothel in the red light district of town. Inside one of these dens might be a collection of small unventilated cubicles that led off a dark main corridor. Each room contained a cot and a small table for the rest of the paraphernalia, including a spirit lamp with a glass globe and a hole at the top. Many of the dens were virtually hermetically sealed in order to prevent the escape of the tell-tale sweet-smelling fumes of opium smoke that would tip off the law to their exact location. This tended to make the atmosphere somewhat overpowering.

To most Westerners, many of the unfamiliar aspects of the Chinese culture were considered to be strange, mysterious, and objects of curiosity. Chinatowns were mysterious and fearsome yet, at the same time, alluring places. The shacks and crowded slums that were permeated with the smell of opium were considered to be fascinating, yet at the same time repulsive. As a result, slumming parties went to Chinatowns on a lark to gawk at the allure of the exotic and the dangerous. Others went to enjoy the unusual diversions to be found there, such as the Chinese gambling, Chinese prostitutes, and opium smoking.

Smoking opium in sordid surroundings was considered to be a Chinese vice. To fill the need for sleaze and scandal for the reading public, Victorian journalists sought out opium dens, looking for stories of corruption, excitement, and vicarious danger. Looking for the worst, they reported on the dens that were squalid, wretched places. Their sinister descriptions of opium dens appeared in melodramatic newspaper and magazine accounts. Some of these may have been overly melodramatic. H.H. Kane commented that he felt that newspapermen may have embellished the details. He added, "In several instances I have known white smokers, who were acquainted with the business of the visitor, tell him the most silly and most outrageously false stories about the practice, and then laugh heartily at the article when it appeared in print."[6] Articles such as these created and perpetuated the theme of an exotic drug used by the criminal elements and linked it to a feared, outcast part of society. These descriptions were representative of squalid opium dens everywhere and still serve as good descriptions of the types of places found in the Old West. Kane's description of an opium den was this: "These places ... consist of a small, low ceilinged-room, guiltless of all furniture save long wooden bunks, about four feet in width, made of board and covered with matting. There is usually but one tier, raised about two feet from the floor. A long, narrow board, sometimes beveled, running along the wall just above the bunk, or small stools covered with cloth, serve as pillows, or, more properly, headrests for the smokers." His described the actual smoking room: "Upon three sides of this place are arranged bunks, in the rear there being two tiers of them, the upper one, however, being seldom used. Light — or semi-gloom — and air are furnished by one small window close up to the ceiling, and so placed that proper ventilation is an impossibility."[7]

Opium dens became one of the staples of sensationalist Victorian literature. In Arthur Conan Doyle's Sherlock Holmes adventure "The Man with the Twisted Lip," Dr. Watson searches for a particular opium den in London as he tries to find his missing friend Isa Whitney. Watson finds the place in Upper Swandam Lane, and recounts that "between a slop-shop and a gin shop, approached by a steep flight of steps leading down to a black gap like the mouth of a cave, I found the den of which I was in search." As he reluctantly enters, he finds "the den peopled with the 'dregs of the docks.'"

As he looks for his friend, he gives the following description:

> Through the gloom one could dimly catch a glimpse of bodies lying in strange fantastic poses, bowed shoulders, bent knees, heads thrown back, and chins pointing upward, with here and there a dark, lack-lustre eye turned upon the newcomer. Out of the black shadows there glimmered little red circles of light, now bright, now faint, as the burning poison waxed or waned in the bowls of the metal pipes. The most lay silent, but some muttered to themselves, and others talked together in a strange, low, monotonous voice, their conversation coming in gushes, and then suddenly tailing off to silence, each mumbling out his own thoughts and paying little heed to the words of his neighbour.[8]

Though opium dens were portrayed as dark, mysterious, and exotic places, the reality was more like that described by Mary Matthews: "A table sets [sic] in the center of the room, a dish of opium on that, and long pipes for each smoker is [sic] dipped in this, and they lie on bunks around the table and smoke till they become unconscious."[9] Reporter Forbes Parkhill, who worked for the *Denver Post*, described a typical opium den he visited like this: "On either side of a dim, narrow corridor the visitor found tiny, windowless, board-partitioned cubicles, barely large enough for a cot and a taboret containing the opium-smoking layout."[10] He also commented that "once smelled, the sweet odor of opium smoke is never forgotten." One observer in the late 1800s said, "Smokers while asleep are like corpses, lean and haggard as demons."[11]

Another boost to the lurid side of opium dens everywhere came from London and the pen of a young writer by the name of Arthur Henry Ward, who wrote under the pen name of Sax Rohmer. Between 1913 and 1917, in the wake of the fascination with the Far East and the perceived fear of the Chinese, Ward wrote three very popular novels about a mysterious Chinese scientist named Dr. Fu Manchu, who was the embodiment of evil. Fu Manchu planned to dominate the world, which in late Victorian times was perceived by Ward to be the British Empire. The novels revolve around melodramatic action-filled threats from the devil doctor's array of deadly rats, spiders, fungi, and centipedes, all of which were guaranteed to revolt — yet fascinate — staid literary audiences. In reality, the Chinese population of Britain was only 147 in 1861, increasing to 665 by the early 1880s.[12] By contrast, the Chinatowns of America contained thousands.

Locations for these Victorian pot-boilers included, of course, obligatory opium dens. In Rohmer's first book, titled *The Mystery of Dr. Fu-Manchu*, published in 1913, the hero, police commissioner Nayland Smith, and his faithful companion Dr. Petrie go to an opium den by the River Thames in search of a missing undercover policeman. Their destination is Singapore Charlie's, "a dope shop in one of the burrows off the old Ratcliff Highway." When they are greeted at the door by a little Chinaman, Smith roars out in typical contemporary treatment of the Chinese, "Get inside and gimme an' my mate a couple o' pipes. Smokee pipe, you yellow scum — savvy?"[13] Dr. Petrie picks up the narrative and describes the den into which they were led: "The next moment I found myself in an atmosphere which was literally poisonous. It was all but unbreathable, being loaded with opium fumes. Never before had I experienced anything like it. Every breath was an effort. A tin oil lamp on a box in the middle of the floor dimly illuminated the horrible place, about the walls of which ten or twelve bunks were ranged and all of them were occupied. Most of the occupants were lying motionless, but one or two were squatting in their bunks noisily sucking at the little metal pipes."[14]

His further description adds to the lurid and grotesque image of an opium den: "The smoky lamp in the middle of the place afforded scant illumination, serving only to indicate sprawling shapes — here an extended hand, brown or yellow, there a sketchy corpse-like face; whilst from all around rose obscene sighings and murmerings in far-away voices — an uncanny, animal chorus. It was like a glimpse of the Inferno by some Chinese Dante." The description of the Chinese proprietor is outlined in the same flowery Victorian prose: "But so close to us stood the newcomer that I was able to make out a ghastly parchment face, with small, oblique eyes, and a misshapen head crowned with a coiled pigtail, surmounting a slight hunched body. There was something unnatural, inhuman, about that mask-like face, and something repulsive in the bent shape and the long, yellow hands clasped one upon the other."[15] To further titillate horrified readers, the "Chinaman" eventually turns out to be a beautiful slave girl dressed for no logical reason in a hideous disguise.

For the attraction and repulsion of Victorian audiences, opium dens played a part in other Victorian literature. In Charles Dickens' novel *The Mystery of Edwin Drood*, which was published in 1870, smoking opium plays a pivotal role at several places in the plot. Dickens was already ill when he started work on the book in the summer of 1869. He was in such pain from gout, rheumatism, and vascular problems that he took large quantities of laudanum in order to sleep. The novel starts out with a scene in an opium den. Part of the novel describes the altered state of consciousness of one of the main characters, John Jasper, when he is under the influence of opium. Dickens actually visited an opium den located by the river Thames in Bluegate Fields in London, where he may have gained inspiration for the old woman who supplies the opium in the opium den scenes. Just before the end of the book another scene of several pages occurs in the opium den.[16]

Another popular Victorian novel that used an opium den as part of the theme was Oscar Wilde's *The Picture of Dorian Gray*. The original story was serialized in *Lippincott's Monthly Magazine* in 1890. An extended version of the story added additional material that raised controversy about the book's plot and the author's morality and was published in book form in 1891. As early as the second page Wilde writes, "Lord Henry elevated his eyebrows, and looked at him in amazement through the thin blue wreaths of smoke that curled up in such fanciful whorls from his heavy opium-tainted cigarette."

At one point in the story Gray is seized by "a mad craving" and he retrieves a hidden black-lacquered Chinese box with elaborate designs on it from a secret drawer. The box contains a green paste with an "odor curiously heavy and persistent." This may not be describing opium, because opium resin was typically brown, but the context and the following chapter implies that he wants to smoke opium. As he puts the box away again and goes out into the gloom of night to the docklands district of London to visit an opium den, Gray describes the sensation of how the "hideous hunger for opium began to gnaw at him." Wilde described the scene in the opium den through Gray's eyes: "Dorian winced, and looked round at the grotesque things that lay in such fantastic postures on the ragged mattresses. The twisted limbs, the gaping mouths, the staring, lusterless eyes, fascinated him. He knew in what strange heavens they were suffering, and what dull hells were teaching them the secret of some new joy." While there, Gray accidentally runs into a friend who says, "As long as one has this stuff, one doesn't want friends."

One newspaperman who actually visited a Chinese opium den in the Old West and later wrote about the experience was Mark Twain (Samuel Clemens) while he was a reporter for the *Territorial Enterprise* of Virginia City, Nevada, during the city's boom days in the early 1860s. He and a fellow reporter visited Virginia City's Chinese quarter, after which Twain reported the following: "In every little cooped-up, dingy cavern of a hut, faint with

Opium dens tended to be concentrated in the red light districts and Chinatowns of larger towns. In this den in San Francisco (portrayed in *Harper's Weekly* in 1888) both Chinese and American patrons could find a place to smoke a pipe of opium and sleep it off afterwards. The sensationalist Victorian press, looking for scandalous stories, portrayed opium dens as sordid places populated by sinister Chinese proprietors who lured white women into vice and decadence (National Library of Medicine).

the odor of burning Josh-lights and with nothing to see the gloom by save the sickly, guttering tallow candle, were two or three yellow, long-tailed vagabonds, coiled up on a sort of short truckle-bed, smoking opium, motionless and with their lusterless eyes turned inward from excess of satisfaction — or rather the recent smoker looks thus, immediately after having passed the pipe to his neighbor — for opium-smoking is a comfortless operation, and requires constant attention." Probably telling his audience of readers more than they wanted to know, he added that "the stewing and frying of the drug and the gurgling of the juices in the stem would well-nigh turn the stomach of a statue. John [Chinaman] likes it though; it soothes him."[17]

In another example, the *London Daily News* in 1864 described a real opium den in an area called Palmer's Folly: "We push at a half open front door, and at once find ourselves in a small, half-lit, shabby room on the ground floor, in which a large French bedstead occupies the most conspicuous place." The reporter continued: "The old Chinaman on the end of the bed nearest the window seems in a half trance, though he smokes vigorously, and in his cadaverous face, painfully-hollow cheeks, deeply-sunken eyes, open vacuous mouth, and teeth discolored, decayed, and, it seems, loose as castanets, you read the penalties of opium smoking." In an unusual approach for a Victorian reporter, the writer likened the den to the social equivalent of an English pub rather than a vice-ridden den of iniquity for the Chinese. At the same time, public opinion equated opium with everything evil, and it was the primary symbol of degeneracy and corruption.

Tales from a Few Opium Dens Around the West

The larger Chinatowns that sprang up around concentrations of Chinese immigrants were typically located in larger cities of the West such as San Francisco, Denver, and Tombstone.

SAN FRANCISCO, CALIFORNIA

As the primary port of entry for Chinese immigrants on the West Coast, San Francisco soon had an extensive Chinese community. In 1885, the San Francisco Board of Supervisors reported that there were twenty-six opium establishments operating in San Francisco's Chinatown, which was an area bounded by Stockton, Washington, Dupont, and Pacific streets. In them were 320 bunks that were open to the public.

Thrill-seekers looking for the unusual went to the Barbary Coast, San Francisco's red light district, and to Chinatown, hoping to experience depraved opium dens, houses of Chinese prostitution, and gambling dens.[18] Some of these places were fakes and were run to provide excitement and titillation for tourists, but others had real opium along with Chinese prostitutes and gambling. Those looking for a vicarious thrill could go on tours of Chinatown in complete safety with professional guides licensed by the city as the Chinatown Guides Association. Bogus opium dens were set up in dank and dreary cellars and were constructed so that the tourists thought they were creeping through dimly-lit secret passages and deep underground tunnels. The experience was enhanced by the presence of Chinamen carrying evil-looking knives and hatchets, slinking around just at the edge of the group. These villainous-looking men, who were actually employed by the guides, made the tour seem like Chinatown was connected by a network of secret underground passages. In reality, however, the area was thoroughly explored after the earthquake of 1906, and no evidence was ever found of these supposed deep and tortuous passages.[19]

In spite of the tourist attractions, the real thing was there, hidden from the public's view. Author Benjamin Lloyd commented, "The Barbary Coast is the haunt of the low and vile of every kind.... Opium dens, where heathen Chinese and God-forsaken women and men are sprawled in miscellaneous confusion, disgustingly drowsy, or completely overcome by inhaling the vapers [sic] of the nauseous narcotic, are there.... And Hell, yawning to receive the putrid mass, is there also."[20]

Sailors on the West Coast were subject to a particular kind of violence due to drink, opium, and other drugs. Up and down the West Coast, sailors exposed themselves to peril when they drank in low dives and risked being kidnapped. One of the worst towns was San Francisco. Representatives of various saloons and dives on the Barbary Coast came out into the bay in small boats, armed with liquor and vulgar pictures, to meet incoming ships in an effort to entice sailors to sample the supposed pleasures of their particular saloon. Ships' captains encouraged the practice, as they were glad to have the men off the boats and in town so they could avoid paying an idle crew while in port and thus save money. The result was that many of the sailors were drugged, robbed, kidnapped — and sometimes murdered — in the haste of saloon owners to relieve them of any money.

One of the most notorious dives on the Barbary Coast was Shanghai Kelly's saloon on Pacific Street, right in the heart of the red light district. Kelly had a sideline of supplying crews for outbound ships that were unable to find enough men to sail with them through normal recruiting procedures. He gave unsuspecting likely customers a powerful cocktail of schnapps and beer laced with opium. When the alcohol and opium took effect, he dropped them through a trapdoor into a waiting boat which took them out to a ship. This practice was known as "shanghaiing," as most of the ships were bound for Shanghai, China. Another of Kelly's techniques was to give a man a cigar that was heavily laced with opium. When the man had smoked enough to pass out, he was taken by boat out to a departing ship in San Francisco Bay and became part of a forced crew sailing for the Orient. These cigars were specially made for him by a Chinese cigar maker and were known as "Shanghai smokes." Kelly's reputation for shanghaiing customers was well known, but still they kept coming. His standing offer of free women and free beer was too great a temptation. Another drug used for shanghaiing sailors or for rolling drunks was chloral hydrate. The drug acted fast, within ten or fifteen minutes, and produced a period of sleep that lasted five hours or more. It was an ideal drug for men with crooked intentions because it could be readily dissolved in whiskey, where it produced an additive effect to the depressant effect of the alcohol.

As one story goes, Kelly had an order to fill three ships anchored outside the Golden Gate at the same time and had run short of likely victims. He came up with the ingenious idea of chartering an old paddle-wheel steamer and advertised that for his upcoming birthday he had organized a cruise with free liquor for everyone. As he fully expected, ninety of San Francisco's riff-raff showed up. As promised, he gave them free beer and whiskey, but both were loaded with opium. After all the men fell asleep, Kelly steamed out to his three customers and delivered three crews to them.[21]

The business of selling unwilling sailors to ships departing for the Orient that were short of crew members was a flourishing business in major seaports on the Pacific Coast in the late 1800s. The ships that transported lumber around the world from the Northwest, for example, often found it difficult to attract sufficient crew members. As a result, crooked bartenders, pimps, and prostitutes teamed up to lure sailors to an unpleasant fate on an outbound ship. The men who carried out the dirty work were called "crimps." A system similar to that in San Francisco was used and likely victims who had drunk too much were hauled senseless out to departing ships. If the man was not drunk enough, a few drops of chloral hydrate in his drink would do the trick.

One establishment that was notorious for the practice of shanghaiing was the Bucket of Blood Saloon in Everett, Washington, which was built on stilts over the river. A convenient trapdoor dropped a drugged or drunk unsuspecting victim into a boat or to the mudflats below, depending on the tide, and then to the expectant hands of a crimp who transported him to a nearby waiting lumber ship. If the victim was not needed to fill a quota of crewmen, he might simply be robbed and left to drown. Similar arrangements operated in Port Townsend and Aberdeen, Washington, and Portland, Oregon. The Gray's Harbor area in southwestern Washington was so notorious for shanghaiing that it was known as the "Port of Missing Men." The routine kidnapping and disappearance of sailors became so bad that in 1906 Congress passed an act to prohibit the shanghaiing of sailors in the United States.

This was often the treatment handed out by sinister Chinese in opium dens to sailors who were kidnapped to form part of a forced crew sailing to the Orient. After suitable drugging with alcohol or opium, the unfortunate was dropped through a trapdoor into a waiting boat and ferried out to a departing ship. Note that with typical Victorian sensationalism most of the smokers in this illustration are depicted as white women being debauched by opium (Library of Congress).

DENVER, COLORADO

As one of the few large cities in the Old West, Denver soon had a Chinese district called Hop Alley that was literally in an alley behind the bordellos of the main red light district on Holladay Street. Many of the buildings in the alley were said to be connected by tunnels and secret rooms. By 1880 Denver had seventeen known opium dens, twelve of them in Hop Alley. Most of them offered morphine, cocaine, and opium. Unlike San Francisco, Denver had very few Chinese prostitutes, tong wars were unknown, and crimes of violence in Chinatown were rare. Prejudice against the Chinese was high, however, which later resulted in a major race riot.

Denverites who drank were often prejudiced about using opium. There was no federal or state law forbidding its use until the 1914 Harrison Narcotic Act; nevertheless, Denver city fathers had a local ordinance against its use. This was used to harass owners of the dens, but local white customers were seldom arrested. The white patrons were viewed as innocent victims of an evil Chinese practice.

Morbid fascination with opium dens was high. The *Rocky Mountain News* of October 27, 1880, reported that "a visit to the den on Arapahoe street showed it to be full of smokers, a large portion of whom were women, in the several stages of stupefaction produced by the drug. There seemed to be no secrecy about the matter.... Very few men were seen excepting the Chinese, but all of the women were Caucasians." The newspaper reported with apparent glee that the manager of the den said that a higher proportion of women than men made up their customers, by as much as ten to one. In Central City, which was located in the mountains about thirty miles west of Denver, the *Weekly Central City Register* published an article in 1874 titled "The Opium Pipe: The Heathen Chinese and the Narcotic of Death: How John Smokes His Pipe."

The drug of choice for Denver's middle-class and upper-class white women was opium. They thought it was daring to gather in a darkened opium den to socialize and smoke, then doze. Opium was also popular among criminals, gamblers, and prostitutes of the red light district. Like the Barbary Coast in San Francisco, for a while Denver's Hop Alley was a tourist attraction and visitors could even go to the central police station to find a guide. In 1881, Denver passed a law prohibiting opium dens. The law was backed up by a fine of $50 to $300. Interestingly, at the same time, the fine for operating a bawdy house was only $5 to $100.

VIRGINIA CITY, NEVADA

Virginia City, the site of the fabled Comstock Lode, had its own Chinatown. In September of 1876 the aldermen of Virginia City passed an ordinance banning opium dens and levied fines on those who were caught smoking. In 1877, the Nevada state legislature restricted opium to the medical profession and dispensing was by prescription only. The ownership of opium pipes and related paraphernalia for smoking was made illegal. Such a law was, however, difficult to enforce. In an initial burst of civic enthusiasm, several Chinamen were arrested and fined, but after a few weeks business was back to normal.

SILVERTON, COLORADO

Most mining towns such as Silverton, which boomed in the 1870s and 1880s, had opium dens. The *Silverton Democrat* of August 4, 1883, reported on the trial of five Chinamen from town on charges of smoking opium. Three were convicted and paid fines of $15 and court costs. The other two were discharged. As a follow-up, on August 25 the paper pointed out that the Chinese were not the only ones who frequented opium dens, and that if the city marshal really wanted to suppress the dens he should arrest "a lot of white trash."

DEADWOOD, SOUTH DAKOTA

Deadwood's relatively large Chinatown was located on lower Main Street. Pine Street in the nearby mine town of Lead was that city's tenderloin with most of its dance halls, brothels, and opium dens. The Chinese were not allowed to engage in mining, but operated laundries, restaurants, and shops instead.

Opium arrived in the Black Hills during the gold rush of 1876 and quickly became one of the most popular drugs in town. It was used by many for its medicinal benefits. Others were mainly interested in the pleasant feelings they could get from it and used it as a cheap substitute for alcohol. The cost for one pipe was 20¢; or for $1 the addict could smoke as much as he wanted until he fell asleep. In November of 1883, three opium dens were in full operation in Deadwood.

Estelline Bennett, who lived in Deadwood with her parents in the boom days of the late 1870s, claimed that judicial and public opinion were not strong about smoking opium. She said, "If a Chinaman wanted to smoke who cared? They rarely were in trouble about anything else."[22] But the local newspaper, ever vigilant to report any sensational aspects of the news, sent reporters frequently into Chinatown to tease out any lurid tidbits they could find. For example, a reporter for the *Black Hills Daily Times* visited a Chinese doctor on August 1, 1877, and found a room with several Chinese smoking opium and sleeping off the effects. The *Black Hills Daily Times* on July 16, 1878, reported observing some other smokers and commented that "the victims are reduced to a semi-unconscious state when all is placid, calm, serene, no hilarity or mirth is observable, and if there is any enjoyment in its effect it must be in the mind or imagination of the smoker."

In 1878, in an attempt to regulate the practice of smoking opium (and gain some revenue at the same time) Lawrence County (Deadwood) instituted a licensing fee of $300 for an opium house. "Respectable" people looked on smoking opium as another vice of the heathen Chinese. Major complaints were that unsavory characters hung around these houses and the neighbors complained of second-hand opium fumes. In fact, those who could not afford to purchase a pipe often hung around opium dens hoping to suck up some of the pleasurable effects by inhaling the errant smoke of others. Police raids did shut down dens from time to time, but then smokers simply moved to dens in private houses, so the problem did not stop.

Many of the residents of Deadwood did not agree with Estelline Bennett's view of opium smoking and looked upon it with suspicion and concern. The *Black Hills Daily Times* of April 23, 1878, commented that it was cheaper for those seeking solace to render themselves oblivious with opium rather than whiskey. The paper did back off a little on May 5 and commented that smoking opium was a greater evil than drinking whiskey.

A law passed by the Dakota Territorial Assembly in 1879 instituted a fine of up to $100 for opium smoking, along with imprisonment in the county jail of up to thirty days. The difficulty of catching someone in the act of smoking, along with claims of a lack of evidence, lenient judges, and juries unwilling to convict their peers made it difficult for any charges to stick.

CRIPPLE CREEK, COLORADO

Cripple Creek, which boomed as a gold-mining town in the 1890s, had several well-patronized opium dens. They were located in the alleys behind Myers Avenue, which was the main red light district of town and was lined for several blocks with brothels and cribs. One den was in a small brick building behind the Red Light Dance Hall. Another was in the apartment of Lizzie Moore.

BUTTE, MONTANA

Butte had an extensive Chinatown that was located on lower Main Street. Here were gambling houses, opium dens, and tiny cribs occupied by prostitutes, along with noodle parlors, laundries, and tailor shops. Not all the dens were large-scale operations. One of the most popular ones in Butte was Oolu Jack's place, which had only four bunks. The cost for a smoke was from 25¢ to 50¢ a pipe. On the shadier side was the Clipper Shades concert hall and bordello run by Pete Hanson, which in 1887 had a bad reputation for drugging and robbing patrons who displayed large amounts of cash.

Though there was some concern about the actual opium dens, there was more concern that white men and women were being corrupted by the habit. In nearby Helena, a twenty-six-year-old journalist named Joseph E. Hendry took it upon himself to publish an expose of Chinese opium dens in the Helena *Daily Independent*. In true sensationalist fashion, he reported them to be a dangerous threat to white womanhood. His series of articles immediately created outrage from the general public and forced a police raid on the local opium dens. To Hendry's chagrin, these efforts did not find the young white wanton women that he had reported. The result, however, was the banning of prostitutes from the city and the establishment of a series of fines for prostitutes, though how they could be fined if they had been banned was not made clear. Hendry had hoped instead for a total shutdown. In 1887, the city council ordered another raid, which did result in the arrest of sixty-five white and Chinese prostitutes. The city attorney, however, refused to prosecute. Hendry died unexpectedly in December, and the entire morals campaign died with him as the city council turned their attention to what they considered to be more important matters.

THE DECLINE OF THE DENS OF INIQUITY

Ordinances were eventually enacted in most cities to try to get rid of opium dens. Most were unsuccessful.

In 1875 San Francisco passed an ordinance banning the smoking of opium outside an opium den and the possession of opium within the city limits; however, it was still smoked in semi-clandestine fashion in Chinatowns dens. Virginia City, Nevada, whose fortunes were closely allied with San Francisco, did the same in 1876. Again, the trade continued, but in clandestine fashion. The dens continued to operate even after they were banned by the Nevada state legislature in 1877 and druggists were required to obtain a physician's prescription before dispensing. In 1877 the Virginia City board of aldermen passed an ordinance declaring opium dens a nuisance. This only drove the trade underground. Nor did raising the tax on opium work, even when it was taxed as heavily as 75¢ per ounce. In 1881, Denver passed an ordinance banning opium dens.

In 1909, the Smoking Opium Exclusion Act was passed by the federal government, banning the importation of opium for smoking and providing for stiff penalties for traffickers. This did not stop the trade, however, as had been hoped. Instead, it had the undesired effect of increasing opium smuggling, which of course simply led to substantially higher prices for the consumer.

Smoking opium reached a high point in 1896, with 157,061 pounds of the drug prepared for smoking.[23] Then a decline in smoking opium started in the late 1890s when Chinese immigration declined severely due to restrictive immigration regulations and many of those already in the Old West went back to China. By the early 1900s, the demand for smoking opium had declined sharply, though even then it did not disappear fully.

CHAPTER NINE

The Horrors of Addiction

By the 1860s, the nonmedical use of opium had become a major social issue in America. Imports of opium into the United States had increased from 40,885 pounds in 1851 to 119,525 pounds in 1860.[1]

By the latter half of the nineteenth century, physicians knew that opium and morphine provided fast relief from many symptoms of pain and illness and accordingly prescribed them widely. Both were easily and legitimately available without a prescription at a drugstore or other supplier that dealt in medicines. Hypodermic syringes were readily available from drugstores without a doctor's orders.

As early as the 1860s, physicians vaguely realized that some people who used opium regularly developed a craving for continued use of the drug and exhibited a series of strange symptoms when the drug was withdrawn. They did not, however, understand what a physical addiction to opium involved.[2] Though physicians had inklings that opium was an addictive substance, the reason why certain people became addicted to opium was not understood. One early explanation for addiction was that the opium or morphine addict became "hungry" for the drug in the same way that an individual became hungry for food. Therefore, physicians reasoned, taking opium by mouth would eventually lead to this "hunger." They thought that if the stomach could somehow be bypassed, then the possibility of addiction would be diminished.

Another significant problem with administering opium by mouth was that it often produced nausea and other undesirable side effects in the stomach. Physicians therefore theorized that if they could administer the drug without the patient having to eat it, she could tolerate it better and would not become addicted. The breakthrough that appeared to solve the problem was to deliver the drug under the skin using a hypodermic syringe with an attached hollow needle.

The Hypodermic Syringe

The hypodermic syringe allowed direct injection of substances into unbroken tissue at the site of the pain or into the bloodstream, instead of the earlier methods of dusting, eating, or smoking opium.[3] Morphine was poorly absorbed by the body when taken by mouth or dusted into a wound, and it was not until after the development of the hypodermic syringe that the full benefit of morphine as a painkiller became apparent. At the same time, however, the hypodermic syringe made morphine abuse worse.

With an obvious lack of understanding, physicians felt that administration of morphine by hypodermic injection was safer than by mouth. They reasoned that because less of the drug was required in this manner to reach the same level of pain relief, there should be a lower likelihood of addiction. The reality, of course, was the reverse. Morphine was simply a more concentrated version of the active material contained in opium. Because morphine injected with a hypodermic syringe went straight into the bloodstream, there was actually a higher probability of addiction. Physicians soon noted that even in small doses morphine depressed the respiratory system and tended to cause nausea, vomiting, and diarrhea. And even worse, small doses led rapidly to large doses, as morphine lost its effect unless the dose was constantly increased.

Before the development of the hypodermic syringe, the methods of delivering opium into the human body were limited. Nevertheless, doctors experimented with various methods of administration to try to find the best one. One method was to inhale a vapor containing the drug — similar to smoking opium — and hope that enough of it was absorbed into the body from the lungs to be effective. This method did work; it was found to be too time-consuming for practical use.

As the stomach was often upset when taking opium by mouth, even though the patient needed to sleep or be sedated, another method was to administer the opium at the other end of the intestinal tract. As far back as the Middle Ages, Monsieur Pomet, the chief apothecary to Louis XIV, had noted that opium acted faster when administered by this method than by mouth.[4] One typical medical text of 1837 recommended mixing sixty drops of laudanum into a half-pint of flaxseed tea and administering it as an enema.[5] A similar method of administration was to use suppositories containing opium. These methods, however, were time-consuming, slow to act, and unpleasant for the patient.

Physicians knew that it was effective to deliver the drug under the skin, but they had not yet determined a simple, practical method for achieving this. During the Civil War, surgeons often dusted a wound with morphine or pushed the drug into damaged flesh with their fingers.[6] Sometimes they moistened a finger with their own saliva to make the powder stick during the transfer. When this method was used, the correct dosage was considered to be the amount of morphine powder that adhered to the wet finger. The problem was how to get the drug into a patient who did not have a gaping wound. In one early method of administration, a small cut was made in the skin and then a probe was pushed into the wound to create a hole that was packed with morphine powder to allow the drug to penetrate the tissue beneath.[7] The dose of morphine used was on the order of one to three grains.

The first methods of hypodermic injection were crude. In the earliest attempts, surgeons made a small incision in the skin then forced the drug into it with a glass piston syringe that had no needle. Physicians such as Dr. Isaac Taylor in the United States, for example, pushed drugs into an incision in the skin by using a glass syringe whose injection end tapered down to a blunt nozzle. An advance on this method was made in 1844 when physician Francis Rynd in Ireland dissolved fifteen grains of morphine in one drachm of creosote and injected it through a needle directly into the nerve of a woman who had been suffering from severe pain. He did not use a hypodermic syringe as we picture it today, however. His equipment consisted of a hollow needle attached to a length of tubing that in turn attached to a glass bottle that acted as a reservoir for the drug. His apparatus looked more like today's system for injecting intravenous fluids in hospitals. The drug flowed into the patient via gravity, rather than being forced in by a plunger.

The development of a usable syringe to inject morphine under the skin directly into the site of the pain is generally credited to Dr. Charles-Gabriel Pravaz in France in 1851. This type of hypodermic syringe, which used a plunger to force the drug from a glass barrel through a hollow needle, was further perfected by Dr. Alexander Wood in Edinburgh, Scot-

This is an early form of syringe used for "hypodermic" injections. The blunt end was inserted into an incision in the skin and the contents of the syringe injected. Note that there is no needle. Twine or cotton wool was typically wrapped around the end of the plunger to seal it to the barrel and prevent the contents from leaking out backwards (author's collection).

land, in 1853 to inject morphine under the skin. Wood's first published account in 1855 described a syringe with a barrel and plunger made out of glass, with cotton wool wrapped tightly around the plunger in order to seal the piston to the barrel and prevent leakage of the drug around the sides. The syringe was developed by a precision instrument-maker named Ferguson in London. Wood's improvement over Pravatz's syringe was to make a better cutting point that made the needle smaller and sharper.[8] The hypodermic syringe was used for the first time in America in 1856 by physician Fordyce Barker — one that he obtained in Edinburgh.

The technique used for hypodermic injections was not perfect in the beginning. Repeated injections at the same site, for example, produced infection, abscesses, and ulceration of the skin. Another practical problem was that the injection needle became blunted after several uses and thus created pain when forced into subsequent patients. How traumatic this whole procedure was for the patient can be judged by the fact that early hypodermic syringes were known as "the painful point." Cleaning and sterilization of the syringe between injections were not commonplace. Syringes were not disposable, as today, but were reused and (ideally) cleaned after each use.

For all this, even after workable hypodermic syringes became readily available they were not widely used by doctors, the majority of whom still dusted morphine into wounds or administered opium as pills. Even addicts did not always use the newly invented syringe. In the late 1880s in San Francisco, some of the opium addicts — known locally as "hoppies" — couldn't afford a hypodermic syringe. Instead, they filled an ordinary glass eyedropper with morphine or cocaine and forced the end through their skin into their flesh to inject the drug. Some eked out enough small change to help to pay for their drug habit by proudly showing the holes in their scarred flesh to horrified tourists.[9]

The Increase in Addicts

Early warnings about opium use and abuse, and reports of addiction, started to appear in medical journals and textbooks in the 1870s. In 1875, the *San Francisco Evening Post* estimated that there were 120,000 opium addicts in the United States, excluding the Chinese. Though cases of addiction came to light in the 1870s and 1880s, many physicians chose to ignore them. Even when addiction was first recognized, it was not looked upon as being particularly evil, but merely as an unfortunate inconvenience associated with a minor vice and an unavoidable consequence of the use of opium.

Addicted opium users were not called "addicts," but rather "habitués" to designate merely a habitual user of the drug. A continued urge to use the drug was lightly passed off as "the opium habit." Similar attitudes existed in Britain, where the *Report of the Royal Commission on Opium* (1894–1895) concluded that the majority of cases were of "habitual and moderate use which causes no health or welfare concerns."[10]

It was not until the 1890s that the problems of addiction started to receive significant attention. Drug addiction didn't receive wide mention until about 1900 and was not really understood until about 1910.[11] By 1900, the number of American addicts was estimated to be 250,000.[12] Whether or not these figures are accurate or are wildly exaggerated estimates is unclear. Other sources claim that the number remained fairly constant from an 1875 estimate, remaining at approximately 110,000 in 1924.[13]

"Drug inebriety," "narcomania," and "morbid cravings" were some of the names that were used to describe the addiction of heavy opium users. Addiction came to be feared and the image of the opium addict changed from that of an innocent and casual drug user to that of a corrupt and perverted menace to society. Even so, rampant "morphinism," as morphine addiction was called, was thought to be less dangerous than alcoholism. Observer John Thomson, in the late 1800s, said, "Opium-smoking throws whole families into ruin, dissipates every kind of property, and ruins man himself."[14] In all fairness, however, it should be pointed out that not everybody was opposed to opium. In 1879, the local newspaper *Butte (BT) Miner* launched a crusade against opium that turned out to be spectacularly unsuccessful.

For a long time it was believed that only certain types of people became addicted to opium. For example, it was theorized that the Chinese were resistant to opium because the plant came from their homeland. In reality, of course, this was muddled thinking, as the opium poppy was not even native to Asia. In an era of extreme class consciousness, Victorian moralists also thought that the lower classes were more likely to be attracted to and perverted by any of the vices, one of which was opium. Some "experts" even theorized that a person became an addict because of a weak character or due to their own moral depravity. Victorians were obsessed with everybody else's morals. One nursing text as late as the 1960s said, "Results vary in different persons, but in general, continued use leads to depression and weakness, not only of the body but also of the mind and morals." The authors added, "Later, he grows nervous and irritable, is unable to work except under the influence of the drug, and may engage in low moral practices."[15]

Many physicians thought that women were more susceptible to addiction, a perception that may have had some basis in fact, as many women regularly used opium and morphine for relief of menstrual discomfort and to treat the nervous afflictions from which women were believed to suffer.

The Road to Addiction

Smoking a pipe that consisted of few grains of opium gave the novice smoker a feeling of euphoria. The first few times that an individual took opium, it produced a sense of well-being. Physician Norman Kerr described it in flowery terms when he said "there is a pleased feeling [among users] of satisfaction, partaking of delight and ineffable composure."[16] Later, when the effects of the opium wore off, the user was overtaken by a sensation of profound listlessness.

As the user continued to eat, smoke, or drink opium, the body adapted to the drug and the effects were lessened. The user quickly developed a tolerance for the drug and found the need for an increasing amount to produce the same pleasant feelings. An article in the *British and Foreign Medical Review* in 1837 commented that "opium eaters generally begin with doses of from half a grain to two grains, and gradually increase the quantity till it amounts to two drachms, and sometimes more, a day."[17] From smoking one pipe a day, the level might have to be increased to three pipes a day to obtain the same feelings of well-being. If drug use was halted, the user felt an intense craving for it.

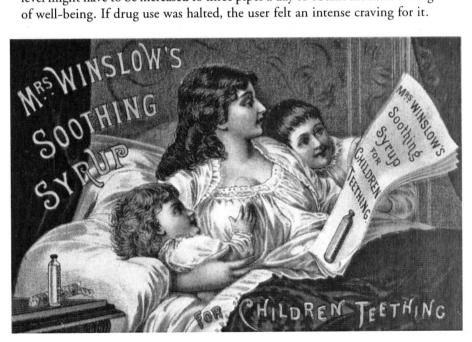

Mrs. Winslow's Soothing Syrup was a patent medicine that contained both alcohol and a grain of morphine in each fluid ounce. This cordial was used for teething infants and to "soothe" fussy children. It was also used by the poor to put babies into a comatose state so that they could be left alone while the mother worked. Addiction was inevitable (National Library of Medicine).

Whether or not the user was liable to become an opium addict at this point depended primarily on the dose of the drug and the frequency of administration. Modern studies have shown that very few patients become addicted after using therapeutic doses of opium to relive pain. On the other hand, one cannot be surprised to learn that Thomas de Quincey, author of *Confessions of an Opium Eater* (1821), was an addict. He first took opium for pain relief, then continued the practice for his own enjoyment, using higher and higher dosages. At one point he took up to 8,000 drops of laudanum a day.[18]

De Quincey made several observations about his opium habit. First, he felt that the creative state of his mind was increased. Second, his dreams were accompanied by anxiety and melancholy. A third observation was that his perceptions of space and time were altered. And, finally, he experienced a heightened ability to recall experiences. He also noted that opium distorted his perception of color.

Signs and Symptoms of Opium Addiction

An increased level of consumption eventually led to addiction and, as the dose increased, so did the accompanying symptoms of addiction. Opium addicts started to experience a physical decline into general weakness, along with feelings of depression and lethargy, when they were not using the drug. They became thin because suppression of the appetite led to a severe loss of weight and eventual emaciation.

Opium suppressed the cough reflex (hence its use as a consumption treatment), but it also depressed the respiratory system. It constricted the pupil of the eye. Other effects included muscle tremors, restlessness, memory loss, an impaired sense of smell, distorted vision, constant sneezing, heartburn, nausea, and inflammation of the mouth and throat that led to a hoarse voice. Other undesirable effects were wild mood shifts, reveries, extravagant thoughts, disturbing dreams, periods of intense energetic activity, lack of concentration, continued inner urgings to feed the drug habit, delusions, hearing voices, despair, irritability, and lapses in consciousness. The erotomania claimed to be induced in women was more wishful thinking than reality.

As drug use progressed, the addict became more and more lethargic and the memory became more impaired. He found it difficult to focus and became more and more forgetful. Hallucinations were not unusual. The body became more emaciated as the appetite for food was lost. The medical benefit of stopping dysentery was so effective that the addict was constantly constipated. Opium induced irregular menstruation and a loss of fertility in women and impotence in men.

Though most bodily functions were depressed, at the same time addicts reported an alteration of the senses and heightened perceptions of hearing and sight. In some cases, noises and light actually became physically painful. Addicts were susceptible to gastric illnesses, circulatory disorders, and difficulty in urination. More serious complications included hepatitis and liver damage, blood poisoning, fungal skin infections, difficulty in breathing, tooth decay, and nervous tremors. In large enough doses, opium depressed the action of the heart muscles and breathing to the point of death.

Though accurate, this description from 1874 sounds most unpleasant: "The habitual opium eater, is instantly recognized by his appearance. A total attenuation of body, a withered yellow countenance, a lame gait, a bending of the spine frequently to such a degree as to assure a circular form, and glossy, deep-sunken eyes, betray him at the first glance. The digestive organs are in the highest degree disturbed, the sufferer eats scarcely anything, and has hardly one evacuation in a week; his mental and bodily powers are destroyed; he is impotent."[19] This description is consistent with newspaper accounts given by reporters who visited opium dens in the Old West.

DRUG WITHDRAWAL

At this point in addiction, if the opium or morphine was stopped — even for a day — the user experienced severe withdrawal symptoms, which included dizziness, watery eyes, prostration, and torpor. If the addict did not resume consumption of opium, then chills, aches, diarrhea, and depression would follow quickly. When the drug was stopped, the addict underwent symptoms of restlessness, abdominal cramps, diarrhea, vomiting, difficulty breathing, muscular twitching, sweating, and an inability to sleep. Other withdrawal symptoms included a craving for the drug, depression, insomnia, yawning, sneezing, heavy perspiration, heavy tearing from the eyes, a runny nose, tremors, goosebumps on the skin, muscle twitch, mental confusion, muscular aches and pains, hot and cold flashes, chills, and some loss of control of the arms and legs.

As the process of withdrawal continued, the symptoms became even more unpleasant. With initial use, the opium affected the smooth muscles of the intestines, reducing contractions. As the addict went into withdrawal, the serious constipation problem that was brought on by the ingestion of large amounts of opium reversed itself and violent diarrhea accompanied the other withdrawal symptoms. This was a rebound effect, where the body reacted as if the drug was still present. Because it was not, the body overcompensated, which led to fearsome diarrhea.

After about a day and a half, the addict presents a dreadful appearance. The following description is by physician John Hawkins, himself a morphine addict after treatment for accidental burns: "Yawning may be so violent as to dislocate the jaw, watery mucus pours from the nose and copious tears from the eyes.... Now to add further to the addict's miseries his bowels begin to act with fantastic violence; great waves of contractions pass over the walls of the stomach, causing explosive vomiting.... The abdominal pain is severe and rapidly increases. Constant purging takes place ... and as many as sixty large watery stools may be passed in a day.... The quantity of watery secretion from eyes and nose is enormous, the amount of fluid expelled from stomach and intestines unbelievable."[20] Hawkins added that "even a physician, accustomed to the sight of suffering, finds it an ordeal to watch the agonies of patients in this condition."

Cocaine Addiction

Opium and morphine were not the only drugs that created addiction. Another common narcotic drug of the late 1800s with a high potential for abuse was cocaine. Frequent use, whether recreational or medical, led to cocaine addiction. Unlike opium and morphine, however, cocaine was not physically addictive, but it did produce a high level of psychological dependence. A moderate dose of the drug created stimulation. The user's respiration and pulse rate were raised, and brain activity was increased, leading to a feeling of well-being and mental alertness. However, these sensations faded away rapidly and were followed by feelings of deep depression. The solution for the addict was to continue the cocaine intake. This started a vicious cycle of mood swings between ecstasy and depression.

A pharmacist interviewed by a reporter for the *Denver Times* on October 21, 1900, commented, "The cocaine habit invariably starts with its use for aches and pains, and while it is a certain remedy for temporary relief, my experience is that many never stop using it, becoming so fond of it as a drug that they cannot and will not break off, and at the same time would be insulted if you were to suggest that they were slaves to the drug."

The coca alkaloid was extracted from the dried leaf of the *Erythroxylon coca* plant that grew in the mountainous areas of Peru. It had been used for centuries by indigenous Indians, stretching back to the Inca period, to reduce the fatigue and hunger intensified by high altitude. The coca leaves provided cheer and strength, but eventually turned the teeth black.[21]

Cocaine was first isolated from the plant in 1859, and by 1860 the Merck Company had started to manufacture cocaine commercially. It was originally promoted as "nourishment for the nerves" and a "harmless way to cure sadness."[22] And, admittedly, use of the drug did make people feel confident and happy. Cocaine overdose, however, led to dizziness, fainting, and convulsions. Continued long-term use of the drug led to tremors, delirium, and insanity.

Purified cocaine became available in the United States in 1884. Within a year, the Parke-Davis Company had introduced cocaine in fifteen forms, including cocaine-laced cigarettes, cocaine solution for injection, and a variation that could be used for sniffing.[23] They also sold a handy cocaine kit for home use that included a hypodermic syringe along with a supply of the drug. Cocaine was freely available and was commonly used for ailments that would today be treated with aspirin. It was so commonly stocked in drugstores that occasionally the owner had to run a special sale because the drug had a limited shelf life and it was necessary to sell overstocked supplies.[24]

On the other hand, cocaine did have medical uses. It was not absorbed well through unbroken skin, but was rapidly absorbed through mucous membranes such as those of the mouth and nose or through an open wound. In 1884 in Vienna, physician Carl Koller used cocaine as a local anesthetic during eye surgery to dull the pain and to prevent the eye from moving. It was also used to treat hay fever because it shrank inflamed tissues, though, unfortunately, continued use often led to gangrene of the inside of the nose. Cocaine in the form of Lloyd's Cocaine Toothache Drops was used to relieve toothache. Suppositories containing cocaine were used to successfully shrink inflamed tissues in cases of rectal, uterine, and urethral diseases. But the dark side to cocaine was that early experiments with the drug resulted in many doctors and medical students becoming addicted.

Cocaine was even a popular ingredient of soft drinks. Around 1890 there were more than a hundred beverages that contained either extracts of the coca plant or pure cocaine. This included "tonics" such as Koka-Nola and Celery Kola. One of the most famous of the cocaine-containing soft drinks, and the one that outlasted the others, was Coca-Cola. It was first concocted and commercialized in 1885 by John Sith Pemberton, a pharmacist from Atlanta, Georgia, as a carbonated alcohol-based patent medicine.[25] Pemberton was a morphine addict due to injuries received in the Civil War and originally sold the "medicine" to cure morphine addiction and neurasthenia. He conceived the idea from a similar drink that had been popular in France for the preceding thirty years or so, and he originally called the drink Pemberton's French Wine Coca. It contained wine and extracts of coca and flavoring from the kola nut. The *Atlanta Journal* of March 10, 1885, called it "a wonderful medicine." The drink was first sold at Jacob's Pharmacy in Atlanta in May 1886.

Pemberton lost money on the venture and sold an interest in the formula to another druggist, Asa Grigs Candler, who eventually became the full owner of the company for $2,300 in 1889. Candler was apparently a better businessman than Pemberton. He sold premixed syrup to bottling companies to create an independent soft drink under license. A typical 1890s poster advertising Coca-Cola trumpeted "it relieves fatigue and excitement, and induces a spirit of thorough restful satisfaction as delightful to the senses as Coca-Cola is to the sense of taste."

At the time, cocaine was still thought to be nonaddictive. Dr. William Hammond of New York, a prominent neurologist, assured users that cocaine was harmless. He developed his own tonic that consisted of two grains of cocaine in a pint of wine. He assured readers that cocaine users could stop whenever they wanted.[26] It was not until the 1890s that physicians realized that there was such a problem as the cocaine habit. (Caffeine replaced cocaine as the active ingredient of Coca-Cola in 1903.)

Cocaine was sometimes combined with other types of alcohol. For example, it was sometimes added to whiskey to give a drink an additional boost. In Denver cocaine was sold by the pinch in a shot of whiskey. This was not a very safe practice. The combination of alcohol and cocaine produced cocaethylene, which was a very toxic compound. As a result, red wine with cocaine added produced a higher state of euphoria, but it also carried a higher potential for harmful effects.

By the beginning of the twentieth century cocaine had run the gamut of opinions. Some believed that it was deadly. Some believed that it was therapeutic and rarely abused. Others considered it useful for certain conditions and people.

Unintentional Addiction

It was not unknown for individuals to become addicts without knowing it or desiring it. One way was when a patented "cure" for alcohol addiction were given to an unknowing loved one. For example, if a husband drank to excess and appeared to be on the road to alcoholism, a wife might slip one of the patent medicine cures into his coffee or tea. As most of these "cures" contained opium, morphine, or codeine, it was possible that the man might unwittingly become addicted after continued use. One such "cure" was the White Star Secret Liquor Cure sold by Sears Roebuck. The "cure" was basically an opium-based tonic. To counteract this, Sears sold a cure for opium and morphine addicts that contained alcohol. For fussy babies, the company also sold a "soothing syrup" that contained both opium and alcohol.

The real-life behavior of these "cures" was satirized in the motion picture *The Road to Wellville* (1994), in which Eleanor Lightbody (Bridget Fonda) unintentionally addicts her husband, Will Lightbody (Matthew Broderick), to opium. She says to a friend, "He used to take Hostetter's Bitters for his stomach." Then he progressed to large amounts of alcohol. In retaliation, she put White Star Liquor Cure in his coffee every day so that he would sleep and not go out and get drunk. She realizes afterwards what she has done and has terrible feelings of guilt. "I turned him into an opium addict," she confesses tearfully to her sympathetic friend.

Many women were also responsible for unknowingly creating addiction in their children. Mothers gave soothing syrups to their babies to keep them quiet. Mrs. Winslow's Soothing Syrup, for example, which was widely advertised and consumed, contained one grain of morphine in each fluid ounce. Contrast this to the dosages in Illustration 1 in chapter 4, which recommends ¼ of a grain *for an adult*. Infants dosed with this powerful opium solution were certainly kept quiet. They were, in fact, kept in a semi-comatose state. Opium was also given to children in poor families to suppress the appetite so that they were not as hungry, thus economizing on food. Another cause of unwanted addiction was military service. Many veterans who had been wounded and treated for pain or suffered from chronic dysentery from unsanitary camp conditions left the army addicted to opium. This type of addiction was commonplace after the Civil War.

This is the hospital at Fredericksburg, Virginia, which was used to treat injured soldiers during the Civil War. So many wounded men were treated with opium and morphine for pain that they became addicted to the drug. Addiction was so common that it became known as "old soldier's disease" or "army disease" (National Library of Medicine).

Treatment of Addiction

The physical tribulations of the opium addict were bad enough; however, some of the "cures" used to treat addiction weren't very pleasant either. Addiction treatments of the day typically prescribed strong laxatives and other drugs to counter the effects of addiction withdrawal.

The following dreadful-sounding treatment was described by physician Alexander Lambert in 1909 in the *Journal of the American Medical Association.* The basic medicine used for this treatment was a tincture of belladonna and prickly ash. Lambert outlined the course of action as follows: "While this specific is being given, the patients do not suffer from the intense diarrhea which usually accompanies the withdrawal of morphin [*sic*]. On the contrary, the most energetic, drastic, cathartic medication is necessary to obtain the desired elimination and to make their bowels move satisfactorily." He recommended starting treatment with a five-grain dose of blue mass. He followed this with doses of purgative pills (which he called a "compound cathartic") that contained colocynth, jalap, podophyllum, capsicum, and croton oil, at the same time administering a soapsuds enema. He recommended giving the tincture until signs of belladonna intoxication were noted (such as dilated pupils, a red rash, or the beginning of delirium). He waited until after the symptoms subsided then started again with the pills, along with half the patient's usual dose of opium or morphine. He continued with the compound cathartic and blue mass pills, perhaps adding a dose of castor oil.[27] Lambert added that "after the patient has been under treatment for thirty hours, one should begin to give some cardiac stimulant, such as strychnin [*sic*] ... or digitalis.... These tend to overcome the relaxation of the vascular system, which in these patients often produces a feeling of exhaustion."

This must have been heroic treatment indeed and a "feeling of exhaustion" would seem to be a gross understatement. Blue mass was the common name for a chunk of calomel (mercurous chloride), which was used as a powerful purgative. The components listed for his cathartic pills — colocynth, jalap, podophyllum, capsicum, croton oil, and castor oil — were all powerful evacuants in their own right. After thirty hours of this "treatment," the addict who survived should have been "purged" of his addiction and, it was hoped, should certainly have been cured. The treatment was also recommended for alcoholism and was claimed to cure neurasthenia.

A powerful cure for addiction was promoted by Charles B. Towns, a former insurance salesman and stockbroker. His "secret" cure was a mixture of the addictive substance combined with extract of prickly ash bark, hyoscyamus (a narcotic), and tincture of belladonna (deadly nightshade, used as a sedative), topped off with castor oil and strychnine. Towns claimed that the addict would be cured after three days of treatment. Needless to say, though this mixture had a substantial effect on the addict as described above, it had no particular effect on his addiction and Lambert withdrew his support. Towns, however, retired a rich man.[28]

One of the best-known of the cures for the treatment of alcoholism and opium addiction was the Keeley Double Chloride of Gold Cure, which was developed and promoted by Leslie E. Keeley through his Keeley Institute. Keeley, a surgeon for the Union army during the Civil War, was not bashful, advertising in huge letters that it would "absolutely cure anyone." Keeley claimed that cures for addiction were made between eight and twenty days, "without pain or nervous shock."[29] The treatment consisted of intravenous injections of his proprietary gold formula, accompanied by healthy doses of exercise, fresh air, good diet, and adequate sleep. With irrefutable, but convoluted, logic, Keeley claimed that if patients continued to drink after his treatment, it was because they wanted to and not because they were still addicted.

Keeley advertised heavily and sold his medicine, called "bichloride of gold" or "double chloride of gold," through mail order and at a series of over two hundred franchised sanitariums.[30] In the 1890s, there were 118 franchised Keeley Institutions in the United States, as well as in Canada, Mexico, and Europe. Patients at Keeley's sanitariums paid $25 a week for a four-week cure, which eventually made Keeley a millionaire. By 1895, the Keeley League claimed to have 30,000 members in chapters across the country. Keeley's followers also met at an annual convention. By 1918, an estimated 400,000 Americans had taken the Keeley Cure. The last Keeley Institute closed in 1966.

Keeley never revealed the formula for his medicine, but a government study found that it didn't cure addiction and a chemical analysis showed that it didn't contain any gold.[31] Instead, ingredients of his cure included atropine (a circulatory stimulant), strychnine, arsenic, cinchona (the source of quinine), ammonium chloride, and glycerin.[32] One of Keeley's theories was that alcohol poisoned nerve cells, so his medicine was supposed to purge these toxins by increasing elimination. Experts, however, found that it could also damage the kidneys.

Nevertheless, physicians correctly continued to try what they considered to be scientific methods to combat alcoholism, rather than the older ineffectual moral persuasion and guilt approaches to sobriety. When morphine was first isolated, it was hailed as a cure for opium addiction. Among the many "cures" offered to addicts, most contained morphine disguised by sugar or other sweeteners. When twenty of these "cures" were tested and reported by the Massachusetts' Board of Health in 1872, nineteen of them were found to contain morphine.[33] Physicians sometimes treated alcoholics with morphine and addicted them knowingly and on purpose to drugs, thinking that morphine addiction was the lesser of the two evils. With modern hindsight, of course, it was not. In some parts of the country, particularly the rural West, this technique to treat alcoholism was still used into the late 1930s and early 1940s.[34]

Perversely, medical treatments for opium addiction often used opium, morphine, codeine, or cocaine to try to "cure" the unfortunate addict. To compound the problem, morphine was often used to treat a hangover after alcoholic overindulgence. Alcohol addiction and the resulting delirium tremens were treated by the use of opium, and morphine addiction was treated by the use of alcohol. Conventional physicians finally realized that opium addiction was a disease with no cure and treated the symptoms rather than the cause.

HEROIN AS A CURE FOR ADDICTION

Scientists continued attempts to find other nonaddictive substances that would cure the opium addiction problem. A powerful drug that was initially hailed as a nonaddictive pain reliever, a substitute for morphine and codeine, and a "cure" for morphine addiction was heroin. Doctors soon realized, however, that this new substance was even more addictive than morphine; the "treatment" still replaced one addictive drug with another and the addict was never cured.[35]

Though distantly related to opium through chemistry, heroin did not occur naturally in the opium poppy but was artificially produced. In 1874, British scientist C.R. Alder Wright discovered a process to chemically alter morphine into a variation called tetra-ethyl morphine, later renamed diacetyl-morphine. His work was duly noted by other chemists, but nothing was done with the substance for a number of years.

In 1898, Heinrich Dreser, a chemist at Bayer Laboratories in Germany, conducted clinical tests with diacetylmorphine and found that it had powerful pain-relieving properties. Dreser noted that heroin was about five times more active than morphine. In terms of the strength of opium administered to a patient, then, this meant that about fifty times as much opium would have to be used to produce the same amount of pain relief. Noting this, Bayer therefore mass-produced and marketed this product as new pain reliever. The brand name chosen was "heroin," from the German word *heroisch*, which means "heroic," as that is how Bayer viewed it.[36] As a result, heroin was nick-named the "heroic drug."

Opposite: Opium and morphine abuse was so common that many cures for addiction were widely advertised. Ironically, opium addiction was often treated by morphine or whiskey, and alcohol addiction was treated by opium or morphine. Heroin was initially considered to be a cure for morphine addiction until physicians realized that they were trading one type of addiction for another. Pictured here is the Dr. Collins Opium Antidote Laboratory in La Porte, Indiana, which manufactured a self-proclaimed "painless cure" named Theriaki (National Library of Medicine).

THERIAKI !
Painless Cure for the Opium and Liquor Habits.

DR. COLLINS' ANTIDOTE enables the patient to discontinue the use of Opium in any form at once, without pain or inconvenience, and without any interruption of ordinary business. It rebuilds the broken constitution, and restores the nervous energies. Discovered in 1868—the only painless cure ever discovered.

Persons interested are respectfully referred to the following parties: T. M. Endicott, Shelbyville, Ind. Chas. Beardsley, New Berlin, N.Y. W. W. Hightower, Memphis, Tenn. F. F. Taber, M.D., Atlanta, Ga. W. L. Towner, Lake Station, Ind.

Miss. S. G. Gates, Wallingford, Vt. R. F. Scott, San Francisco, Cal. S. P. Guin, Jacksonville, Ill. Robt. McNeil, Pierceton, Ind. Wm. Sanderson, Prophetstown, Ill. A. P. Andrew, Jr., LaPorte, Ind. W. Y. C. Hannum, Marysville, Tenn.

A Magazine of 80 Pages Sent Free to Any Address.

Address, **Dr. S. B. COLLINS, LaPorte, Indiana.**

Heroin could be smoked or eaten, but the primary method of administration was by hypodermic injection. Heroin acted rapidly, perhaps even a hundred times faster than morphine, and its effects were felt in only a few seconds. Overdose, though, depressed respiration. The victim fell into a coma and eventually stopped breathing. Ironically, heroin was used initially to treat respiratory problems, such as coughs and colds, until the problems of addiction were understood. By the late 1800s, heroin had overtaken the use of opium by addicts. The use of heroin was discontinued in the early 1900s, though heroin continued to be sold freely after opium and morphine became controlled substances.

Overdose and Suicide

Opium and morphine poisoning were common in the Old West due to either an accidental overdose or deliberate suicide. In large enough doses, opium, morphine, and laudanum were used to commit suicide by disillusioned prostitutes. During the boom mining years in Virginia City, Nevada, there were forty reported suicide attempts, of which nineteen were successful.[37]

One of the best-known suicides in the West was Eleanor Dumont, also known as "Madame Moustache," who gambled her way from Nevada City, California, to mining towns around the mountain West in the 1850s and 1860s. Disillusioned as she aged and her situation in life declined, she drank an overdose of morphine and was found lying by the roadside a few miles outside Bodie, California, on the morning of September 8, 1879.

OVERDOSE

Prostitutes commonly took opium or morphine to sleep. Part of this habit was due to their working hours, which required them to work all night and then sleep during the daylight hours. In Nevada's Comstock mining district, for example, prostitute Capriana Avila was in the habit of taking morphine every day. However, the difference between the size of the dose that created sleep or euphoria in an addict and the dose that would kill the user was a fine distinction. To a novice who was not accustomed to opium, one grain of the drug might be a toxic dose. A lethal dose of the drug might be as little as four grains (this is less than a quarter of a gram, or eight *one-thousandths* of an ounce). As a result, some suicides may well have been accidental overdoses. As most prostitutes used drugs and alcohol freely, police officials often didn't know if suicides were intentional or not. As one example, when Nellie Rolfe was found dead in her room in the red light district of Cripple Creek, it was not clear if she had committed suicide. The *Cripple Creek Times* of January 3, 1903, commented, "The woman was a victim to the morphine habit. Three small bottles of the drug and two hypodermic syringes were found on the dresser of her room."

As tolerance to opium by the user increased, higher and higher dosages were required to achieve the effect desired. Thus addicts could take doses that would kill a novice. However, even for them, the lethal dose was still close to the effective dose, making the likelihood of accidental death quite high. In small doses, morphine exerted a depressing activity on the brain, which resulted in sleep and relief from pain. Morphine also desensitized the part of the central nervous system that regulated breathing and forced it to slow down. In moderate doses, this was not a problem. In large doses, morphine depressed the breathing so much that death occurred due to respiratory failure. If combined with another depressant, such as alcohol, it was often fatal.

In India, early rulers used this fact and employed opium to get rid of political rivals by making them drink poppy seeds in water. After continued doses, the victims became emaciated, lost their strength, and eventually died. This method was also reportedly used by East Indian women to commit suicide to escape from male domination.[38] (Given that poppy seeds alone are harmless, the stories probably refer to use of the entire seed pod, which, properly processed, would produce the desired effect.)

The first line of treatment for a drug overdose, either intentional or accidental, was to pump out the stomach in hopes that the drug had not fully taken effect. Another emergency remedy might be to make a semiconscious victim swallow olive oil to coat the stomach and slow absorption of the drug, or make them drink mustard in water to induce vomiting. Among the more extreme nineteenth-century methods of treatment to induce and maintain consciousness after drug overdose were severe whipping of the semiconscious victim, the application of red-hot irons to the feet, and beating with a club. Professor H.C. Wood at the University of Pennsylvania commented, "I have seen the whole body of a woman almost as black as a man's coat from the beating she had received to keep her awake in narcotic poisoning."[39]

If the time between the overdose and the treatment was delayed, and too much of the drug had been absorbed, nothing much could be done. One such unfortunate was Pearl de Vere, madam of the Old Homestead parlor house in Cripple Creek, Colorado. Whether she took morphine before going to bed to calm her nerves and took an accidental overdose or whether she intentionally tried to commit suicide was never satisfactorily determined. Whatever the case, Pearl was found on the morning of June 5, 1897, breathing heavily but unconscious. A local physician, Dr. Hereford, was summoned immediately, but the drug had been at work too long. He was unable to revive her and she died several hours later. The *Cripple Creek Times* for June 10, 1897, concluded that the death was not intentional. As the newspaper reported, "There is no evidence that the act was intentional, and it is the opinion of all her friends that in taking a sleeping potion she had carelessly taken too much of the drug."

Some women were luckier. Two of them were 16-year-old Hattie Willis and 21-year-old Katie Thompson, who worked as prostitutes at Rose Benjamin's bordello on D Street, the red light district of Virginia City, Nevada. In August 1872, they tried to commit suicide together, using a combination of morphine and laudanum. Three doctors were called and, due to quick action with a stomach pump, the two women survived. Twenty-year-old Laura Steele at Rose's was not so lucky and succeeded in taking her own life with an overdose of laudanum in 1875. Another was twenty-one-year-old Sallie Talbot in Cheyenne, Wyoming, who took too much laudanum in 1883 and died a few hours later, in spite of the valiant efforts of Dr. W.A. Wyan.

The progression after taking an overdose was downhill. First came a deep sleep, then stupor from which it was difficult to awaken the victim, followed by a coma from which there was no awakening. Finally death occurred from respiratory failure.[40] Death often came in less than an hour, though the victim might linger for as long as six to twelve hours.

A combination of alcohol and opium was often fatal. Many of these women may have crossed the fine line between an effective dose and a lethal dose unintentionally, especially if they had been drinking heavily. The *Butte Miner* reported in 1896 that Dora Forrest, a prostitute from Butte, Montana, was found dead in bed from an overdose of morphine at Lillie McGraw's brothel in Helena. She was with another prostitute, Madge Dawe, who was almost dead. Dawe was in the habit of taking morphine, but the two had been drinking heavily the previous evening. Dawe eventually recovered.

Accidents certainly did occur. In May of 1891, thirty-year-old William Clark, a banjo player at the Crystal Palace Theater in Cripple Creek, Colorado, went on a drinking spree. Afterwards, when he couldn't sleep, he took a large dose of morphine that turned out to be an accidental overdose. The doctor who came to attend him did not realize that the man had been previously drinking. He diagnosed Clark as suffering from "brain fever" and gave him more morphine as a treatment. This turned the overdose into a lethal one and Clark expired.[41]

Other cases were more clear-cut and contemporary newspapers are full of reports of suicides in red light districts across the Old West. The following are just a few of the many. The *Colorado Weekly Chieftain* reported in 1872 that Kitty Austin died at the Stranger's House in Pueblo. The *Pueblo Chieftain* of August 16, 1878, reported that Mamie at Esther Baldwin's bordello died of an overdose of laudanum. The *Denver Times* reported on December 15, 1886, that a Mrs. Winger had swallowed a dose of morphine in a house on Holladay Street.

Nellie Davis overdosed with morphine at Mrs. Gray's lodging house on B Street in Virginia City, Nevada, in the spring of 1864. An anonymous Chinese woman who cost her owner $800 overdosed with laudanum in the back of Stern's store in nearby Gold Hill, Nevada. Anna Parker tried to commit suicide by drinking a large dose of laudanum. Dutch Leina committed suicide with a dose of morphine. In January of 1891, a woman named Clara who worked for madam Laura Bell McDaniel in Colorado City, Colorado, committed suicide with eight grains of morphine. A customer sleeping with Ida Vernon, one of the girls at Jenny Tyler's Bow Windows brothel in Virginia City, Nevada, woke up the next morning to find that the woman lying beside him was dead from an overdose of morphine. The list goes on and on. Inez Mayberton killed herself at one of the brothels on Park Street in Butte, Montana, in 1881 after a drinking spree of several days which included suicide by taking an ounce of morphine. As she lay dying, bitter at the boyfriend she said had mistreated and deserted her, she said, "If there is any such thing as haunting, I will haunt him to his deathbed."[42]

Some survived after their brushes with death, but not all efforts to save suicide victims were so successful. On March 6, 1892, Effie Pryor and Allie Ellis tried to commit suicide by using morphine at Mattie Silk's bordello in Denver. Effie was saved, but Allie later died despite efforts by physicians to pump her stomach.

Not only prostitutes and other whites used opium and morphine for suicide. Chinese who were badly injured or irrecoverably ill took "the black pill," which consisted of an overdose of opium. Alcohol by itself was also responsible for deaths. In 1880, a prostitute with the last name of Pennybacker died in Arizona from drinking too much whiskey. In Butte, Montana, prostitute Josie Davis died after drinking a pint of whiskey and Jamaica ginger.[43]

CHAPTER TEN

Inebriety

Author Mark Twain once said "sometimes too much drink is barely enough." Drinking was so commonplace in the Old West that "how much alcohol was too much" was relative and a matter of opinion. In most towns of the Old West, "drunk and disorderly" was the commonest "crime" most law officers had to deal with. Heavy drinking was thought to be an expression of manliness and males were expected to assert their manhood by showing that they could drink to excess with the best of them. The opinion of one old-timer was that no man should be considered drunk in the mountains if he could still make a noise.[1]

Even the police, whose job it was to arrest drunks, were not immune to heavy drinking and sometimes law officers and firemen were too drunk to perform their duties. The *Denver Times* of November 12, 1885, reported, "A policeman under the influence of liquor and a bountiful supply of it, at that, was gyrating around and enjoying himself to the annoyance of respectable passers-by. He reached a climax when he laid hands on a woman who resisted his attack and the pair soon were rolling in the muddy ditch in a sort of cat and dog struggle."

On December 10, 1894, the *Denver Republican* reported, "A jag entered into Policeman Thomas P.S. Robinson and made him do things altogether unbefitting a guardian of the peace. After a wild and uproarious day, he wound up by arresting Alderman Thomas E. McNulty, three respectable women, [*and*] a saloon keeper who refused to supply him with liquor."

Interestingly, most saloon bartenders in the Old West drank very little, didn't drink on the job, and were typically not in favor of customers who were very heavy drinkers. If they were offered a drink by a customer or forced to join in when someone bought a round for the house, they would take the money and say that they would have a drink later. Other ways to avoid drinking would be to discreetly pour the drink back into a bottle behind the bar, to pour their drink into a special glass that was so small that it held almost nothing, or to fill their glass with cold tea the color of whiskey.

On the other hand, the urge to drink whiskey for some alcoholics was high. Alcohol was forbidden for the inmates of the Coconino County Hospital for the Indigent (the county poor farm) near Flagstaff, Arizona, in the early 1900s. Not to be deterred, however, they drank anyway and then threw their empty beer and whiskey bottles into the crawl space under the building, where they were not discovered until the building was turned over to the Arizona Historical Society as a museum years later.

What They Drank

As the 1900s dawned, one historian commented, "All the early theorists, and that of practical judges, too, agreed that the whiskey Denver consumed in her youthful days was that of an exceeding bad quality. It was colored and otherwise doctored to suit the fiery tastes of various grades of customers, and retailed from bottles bearing popular nick-names, one virgin barrel usually serving as the base of all these operations."[2]

The basic drink of the Western saloon was whiskey, with beer as a popular favorite. In early tent saloons, the selection of drinks was

Speaking trumpets were used by firemen to shout commands and facilitate communications during a fire. A lesser-known use was that after a fire was successfully extinguished, a cork was often secured in the mouthpiece and the trumpet inverted for use as a celebratory beer stein (author's collection).

usually limited to whiskey because bottles, jugs, or small kegs of liquor were easy to transport. The thirst of the early settlers could indeed be prodigious. One typical wagon train carried 1,600 barrels of whiskey and 2,700 cases of champagne to Denver in 1864. Eighty wagons were required to transport this over-abundance of liquor.[3]

The name "whiskey" in the West usually referred to bourbon whiskey, and it was sometimes called "red liquor" because of its reddish color. Other names for whiskey with a similar derivation were "redeye," "red ink," and "red disturbance." Occasionally the name "whiskey" also referred to rye whiskey, though rye was more commonly a drink of the East and Midwest. Some Scotch whiskey was served on the frontier but was not commonplace until after the turn of the century. Wine was also a popular alcoholic drink. Claret and champagne were often served at suppers and similar social gatherings.

The vast majority of drinkers in the West drank straight bourbon whiskey. When a town became well-established, most saloons started to offer a variety of liquor. This included several different whiskeys, gin imported from England, rum from the Caribbean, and wines from California and France. Mixed drinks were available in the larger bars and towns, and the hard-drinking saloon patrons might drink martinis, along with various juleps, mashes, cobblers, flips, and sours. Men who ordered mixed drinks, however, were looked down on a bit by serious whiskey drinkers who drank their liquor straight, and they were generally avoided for putting on fancy airs.

There was a certain etiquette to drinking in the West. The drinker tossed back his whiskey quickly, as nursing drinks was not considered to be customary. Being treated to a drink by a fellow drinker meant that the recipient had to buy one in return. All drinkers were expected to buy fellow drinkers a round from time to time. This practice of "treating" one another to drinks was encouraged by the saloon-owner, and bartenders would occasionally set up a free round. They knew that the drinkers would then feel obligated to treat each other, thus substantially increasing the sales of whiskey. These practices promoted almost continuous guzzling. Any scheme was fair game for getting the customer to leave his money with the house. At the Senate Saloon in Portland, Oregon, if a logger came in and offered to buy a drink for a few of his fellow workers, the bartender pressed a buzzer to signal any of the girls upstairs who were unoccupied to hurry down and join them. The bartender knew that the customer would be too embarrassed to refuse to buy them a drink too.

Drinks that were popular locally were served in different areas of the West. A "cavalry punch," for example, was drunk at Fort Laramie in Wyoming and Fort Lincoln in Kansas. This concoction consisted of tea mixed with rum and blackberry juice. Residents of Colorado City and Denver, Colorado, liked a drink called "velvet," which consisted of equal measures of porter and champagne mixed together in a large glass. Germans in the West made a specialized drink called "rumtopf," which consisted of rum, fruit, and sugar.

Mixtures that involved whiskey were understandably popular. A "mule skinner" consisted of whiskey mixed with blackberry liquor. "Grizzly bear's milk" was whiskey laced with milk and sugar. A boilermaker, which is still popular among some modern drinkers, was a shot of whiskey followed by a beer. In San Francisco, the specialty of the house at Warner's Saloon was a drink made by boiling whiskey and gin with cloves. Another popular drink was the Tom and Jerry. The drink was created from a batter of eggs, sugar, rum, and brandy. Hot milk and nutmeg were sometimes added. The Tom and Jerry was originally named as part of the publicity for an 1820 novel by Victorian novelist Pierce Egan — also a British journalist — named *Life in London; or the Day and Night Scenes of Jerry Hawthorn, Esq., and His Elegant Friend Corinthian Tom*. In the late 1880s, both the drink and the novel were extremely popular.

At a saloon in a mature town, nondrinkers who had taken the "Temperance Pledge" could order ginger ale, ginger beer, lemonade, sarsaparilla, or other nonalcoholic beverages. Beer, though popular with many drinkers, was slower to arrive in early Western towns because of the difficulty and expense of freighting it from a brewery. Some ingenious businessmen, however, found ways to get around these limitations. A "lager wagon" followed German troops in the Union army in summer during the Civil War. Lager beer, brought to the United States by German immigrants in the 1860s, became very popular after the Civil War. Normally, beer tended to spoil rapidly and it did not travel well in a wagon. It was also too bulky and inexpensive to make a reasonable profit for the saloon if it had to be shipped for long distances, that is until the arrival of a railroad provided cheap freight rates and fast delivery.

The completion of the transcontinental railroad and the subsequent proliferation of spur railroad branches made it possible to ship beer economically from major breweries in St. Louis and Milwaukee to relatively remote locations in the West. The thirst for beer was strong. After the railroad arrived in Helena, Montana, one distributor sold more that 1,600 kegs of beer between April and July.

Before the arrival of the railroad, when a town reached a reasonable size and showed some stability, an enterprising businessman usually erected a brewery and made beer locally. William Bull erected the Empire Brewery in 1849 in San Francisco, which had grown rapidly from a sleepy seaport to the booming jumping-off point for the California gold fields.[4] Denver, which grew in similar fashion with the 1858 discovery of gold in nearby Central City and Blackhawk, had a brewery as early as 1859. The Rocky Mountain Brewery was started in 1860. The Golden Eagle Brewery in Tombstone, Arizona, started selling beer in 1879 when the town had only 300 inhabitants. Beer, stout, and ale were commonly available to the residents of Leadville in the 1880s, as were gin and French wines. Parkhurst and Company brewed beer as early as 1876 in Deadwood, South Dakota, the same year the town was founded.

In the hotter climates of the Southwest, beer was often served cool but not cold due to a lack of refrigeration and a limited supply of ice. If ice was available, some saloons had a metal ice chest on the floor at the end of the bar to keep the beer cool. In areas of the West such as Montana and the high mountains of the Southern Rockies, ice was more commonly available. Cut from frozen lakes in the winter and stored under sawdust for insulation, ice could provide cooling for drinks throughout the summer.

Whiskey was relatively light in weight and small in volume compared to beer, so whiskey was easy to transport by wagon before the railroad arrived in the Old West. Small wooden barrels like this, nicknamed "hollow wood" by some Navajo Indians, were used to store and transport liquor around the frontier (author's collection).

Intemperance

Not all towns of the Old West, however, embraced liquor. No saloons were allowed within the city limits and all alcoholic beverages were banned when Greeley, Colorado, was founded as the Union Colony in 1870. In fact, the consumption, production, and distribution of liquor was banned in the town until 1969. The nearby town of Longmont, founded by the Chicago-

Colorado Colony in 1870, did not initially allow the sale of alcohol on Colony land. The measure was apparently unsuccessful, as the liquor ban was lifted within two years.

When Colorado Springs, Colorado, was founded by General William Palmer in 1871, all the town deeds contained a clause proclaiming that intoxicating liquor as a beverage could not be manufactured or sold on the premises, or else the property would revert back to the original town company. It was not so much that residents objected to drinking, but rather they were hoping to ban saloons, liquor, and drink that they felt would lower property values. Even General Palmer was not opposed to a drink or two.[5] The situation was resolved to everyone's satisfaction by locating the saloons and bawdy houses in nearby Colorado City, which was about

Whiskey was also stored in ceramic jugs like this, which were commonly refilled and reused due to shortages of containers on the frontier. If a stopper made from cork was not available, a corncob could be used as a convenient substitute (author's collection).

two miles west of downtown Colorado Springs. An estimated twenty-seven saloons were soon in operation there.

Somewhat hypocritically, municipal leaders of Colorado Springs organized a private club, the El Paso Club (which is still in existence today), that allowed members to keep private stocks of liquor in lockers at the club. When the club changed buildings in 1890, the mayor and civic government decided that their "liquor" was not "*the* liquor" covered by the liquor ban and the club opened a member's bar in the new building.[6]

Temperance workers loved to promote the sordid image of a downward spiral into the depths of drink and degradation. A typical story was one that appeared in the *Denver Tribune* of November 8, 1885, which described a vagrant named Lizzie Greer. The paper hypothesized that she had "probably been a factory girl, and it was thought that her employer had been her destroyer." Whether true or not, the image of the seduction of innocent young women, especially servant girls or female factory workers, by an evil employer, then their descent into drink and drugs, was a common and perversely enjoyed voyeuristic Victorian theme. This theme was often used in melodramatic Victorian plays. The article continued: "[s]he drank only what she could from one saloon to another ... tipping up empty beer kegs in [the] back of saloons ... to drain out the last stale drop into her can and drink it with as much relish as if it were nectar."[7]

BUT BY ANY OTHER NAME

In the late 1840s, a new medical term, "alcoholism," replaced the previous name of "inebriety," which was the old-fashioned name for a state of drunkenness or intoxication.[8] Inebriety was the preferred earlier term, with its meaning analogous to addiction. Contemporary medical textbooks talked about alcohol inebriety, drug inebriety, cocaine inebriety, and even tea inebriety. Other older terms for addiction were "dipsomania," for too much to drink, and "narcomania," for drug addiction. "Potomania" was a condition of body fluid and electrolyte imbalance brought on by the consumption of massive amounts of beer. The term "alcoholism" as a disease has been attributed to Swedish physician Magnus Huss in 1849.[9]

Heavy Drinkers

In the late nineteenth century, drinking alcoholic beverages by women was considered to be improper. Women were thought of as the weaker sex, with their primary place being in the home. Respectable women were thought to have superior virtue and strict morality, so being drunk or an alcoholic was a real stigma. Men could — and did — become roaring drunk and still be considered male icons, but women who drank were considered to be debauched and the equivalent of fallen women. But male drunkards were not necessarily looked upon kindly either, even by contemporaries. The editor of the *Daily Miner's Register* of Central City, Colorado, wrote on December 18, 1867; "They are the excrescence of society, and like the fungus which fastening itself upon the trunk of a living, thriving tree, must be speedily removed else they will communicate decay and rottenness to every thing with which they come into contact." All the same, many women in the Old West were heavy drinkers. Estimates place the number of female alcoholics at anywhere between one in three and one in ten, though some abusers could be considered to be innocent, as their alcoholism resulted from drinking patent medicines. By the time they sought help, they had been ignoring or concealing the fact that they were addicts for too long and it was too late for successful treatment.

Prostitutes tended to drink to excess due to their way of life and work, and inebriety was responsible for many of the quirky incidents that took place in the booming mining towns of the Old West. In the mining town of Cripple Creek, Colorado, one rather overweight crib woman named Leola Ahrens, better known by her nickname of Leo the Lion, appeared roaring drunk and stark naked at the corner of Myers Avenue and Fourth Street one day and yelled at the top of her voice, "I'm Leo the Lion, the Queen of the Row." Nobody seem to think this was out of the ordinary and someone simply guided her home and put her to bed to sleep it off.[10] Similar was the incident involving prostitute Mary Murphy, who was drunk and undressed in public in Aspen, Colorado, in 1897. The police of Aspen were not so understanding and she was arrested and hauled off to jail.[11] In Denver, working women Belle Jones, Daisy Smith, and Annie Griffin became carried away by drink and staged an impromptu naked dance on a street corner in the middle of town. They also were arrested.[12]

This type of woman was always blatant, but many became drunk in public nonetheless. The *Black Hills Daily Times* of Deadwood for July 7, 1880, reported that "a disgusting sight was presented the morning of the Fourth by the two young men and one of the soiled doves of Lead, who were picked up out of the mud in a state of helpless intoxication." In the same town, the *Black Hills Times* of May 22, 1877, stated that one of their reporters had counted fourteen drunks in the streets. In Virginia City, Nevada, the *Territorial Enterprise* of February 2, 1868, reported that a prostitute named English Gussie became so drunk that she fell from an upper box at McGuire's Opera House and broke a hole in the floor. She was charged by the police as "drunk and disorderly."

This type of behavior was not limited to women. On one occasion gunfighter Clay Allison lurched drunkenly out of a saloon in Canadian, Texas, wearing nothing but his hat, boots, and gunbelt, and marched up and down the street challenging anybody to a fight. Nobody took him up on it. Showman and occasional army guide William F. "Buffalo Bill" Cody was known to be a heavy drinker and his binges between show stops were legendary. When drinking started to affect Cody's *Wild West* performances, his manager, Nate Salisbury, is reputed to have made Cody limit himself to one drink a day. Supposedly Cody agreed, but poured his allowance of whiskey into a beer schooner so that it would last him all day.[13] In spite of the stories of raucous drinking bouts, Cody never missed a performance due to drink. Under doctor's orders, Cody ceased drinking during the last few years of his life.

The Dreaded Hangover

Hangovers from too much drink have been the curse of the drinking man from time immemorial. Medical understanding of hangovers is as yet incomplete, but two primary mechanisms are thought to produce this unhappy state for the drinker. One is dehydration caused by the diuretic effects of alcohol. This reduction of fluids affects the brain and produces a fearsome headache. The other major effect is due to a build-up of poisonous by-products during the elimination of alcohol from the body. Alcohol is metabolized by the liver, where it is converted to acetaldehyde. If the acetaldehyde, a toxic substance, is not further removed from the body, the results are a hangover. In most drinkers the symptoms of a hangover are an increased heart rate, nausea, diarrhea, bad breath, flatulence, lethargy, and a pounding headache, along with a heightened sensitivity to loud noises and sudden movements.

Approximately 50 percent of the population of East Asia, which includes the Chinese, Japanese and Koreans, have difficulty metabolizing acetaldehyde, and so do members of some American Indians tribes.[14] This results in a build-up of the level of acetaldehyde in the body, which leads to rapid and severe symptoms of a hangover.

Part of a hangover occurs when the drinker's blood alcohol level drops precipitously as the alcohol is being metabolized and excreted from the body. Bringing the alcohol level back up with another drink is the basis for the time-honored old wives' tale that a good stiff drink will cure a hangover.[15] Other recommended remedies for a hangover have been many. The old standby has always been to drink plenty of coffee. This does not cure or lessen a hangover, but does result in a very wide-awake drunk. One suggested "cure" for a hangover in the Old West was to eat canned tomatoes. Another old-time remedy was claimed to be raw egg yolk mixed with Worcestershire sauce, Tabasco sauce, salt, and pepper. Oddly, a bacon sandwich has been claimed to effectively relieve hangovers. Among the more bizarre "cures" in the history books is the recommendation from Roman Pliny the Elder in the first century A.D. to eat two raw owl's eggs or a fried canary.[16]

In spite of many old wives tales and "cures" promoted by folk medicine, a recent paper in the *British Medical Journal* concluded that "no compelling evidence exists to suggest that any conventional or complementary intervention is effective for preventing or treating alcohol hangover. The most effective way to avoid the symptoms of alcohol induced hangover is to practise abstinence or moderation."[17]

Delirium Tremens

After a drinker had established his pattern of alcoholism, sudden withdrawal from liquor resulted in restlessness, irritability, agitation, loss of appetite, nausea, vomiting, elevated heart rate, increased blood pressure, insomnia, nightmares, impaired memory, increased sensitivity to light and sound, hallucinations, and paranoid delusions of persecution.[18]

Withdrawal for the advanced alcoholic resulted in a complex group of further symptoms that were collected under the name of delirium tremens, or the DTs. Who could read the following description by temperance crusader Frederick Powell and not shudder: "Gaze upon the poor drunkard, when under the power of that terrible madness, *delirium tremens*! What hideous imaginings! What foul fiends and grim spectres torment him! Scorpions glare upon him, with jaws like sepulchres and eyes like fire! Fanged serpents hiss at him, and all terrible shapes, creatures of a distorted imagination, gather around to inflict upon him the torments of the damned."[19]

The temperance book *Autobiography of a Reformed Drunkard* was written in 1845 under the pseudonym John Cotton Mather and contained the following: "We have had the past week a horrible case of delirium tremens in the house. The poor fellow chased dogs, cats, rats, and devils incessantly for several days and nights: and just before he died he thought he was in hell, and the devils were all around him, with all sorts of instruments of torture. 'I'm in hell, in hell!' he would cry. 'O! O! don't burn me so!—how that devil bites!'" The editor of the book commented, "Although the book takes the form of a temperance narrative, it is probably a fiction, whole or in part."[20] This description, however, was not inaccurate.

Delirium tremens was also known in the Old West as the "jim-jams," "the rams," or "the horrors." The DTs manifested itself in trembling hands and legs, sweating, and hallucinations. The victim imagined that snakes or spiders were crawling all over him and he shook constantly as he tried to fight them off. *An Autobiography by John B. Gough*, also written in 1845, described Gough's experience with delirium tremens: "Hideous faces appeared on the walls, and on the ceiling, and on the floors, foul things crept along the bed-clothes, and glaring eyes peered into mine. I was at one time surrounded by millions of monstrous spiders, who crawled slowly, slowly over every limb, whilst the beaded drops of persperation [*sic*] would start to my brow, and my limbs would shiver until the bed rattled again."[21]

Other symptoms were tremors, disorientation, and vomiting. If the drinker reached this point, the DTs carried with it a 4 to 5 percent chance of death. Diagnosis of an alcohol-related fatality that appeared on a death certificate death might be "the jim-jams," "black-tongue disease" ("black tongue" was actually the name for blood poisoning that originated in the mouth), "congestion of the brain," "general dissipation," or simply "high altitude."[22] In Lawrence County, South Dakota, which included Deadwood, out of 1,929 deaths between 1877 and 1898, alcoholism accounted for 0.1 percent, as opposed to homicides, which totaled 3 percent.[23]

Alcohol-related deaths also occurred. In 1877, an army captain stationed on the Northern Plains was found dead with his neck caught between two pickets of a fence. The post surgeon speculated he was so drunk that when he bent over the fence to vomit, he fell onto the wire and strangled to death.[24]

The Perplexing Legend of Spontaneous Combustion

According to temperance advocates, strong drink was supposed to take a man straight to hell. Hellfire and brimstone speeches like the following excerpt came from the podium[25]: "The alcohol drinker has his hell also — a hell scorching his veins and consuming all his joys. Terrible as is the hell of the opium eater, still more terrible is the hell of the alcohol drinker."[26]

One manifestation of this hellfire that the drinker was supposed to be consigned to baffled even the most avid temperance enthusiasts. This strange aspect of nineteenth-century drunkenness took the form of a series of reports of unexplained cases of supposed spontaneous human combustion. Contemporary newspapers reported on cases of people in both America and Europe innocently sitting around in their homes when they suddenly burst into flames. The victims were supposedly badly burned or, in some cases, even reduced to cinders. Attempts to douse the fierce flames were said to be unsuccessful and the unfortunate victims were so totally consumed that only a small pile of white ashes remained. Even more curious, reports said that often the victim's clothing and other nearby combustible objects were untouched by the fire.[27]

One physician who promoted the legend of spontaneous combustion was Benjamin Rush. He once related the story of a man he observed who was a heavy drinker. As the story went, the man belched near the flames of a candle and was at once destroyed by the resulting fireball. While it is difficult to refute a story from one of the leading physicians of the time, the anecdote would seem to be suspect and the product of anti-liquor sentiment. But these stories were perfect for the anti-liquor agitators of the day. In the temperance play *Ten Nights in a Bar-Room*, the character Switchel says, "The fact is, every time I look at old Slade, I'm afraid of spontaneous combustion."[28]

Another series of reports was published in Robert Macnish's book *The Anatomy of Drunkenness*, which contained a chapter titled "The Spontaneous Combustion of Drunkards." In it he mentioned "the case of a Bohemian peasant ... who lost his life in consequence of a column of ignited inflammable air issuing from his mouth and baffling extinction."[29] Macnish also mentioned drunkards having been blown to smithereens after belching too close to a lighted candle.

Though never satisfactorily explained, by the end of the nineteenth century these stories of alcoholic spontaneous combustion seem to have spontaneously disappeared, never to be repeated. For what it is worth, Macnish pointed out that most of these tales seemed to originate on the American side of the Atlantic. Whether these were deliberate tall tales or honest confusion has always remained a mystery. Some temperance advocates theorized that excessive alcohol consumption was to blame for human spontaneous combustion, but considering the levels of alcohol present in even the heaviest drinker, this would seem unlikely.

Drinking and Violence

The two primary causes of fights in the Old West were women and too much to drink, both of which were to be found in saloons. As historian Jerome Smiley has pointed out, "Whiskey was at the bottom of most of the frequent brawls and fights."[30] Some saloon fights resulted in a great many shots being fired but few casualties because the participants were so drunk they could not aim straight. Saloon confrontations were often empty threats fueled by too much whiskey. After drinking too much, two men would face off, pull their guns, strut and posture, and make threats about inflicting injury and harm on the other. The next day, when both had sobered up, the entire incident was often forgotten. Nevertheless, these confrontations did not always peter out and saloon bravado and posturing often led to real violence

In spite of this, in many instances the shooting wasn't at another man. It was a case of cowboys letting off steam and shooting at the moon, the street lights, the oil lamps and mirrors in the saloon, likely looking targets on the walls, or up at the saloon ceiling. This behavior could make the situation dangerous for anyone who happened to be in a room upstairs or next door, as the heavy bullets could easily penetrate wooden walls. This practice was so common and the potential for injury was so great in Panamint City, California, in the 1870s that two of the saloons, the Oriental and the Dexter, installed a sheet of iron between their buildings to prevent injury to the patrons or the furnishings of each of these neighbors.

In Cimarron, New Mexico, which not coincidentally means "wild" or "untamed" in Spanish, times were just as wild. At the St. James Hotel the owner installed three layers of oak planking in the ceiling of the saloon in 1903 to protect guests in the hotel rooms upstairs from injury due to random celebratory gunshots. Bullet holes are visible yet in the tin ceiling of the saloon, which is still open for business today.

Most writing about Western saloons focuses on the bawdiness and violence of frontier saloons, and that image was often justified. Pat O'Brien's saloon at Eighteenth Street and Curtis in downtown Denver, for example, was reputed to be so tough that the house would refund your money if you drank two beers and didn't see a fight.[31] In 1881, the year-end police report for Denver recorded

"Drunk and disorderly" was the commonest "crime" in the Old West. Alcoholism was not understood to be a disease, so habitual drunkards or cowboys celebrating too much on a Saturday night made frequent trips to the local jail, such as this tiny wooden frontier lockup, until they slept it off (author's collection).

1,187 arrests for drunkenness, the most common charge in these arrests being "drunk and disorderly." Fines for this charge were usually anywhere from $15 to $35. In Lake City, Colorado, in 1898, the municipal fine for "intoxication and disorderly conduct" was a minimum of $5 (and jail time until sober) and a maximum of $50. This was the same fine as for running a "disorderly house."

The *Ford County Globe* of June 24, 1879, casually reported on a typical evening in the cattle town of Dodge City when it said, "The boys and girls across the dead line had a high old time last Friday. They sang and danced, and fought and bit, and cut and had a good time generally, making music for the entire settlement. Our reporter summed up five knock downs, three broken heads, two cuts and several incidental bruises. Unfortunately none of the injuries will prove fatal."

Many of the gunfighters of the Old West were heavy drinkers and their deeds were made even more vicious when fueled by alcohol. Gunfighter Clay Allison was known to be a heavy drinker. Doc Holliday drank heavily to ease the pain of his tuberculosis. Billy Claiborne had been drinking heavily in

Tombstone on November 14, 1882, when he unwisely argued with gunman Buckskin Frank Leslie and lost.

A few examples from lesser-known gunfights will also illustrate the point. Baz (also called "Bass") Outlaw was a deputy U.S. marshal, but had a reputation as a mean drunk. On April 5, 1894, he spent the afternoon drinking at various saloons in El Paso, Texas, then went into Tillie Howard's brothel and fired a shot in a drunken fit of pique. When Texas Ranger Joe McKidrict ran to investigate the disturbance and challenged him, Outlaw, who was still in an alcoholic haze, shot him in the head. A town constable returned fire and Outlaw died later that day.

Another man who was a terror when drinking was stage driver Sylvester Powell. In 1877 he spent New Year's Day drinking in Wichita, Kansas. In the afternoon he tried to take a horse from E.R. Dennison. When Dennison protested, Powell hit him with a neck yoke and then made threats about what he would do if Dennison should tell the marshal.[32] Charlie Reed was a cattle rustler who rode into Fort Griffin, Texas, with Billy Bland on January 17, 1877. Both of them were drunk and firing their revolvers at random. They continued shooting after they dismounted and staggered into the Beehive Saloon. During a subsequent shooting inside, two men were killed and two more wounded. As a result, Reed left Texas in a hurry.[33]

The drunks were not always the ones who escaped. In October, 1871, a drunk named Wall Henderson threatened to burn down Joe Stinson's saloon in Elizabethtown, New Mexico. When Henderson persisted, Stinson pulled out a gun and shot him.[34] Wild Bill Hickok was known to drink. While under the influence of liquor he became embroiled in a saloon brawl with five drunken soldiers in Hays City, Kansas, on July 17, 1870. In another of Hickok's fights, on September 26, 1869, known troublemaker Samuel Strawhim and several companions spent the evening drinking and smashing up John Bittle's saloon in Hays City. Hickok, who was a law officer at the time, arrived to restore the peace. In the resulting melee, Hickok did what he felt he had to do and shot Strawhim in the head.[35] Hickok's friend Calamity Jane was a heavy drinker, known for carousing with the boys and using drunken language that would be worthy of a mule-driver.

A more humorous Hickok drinking story concerns the time he was appearing with Buffalo Bill Cody in the stage play *Scouts of the Plains*. As part of the plot Cody and fellow frontier scout J.B. "Texas Jack" Omohundro sat down and swapped yarns with Hickok. As they did so, they passed around and drank from a whiskey bottle to add to the ambience. When the bottle reached Hickok and he took a drink, a look of horror appeared on his face as he spat the liquid right out again. It turned out that the bottle was filled with cold tea instead of the real thing Hickok was expecting. Hickok refused to continue until real whiskey was found and substituted for the tea.[36]

Saloons were the scene of many gunfights because the participants had been drinking. When city marshal Ed Masterson was shot and killed in Dodge City on April 9, 1878, the *Globe* reported, "A party of six 'cow-boys' who had arrived in town in the evening, had been enjoying themselves with dancing and drinking, some of them evidently getting too much liquor for their own and the City's good." Sometimes it took very little to provoke a fight among drunken participants. In December of 1867 in Lawrence, Wyoming, two drunken men argued with each other over whose turn it was to buy the next round of drinks. Lawman Steve Long arrived to investigate the disturbance. The result was that Long shot and killed both men. He also incidentally killed and wounded an innocent bystander, a local bootmaker named Upham Ransfield.[37]

The participants of a gunfight were often so drunk that they did not know what they were doing. As one example, when "Rowdy Joe" Lowe tangled with rival dance-hall owner "Red" Beard in Delano, Kansas, on the night of October 27, 1873, both were roaring drunk. The *Eagle* of October 30 reported that "'Rowdy Joe' and 'Red,' both being mad from the effects of distilled poison and armed with revolvers and shotguns, waltzed into a deadly melee. Rowdy Joe was shot in the back of the neck with a pistol ball.... Red was wounded in the arm and hip by buck shot from a shot gun." Lowe later stated that he was not even sure that he had shot Beard. He had, because Beard died two weeks later from severe wounds to his right arm and hip. Lowe himself was shot and killed in February 1899 in Colorado after he became so drunk and belligerent in a Denver saloon that he unwisely challenged a local law officer.

Similar excessive drinking was the cause of the death of Warren Earp, Wyatt Earp's youngest brother. Warren challenged cowboy Johnny Boyet to a gunfight after a dispute over a woman on July 6, 1900, in a saloon in Willcox, Arizona. Earp was so drunk that he forgot that he did not have his gun with him. Boyet calmly shot Earp in the chest. He was later acquitted as he had not provoked the gunfight.[38]

While revolvers were the primary arms used in these fights, other less-conventional weapons than guns might sometimes be used. When Tommy Ryan decided to settle a dispute with saloon-owner Romeo Dwyer in Deadwood, South Dakota, he tried to hit Dwyer with a chair. Dwyer responded by throwing a beer glass at Ryan, hit him, and split his scalp open. Ryan was arrested for assault with a deadly weapon. Whether it was the result of good luck or excellent aim was not recorded.[39] One Montana cowboy claimed that spittoons were occasionally used as unconventional weapons in saloons. According to him, a man would stick his hand inside a spittoon and then use it as a type of heavy brass glove to hit his opponent.[40] Not a pretty thought, considering what spittoons were used for.

Even the ladies of the saloon fought — though in this case they were no ladies. In Leadville, Colorado, a battle broke out between the women of the Red Light Dance Hall and those of the Bon Ton because the former had heard that the latter were wearing shorter skirts. After a short but violent fight, "one girl had a finger badly bitten, another had about half of her hair pulled out, a third one had an eye that looked as if John L. Sullivan [the famous boxer of the time] had snubbed it."[41]

Men in their cups were fueled up to fight over anything and violence often erupted over competition for a woman. On April 30, 1889, at a dance at Cache Bottom in the Indian Territory of Oklahoma, George Tobler felt that Irvin Richmond was dancing too much with a woman that he was hoping to attract. In a fit of jealousy, Tobler simply pulled out his gun and shot Richmond.[42]

In the case of women, rough-and-tumble fights usually involved fighting over a man. In Tombstone, Arizona, in 1882 saloon women Margarita and

Deadwood, South Dakota, was founded as a gold mining town in 1876. By 1877, the town was lined with saloons, even though the location was technically on an Indian reservation, which made the sale of liquor illegal under federal law. Local residents complained frequently about the sweet smell of opium that constantly hung over the red light district (National Archives).

Gold Dollar fought over gambler Billy Milgreen. Gold Dollar stabbed Margarita and killed her.[43]

On a smaller scale, in 1880, the *Boulder News and Courier* of Boulder, Colorado, reported on a fight between two brothel women that "resulted in the complete demolition of one of the ladies, whose head came in contact with an empty beer bottle."[44] Similarly, the *Black Hills Daily Times* in June 1892 reported on the following incident that occurred in a Deadwood dancehall: "The woman who Tuesday night struck a female companion on the head with a beer bottle, causing her head to swell to such an extent that a shoe horn had to be brought into requisition to enable her to get her hat on, was yesterday brought before Justice Belding."

Though not directly associated with saloon violence, ingenious strikers devised an unusual use for empty beer bottles during the 1894 labor war in Cripple Creek, Colorado. Camped out on the top of a hill, they filled the bottles with dynamite and shot them from a crude crossbow at sheriff's deputies below who were trying to end the strike. When this tactic failed, they loaded more of the dynamite onto a railroad car and rolled it down the hill. The flatcar jumped the tracks and blew up before reaching the lawmen. Unfortunately, the blast killed two cows peaceably minding their own business while grazing in a pasture by the tracks.

Temperance Stirs

Though early saloons were popular as social gathering places, they did not always bring a good image to a town. Episcopalian missionary the Rev. Joseph Cook, commenting on his perception of Laramie, Wyoming, in 1868 said, "I think there are somewhere near four thousand people here — the wickedness is unimaginable and appalling.... Almost every other house is a drinking saloon, gambling house, or bawdy."[45]

The *Rocky Mountain News* in Colorado felt that "if all the villainous whiskey and stale beer held in solution by those resorts [saloons and billiard halls] could be poured into one liquid mass, it would form a reservoir large enough to float the Great Eastern."[46] The *Silverton Democrat* of November 22, 1884, described the scene in their town as follows: "There are 27 saloons in this mining camp, nine of them in the block opposite the hotel.... At night the uproar is hideous. A loud piano in one den runs through three charming chords, drowning a vilely squeaking fiddle from seven in the evening until sleep has mercifully closed one's ears. Farther down the block is heard the singing of a woman whose voice is much too good for the surroundings."

This attitude extended to individuals also. The *Silverton Democrat* further reported on December 13, 1884: "One of the leading citizens ... informs us that Mrs. Ed Gorman ... was making herself a general nuisance again yesterday afternoon, indulging in her usual boisterous and indecent language, greatly to the annoyance and disgust of the ladies living in the vicinity.... Mr. Gorman himself is a quiet, law-abiding citizen, so far as we know, but all who know his 'wife' represent her as a 'howly terror' when she gets intoxicated and makes life a burden to everybody for blocks around."

Frederick Powell in *Bacchus Dethroned* claimed, "The drinking system is a more deadly and demoralizing evil than the opium plague of the far East."[47] Drinking was considered to be a male activity and, except for bar girls and prostitutes, the saloon was a male stronghold and institution. One assumption of temperance was that women were pure and above the coarse lust for alcohol but men were not. The next step in the logic, then, was that decent women didn't drink. Based on that assumption, the logical conclusion was that drinking must be indecent and so drinking must be indecent for men.

Many books were written on temperance, including such typical ones as *Inebriety: Its Source, Prevention, and Cure* by Charles Palmer, published in 1898. In typical florid Victorian prose, Section III is titled "The remedying of the Preinebriate Morbid Conditions and the Strengthening of the Bases of Self Control."[48] A section titled "The Masculine Treatment an Essential in Early Life" contained the following type of advice: "The patient [must be] regarded not as a wilful violator of decency, of religion, and of the sacred home, to be punished for his wilful sinning, but as one who has suddenly developed symptoms of a dangerous mental malady."[49]

Stereotypes abounded in temperance literature. The description of "The Brutal Criminal Inebriate of Our Cities" in Palmer's book reads as follows: "The blackguard drunkard of our streets, big of limb, broad of chest, low of brow, and black of visage; born of the gutters; the braggart and bully of his less offensive neighbors, evil triumph in his eyes; with strong assumption of physical power, but cowardly by instinct; thief and murderer by inherent qualities and only needing an accident to make either or both; at times politic with the lowest form of animal cunning; the woman-bruiser by nature and nurture; his language as polluted as his mind, which reverences nothing but the brute force which overcomes him; always the concentrated living spawn of the accumulating growth of generations of depravity."[50] No wonder genteel ladies who championed the temperance movement flinched when they thought that this was who they were dealing with.

Morals were uppermost in the minds of many temperance crusaders. They were convinced that any drink led immediately to the basest of instincts, but with typical Victorian reticence they couched this in delicate terms, such as man's liability to indulge in "every vice which his surroundings and distempered mind incline him to."[51] Another even more delicate way of putting it was an "irregularity of animal desires."[52] Prohibitionists claimed that once a woman took her first sip of liquor she and her reputation were ruined. A typical quote from a book by the national superintendent of the Purity Department of the Woman's Christian Temperance Union stated in 1898, "The *debauche* knows the effects of wine, and uses that knowledge to lead astray the young girl who, if herself, would find no charm in his blandishments, but who, after the wine supper, has no will to resist his advances."[53]

This thought came from several long-standing nineteenth century views of women. One was that women had the inherent characteristic of being sinful; another was that they were weak-willed.[54] A third was, based on arguments of highly dubious logic, that men were innately superior to women.[55] The combination of these viewpoints mandated, then, that men should be the self-appointed guardians of women's morals.

Temperance crusaders seized on this with their own passion. An Anti-Saloon League poster of 1913 said the following, in part, in emphatic terms, "*Alcohol inflames the passions*, thus making the temptation to sex-sin unusually strong. *Alcohol decreases the power of control*, thus making the resisting of temptation especially difficult.... *Avoid all alcoholic drink absolutely* [italics in the original]."[56]

CHAPTER ELEVEN

The Pathway to Prohibition

At the beginning of the nineteenth century legitimate concerns were raised about increasing levels of consumption of drink, along with fears that the United States was becoming a nation of drunkards. Certainly, excessive use of alcohol was detrimental to the drinker's health and well-being, its use affected personal relationships and family life, and it reflected poorly on the drunkard's social standing. As a result, alcohol immediately became the subject of dissent. On one side were the "wets," who enjoyed drinking. On the other were the "drys," who constantly sought to prohibit drinking and ban all alcohol. At the same time, similar temperance movements sprang up in Europe and the rest of the English-speaking world.

Attempts at prohibition of drink had a long history. In November 1848, the school rules for Port Angeles, Washington, included "Rule Number 12," which said that the punishment for drinking "spirituous liquors" at school was eight lashes. Even this, however, was apparently not considered to be as bad as playing cards in school, which rated ten lashes. Obviously these were not pleasant times for students who liked to drink and play cards. (Only slightly less offensive to the school was "making a swing and swinging on it," which rated seven lashes.)

Temperance workers tried to persuade drinkers to swear off drinking. The pledge of the Murphy Movement, one of the temperance advocates, as administered in Lake City, Colorado, in the 1870s read, "With malice towards none and charity for all, I, the undersigned, do pledge my word and honor, God helping me, to abstain from all intoxicating liquor as a beverage, and I will, by all honorable means, encourage others to abstain."[1]

The Early Temperance Movement

Attempts to limit drinking had been made as far back as the 1700s, but popular resentment was stronger than the authorities' ability to regulate, so efforts were generally abandoned. Further concerns about alcohol abuse arose in the early 1800s, starting what came to be called the "Temperance Movement." The impetus was that more alcohol per capita was consumed in the United States between 1790 and 1830 than at any other time in its history.[2] Until the 1830s, most Americans thought strong alcoholic drinks were a necessary accompaniment to any hard work, as well as a suitable medicine to ward off fevers, illness, colds, and snakebite. Contemporary popular opinion was that any alcohol was good for the health, whether it was beer or whiskey.

After the Revolutionary War, progressive thinkers among the elite promoted the idea that in order to succeed, the common masses needed to be self-disciplined and restrained. And that included their drinking habits. The idea of too much relaxation and pleasure was not acceptable, so the concept of temperance seemed ideal to the cause. National groups such as the Society for the Promotion of Morals and the Society for the Suppression of Intemperance came into existence, along with local temperance groups. The first temperance organization established in Phoenix, Arizona, for example, was the Arizona Order of Good Templars. The Sons of Temperance spread their message in the gold-mining camps of California as early as 1852. Trite temperance slogans abounded: "What key will unlock the door to hell? Whiskey," and, for women, "Lips that touch liquor shall never touch mine."

The initial American Temperance Movement was directed primarily against distilled spirits, and not against beer and wine. One of the prominent early advocates of temperance was Benjamin Rush, who was one of the leading physicians in America at the time. He developed what he called a "moral thermometer," which attempted to show the effects of alcohol in graph form on a scale with water on one end and pepper in rum on the other. A little above the middle were the effects of wine and beer, which included cheerfulness, strength, and nourishment. At the other end of the scale, the effects of distilled spirits were intemperance, vice, and disease. Rush's opinion was that drinking beer and wine was acceptable, but that drinking spirits was the cause of "puking, tremors, and death," along with idleness, swearing, murder, and obscenity.

Rush wrote a series of essays on alcohol and its perceived dangers, including *An Inquiry into the Effects of Spirituous Liquors on the Human Body and the Mind*, first published in 1785 and republished in several versions and revi-

Opposite: Physician Benjamin Rush developed this chart which he called a moral thermometer. He placed water on the top of the scale, equating it to health and wealth. Beer and wine were in the middle, in moderate quantities equated to cheerfulness and strength. Whiskey, at the bottom end of the scale, was equated with disease, vice, and a morally degenerate lifestyle. This version of the "thermometer" is reproduced from a temperance book published in 1811 (National Library of Medicine).

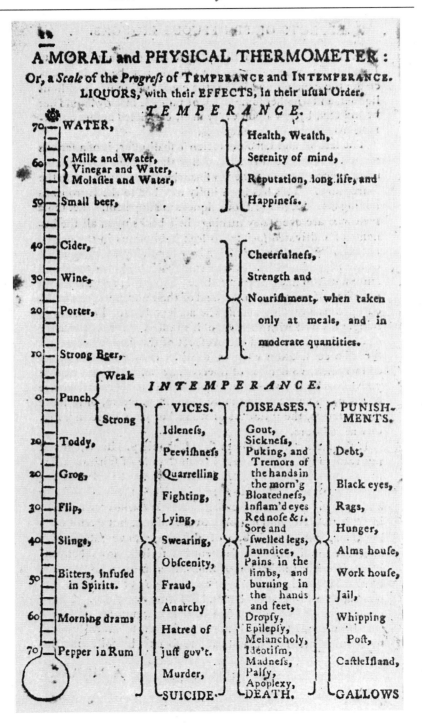

A MORAL and PHYSICAL THERMOMETER:

Or, a *Scale* of the *Progress* of TEMPERANCE and INTEMPERANCE.
LIQUORS, with their EFFECTS, in their usual Order.

TEMPERANCE.

70	WATER,	Health, Wealth,
60	Milk and Water, Vinegar and Water, Molasses and Water,	Serenity of mind, Reputation, long life, and
50	Small beer,	Happiness.
40	Cider,	Cheerfulness,
30	Wine,	Strength and
20	Porter,	Nourishment, when taken only at meals, and in moderate quantities.
10	Strong Beer,	

INTEMPERANCE.

		VICES.	DISEASES.	PUNISHMENTS.
0	Punch { Weak / Strong			
10	Toddy,	Idleness,	Gout, Sickness, Puking, and Tremors of	Debt,
20	Grog,	Peevishness Quarrelling	the hands in the morn'g Bloatedness,	Black eyes,
30	Flip,	Fighting, Lying,	Inflam'd eyes Red nose & f. Sore and	Rags, Hunger,
40	Slings,	Swearing, Obscenity,	swelled legs, Jaundice, Pains in the	Alms house,
50	Bitters, infused in Spirits.	Fraud,	limbs, and burning in the hands and feet,	Work house, Jail,
60	Morning drams	Anarchy Hatred of	Dropsy, Epilepsy, Melancholy,	Whipping Post,
70	Pepper in Rum	just gov't. Murder,	Ideotism, Madness, Palsy, Apoplexy,	CastleIsland,
		SUICIDE.	DEATH.	GALLOWS

sions over the next thirty years or so. Much of what Rush theorized was based on his medical observations and his own opinions, with very little scientific evidence to back most of his claims. Rush offered this description of what happened when someone drank what he called "ardent spirits": "The face now becomes flushed; the eyes project, and are somewhat watery; winking is less frequent than is natural; the under lip is protruded; the head inclines a little to one shoulder; the jaw falls; belchings and hiccup take place; the limbs totter; the whole body staggers." He continued: "He now closes his eyes, and falls into a profound sleep, frequently attended with snoring, and profuse sweats, and sometimes with such relaxation of the muscles which confine the bladder and lower bowels, as to produce a symptom which delicacy forbids me to mention."[3] Obviously, this was not a pretty picture at all.

Women, as usual, were singled out for particular attention. One of Rush's concerns was his fear of the effect of alcohol on women in generating "certain immodest actions" that he also preferred by delicacy not to describe. But he did add, "I am sorry to say, this sign of the first stage of drunkenness sometimes appears in women, who, when sober, are uniformly remarkable for chaste and decent manners."[4] Some of Rush's other opinions were misguided. For example, his advice was to use opium instead of rum to relieve "spasmodic affectations of the stomach and bowels," because he felt that opium was less likely than alcohol to lead to addiction.[5]

The initial meaning of "temperance" was to practice moderation and self-restraint in drinking. But the movement to promote the prohibition of alcohol was not new, and the initial meaning and goals of the temperance movement soon underwent change. During the 1820s and 1830s evangelical preachers roundly condemned sin, much of which was considered to be drinking or that which occurred as a result of drinking. The temperance movement, therefore, changed its focus from moderation to total abstinence. "Temperance" in effect became "prohibition." Prohibitionists were of the opinion that any alcohol was detrimental to good mental and physical health, and they felt that completely outlawing the manufacture and consumption of alcohol would improve American society. The American Temperance Society, for example, which was founded in 1826, changed its definition of temperance to abstinence in 1836.[6] Even the medical community did not escape scrutinizing alcohol, and physicians Gardner and Aylworth made a comment about alcohol-based tinctures in 1836: "They are excellent for administering a great variety of medicinal agents, but in some cases there may be an objection to them in consequence of the spirits they contain."[7]

By the mid–1800s, temperance groups were rapidly trying to propel America along a pathway towards virtue for everybody and many more anti-drink temperance groups sprang up. As a result of their efforts, by 1855, thirteen states and territories had banned the sale and manufacture of alcohol.

Between 1851 and 1865, Maine, Oregon, Massachusetts, Minnesota, Rhode Island, Vermont, Michigan, Connecticut, Delaware, Indiana, Iowa, Nebraska, New Hampshire, New York, and Pennsylvania were among those that declared alcoholic beverages to be illegal. Not everyone was in favor of prohibition, though, and anti-alcohol opinion changed due to popular resentment. Interestingly, as many of these state laws were found to be unconstitutional, were repealed, or were simply ignored, the overall consumption of alcohol jumped by 63 percent.[8]

Temperance enthusiasts were able to reduce American consumption of drink by the 1850s but saw it rise again just before and during the Civil War. By the 1860s, the prominence of the Civil War diverted attention from the temperance movement as the nation became occupied with the conflict between the North and the South, and on more serious issues than drinking. Temperance faded temporarily into the background.

Nevertheless, the prohibitionists saw a few small successes. In 1862 they were able to have the daily ration of rum for enlisted men in the Union navy stopped. It was, however, still allowed for officers.[9] Neither of the armies on either side of the Civil War followed the navy's example. An occasional unofficial whiskey ration was still issued to troops in the Union army.

After the Civil War

After the war was over, opposition to alcohol in the Old West continued, but the pathway to how it should be accomplished underwent a change in direction. Before the Civil War, the focus of temperance advocates was primarily on reforming the individual by trying to get him to stop drinking. Eventually they realized that this was a futile task. After the war, therefore, their strategy gradually shifted and reform activities for the rest of the nineteenth century focused on trying to introduce laws to control the sale and distribution of liquor. In the booming mining and logging towns of the Old West, this was a daunting task. Virginia City, Nevada, in 1876, for example, had 10 liquor wholesalers, 5 breweries, and 137 retail outlets that sold alcohol.

In truth, alcohol and drugs were not compatible with the industrial revolution and the mechanization that was starting to affect urban areas. Drink had previously been considered to be part of the workingman's life, and no hard labor was initiated without suitable alcoholic fortification beforehand. Drugs and alcohol, however, were not compatible with most work that involved operating machinery, such as large-scale mining, industrial logging, or railroad engines, all of which required precision, concentration, and punctuality — not to mention avoiding sticking fingers and limbs misguided by whiskey into the machinery. For example, it was not unknown for a hoist operator in a mine to be so drunk that he did not stop the rising cage in time at the surface and it continued up into the hoist wheel overhead, snapping the cable and sending the cage careening back down the shaft again. In mining terms this catastrophic event was called "overwinding."

Alcohol was estimated to be the cause of many of the 35,000 deaths and 200,000 accidents that occurred every year. Not unusual was an incident in Denver when a boiler exploded at the Gumry Hotel because the maintenance engineer had slipped out to a nearby saloon for fortification. Twenty-two people were killed.[10] By the turn of the twentieth century, Denver police reported that drunkenness was the cause for 20 percent of the city's arrests.

Supporters of Temperance

Activities of the temperance groups slowed during the 1860s, but the movement rebounded with renewed energy during the 1870s and 1880s after women became involved on a large scale. Temperance societies continued to spring into existence. During the 1870s, the residents of Leadville, Colorado, obviously considered their town to have such a drinking problem that they founded the Blue Ribbon Society, the Leadville Temperance Club, the Praying Orchestra, and the Anti-Treat Society. The Prohibition Party of the United States was founded in 1869 to promote temperance. Supporters of temperance were known as "white ribboners" because they wore white ribbons to show their loyalty to the temperance movement.

The saloon was the usual retail outlet for alcoholic beverages in the Old West and was also the place where gambling and prostitution were to be found. For many, then, saloons symbolized drunkenness and irresponsible and destructive behavior. Women across the country attempted to shut down saloons, to persuade owners not to sell spirits, and to pester patrons to sign the pledge not to drink. They held mass meetings, and knelt in saloons and prayed. Those who objected to saloons believed that sober workers were better workers, were happier, and were more prosperous. Other healthy benefits were sure to follow. After all, a preacher with the appropriate name of Areopagus Homily had solemnly pronounced that alcohol caused ulcerated lungs, an ossified heart, cancer, and even hemorrhoids.[11] Nobody wanted that.

Some temperance women thought that saloons were a source of disease and made their husbands wash off all over and put on clean clothing when they staggered home at night from their favorite watering hole. The original temperance movement gradually embraced other social reforms, such as child labor, women's suffrage, and the abolition of slavery. Indeed, the reason that many women were attracted to the temperance movement was that it was linked to the early beginnings of the movement towards women's rights. Ironically, however, the growing movement promoted drug use instead of the "despicable" alcohol. This, of course, produced problems of addiction of a different sort.

Some temperance efforts proceeded with amazing speed and a few states voted to become "dry" states before national prohibition passed into law. Kansas, for example, passed a constitutional amendment to prohibit liquor in 1879. It was ratified in November 1880 and became law on March 10, 1881. The effort, however, proved to be ineffective and illegal drinking behind closed doors started almost immediately. "Medicinal" alcohol in the form of whiskey, wine, and beer, was also freely available by perfectly legal prescription for colds, cramps, biliousness, colic, and the chills, as well as "nervousness" and "general debility."

Other seemingly radical attempts were made to control saloons and drinking. The Kansas cattle towns, which boasted hard-drinking cowboys during the cattle drives, would have seemed to be immune to temperance sentiments. Dodge City, however, passed ordinances banning gambling and brothels, in 1878, and closing saloons on Sundays, in 1879. In 1887 (a number of years after Kansas became officially dry) Dodge City banned the sale of liquor, and in 1896 banned the sale of opium and other narcotics. Radical steps indeed. The net effect, however, was only to slow drinking down, and the sale of liquor in saloons continued until 1903.

THE MODERATE DRINKER

Prohibitionists were so focused on the subject of drinking that they were convinced that any kind of indulgence in alcohol led to problem drinking and alcoholism. Perversely, in the world of the temperance crusader, the moderate drinker was unpopular because he did not fit with the popular drunken image they wished to promote. A beastly drunkard with delirium tremens who spent all the family money on drink and who constantly threw up in the gutter outside the saloon on his way home, then went home and beat his wife was a far more popular image for their purposes. The moderate drinker, in reality, was more likely to be a family man who stopped in at the saloon after work and had a social drink or two with his friends in a quiet corner, then went home to his family and children in a relaxed and mildly intoxicated mood. This type of moderate drinker could have a drink but not beat his wife, wreck his home, and destroy himself with drink as a result.

Much of the image of the drunkard was propaganda. Temperance advocates loved the concept of the drunken wife-beater, but not of the hard-working miner or cowboy having a couple of beers for relaxation after a long day's work. The temperance cause wanted them to be roaring drunks and disgusting alcoholics. And indeed, much of the popularity of the temperance movement was due to the appeal of the scandalous nature of this propaganda image.

In the temperance book *Bacchus Dethroned*, Frederick Powell described a moderate drinker: "is a coarse, brutal-fellow, whose only idea of happiness is the gratification of his passions. The higher joys of life he knows not, and, therefore, has no relish for them. His mental powers are uncultivated, and his moral nature is a barren wilderness. In fact, he is low mentally, low morally, but very strong in his animal nature."[12] This was strong rhetoric, indeed, as Powell's example was that of only a moderate drinker and not even a roaring drunk.

With logic that must have been hard to follow even then, the Rev. Eli Meech of Rhode Island concluded that the respectable, moderate drinker did far more than anybody else "to perpetuate the evil of intemperance."[13] With even odder logic, a Thomas Grimké of Charleston, South Carolina, said, "Temperate drinkers are the parents of all the drunkards who dishonor and afflict our country."[14] On December 18, 1877, the Rev. George Darley cleverly advertised a temperance lecture as "Come Take a Drink." Local lushes who showed up hoping for a free drink were disappointed when Darley preached just the opposite.[15]

Then as now, sinister generalizations were used to further the cause. A circuit-riding Methodist preacher named James B. Finlay darkly stated, without hesitation, "I never knew a man who was in the habit of drinking regularly that did not become a drunkard."[16] This was echoed by Congressman Gerrit Smith from New York, who said, "I would that no person were able to drink intoxicating liquors without immediately becoming a drunkard."[17] Moderate drinkers who could take alcohol or leave it were a nuisance and had to be persuaded to stop.

THE WOMAN'S CHRISTIAN TEMPERANCE UNION (WCTU)

One of the leading temperance groups that crusaded against saloons was the Woman's Christian Temperance Union (WCTU), which was founded in 1874. The group grew to be extremely popular and had branches and meeting rooms all over the West. The woman who worked hardest to move the group forward was Frances Elizabeth Willard. Drink was certainly a problem at the time. When Willard adopted temperance as her cause, a tendency to drink too much by many of the male population had produced a host of personal and family problems, as well as issues for society as a whole.

Frances Willard was born near Rochester, New York, in September 1839. She trained as a teacher and educator, and eventually became president of Northwestern's Ladies College. In 1874 she decided to leave the world of education to pursue the woman's temperance cause and she was elected corre-

As industrialization spread in the Old West, many jobs, such as operating this mine hoist or other large machinery, were not compatible with heavy drinking — or even moderate drinking. Fingers, hands, and whole limbs could easily be caught in machinery by a careless operator. In an era before stringent safety regulations, accidents were common and were only made worse by drinking on the job (Glenn Kinnaman Colorado and Western History Collection).

sponding secretary of the WCTU. As there were no funds in the organization for travel, her job was to write to anyone and everyone she thought might support the cause of temperance. Due to her efforts, paid memberships expanded to 7,500 by the end of the first year. She continued working tirelessly for temperance and was elected president of the WCTU in 1879, a position she held until her death in 1898.

During the 1880s, Willard became one of America's best-known women. She lectured extensively, spending much of her time on the road for a grueling schedule of speaking engagements. She somehow also found the time to write books and pamphlets that expounded on the purported evils of alcohol. Due to Willard's efforts, the union rapidly gained popularity during the 1880s. Membership in the WCTU grew from 27,000 to an estimated 150,000 members in 7,000 branches by 1890.[18]

Some of the WCTU's efforts were unfortunately misguided. In the beginning, the WCTU saw drink as a cause of poverty, but, by the late 1880s, they began to see it as the result of poverty rather than the cause. Unfortunately, also, the results of the WCTU's efforts were not spectacular. From 1864 to 1874, in the decade before the group's founding, Americans drank an estimated 62,000,000 gallons of liquor. In the ten years afterwards, from 1874 to 1884, Americans drank 76,000,000 gallons.[19] As part of their campaign to promote temperance, the WCTU published various inflammatory pamphlets, such as one that loosely claimed that alcohol was a poison. Many of their publications on the "evils of alcohol " were based more on propaganda than factual information.

Under Willard's leadership, the focus of the WCTU shifted and eventually became very diverse. The pathway along which Willard took the group was different from its original goals and this new direction did not always please the members. Willard promoted women's suffrage, allied herself with political groups and labor unions, and promoted Christian Socialism. Among other causes, she and the WCTU opposed gambling, plural marriage, prostitution, cruelty to animals, and tobacco.[20] They also tried to have churches use unfermented grape juice instead of wine in their services. Part of this newer mandate of the WCTU was the reform of inmates of jails and asylums, and the rescue of "fallen women," all of whom were considered to be direct or indirect victims of the saloon.

Similar efforts were made by other organizations, such as the Florence Crittenton Mission, which, by 1879, had fifty-three branches throughout the country trying to reform alcoholic women, prostitutes, and unwed mothers. They were not always successful — or welcomed — either. In 1896 the Florence Crittenton group opened homes in Butte and Helena, Montana, to rescue fallen women and wayward girls. The home in Butte closed in short order, reportedly for lack of interest.[21]

In the ideal Victorian world of the late nineteenth century, the man's world was outside the home, he being involved with business, politics, or a stable job. A woman was supposed to be the wife and mother, the protector of the home, and the nurturer of the children. Women had few legal rights. Women who worked had no control over their wages and no claim on their husband's earnings. From the prohibitionist's viewpoint, a man could — and would — drink up his all wages and also any money that his wife happened to have. Nineteenth century drunkards gained the reputation that they were wife beaters, child abusers, and irresponsible providers. In light of this logic, therefore, moving into other areas of political activities was not unusual for organizations such as the WCTU. By 1874 the temperance movement and groups promoting social reform and equal rights for women were taking similar pathways. So, under the guise of the temperance crusade, many women added other causes including political lobbying and the vote for women.

From 1873 to 1900, the WCTU was both the leading temperance organization and leading women's organization in America. After about 1880, the WCTU was interested in many other reform causes linked only loosely to temperance by Frances Willard, including removing poverty, crime, corruption, and the mistreatment of prisoners. The worst social offense, however, was still considered to be drinking and drunkenness, and the saloon was perceived as the cause of this sin and debauchery. One of the WCTU's allied causes was that opium was a drug that should be suppressed, because smoking opium by whites as well as by Chinese had become widespread in the United States in the 1870s.[22] But when the WCTU started to support issues that were only remotely connected to drink, such as government control of the railroads, universal suffrage, a wealth tax, equal pay for women, and the abolition of lynching, they lost their focus as the primary temperance organization.

Willard worked so hard that she died exhausted in 1898 at the age of 59, probably partly due to the grueling schedule of work she had undertaken.

CARRIE NATION AND HATCHETATION

One of the best-known of the crusaders against alcohol, and certainly the most flamboyant, was Carry Nation. Contemporary critics ridiculed, lampooned, and satirized her temperance activities and generally treated her as a figure of fun. Even her sanity was questioned. Some of her actions were perhaps fanatical and a bit peculiar; however, it appears that she felt a calling and her religious zeal led her on a single-minded mission. She felt that she was God's instrument in opposing drink and she wanted to totally outlaw alcohol.

Carry Nation was born Carry Amelia Moore in Kentucky in 1846. She came from a peculiar family. Her mother thought herself to be Queen Victoria, and Carry had an aunt who believed that she was a weather vane. Carry herself experienced visions and strange dreams. She was named Carry by her father, but until 1903 she spelled it Carrie, as was the current fashion. In 1903 she legally changed her name to Carry A. Nation, as she said she was told from above to "carry a nation" towards prohibition.

She married Charles Gloyd in 1867 and had one daughter. Gloyd had studied medicine and was a physician during the Civil War in the Union army. After the war he tried to set up a medical practice and at the same time owned a drugstore. Gloyd was a heavy drinker and a cigarette smoker. He died in 1869 either from alcoholism and the DTs or from pneumonia brought on by excessive drinking.

Moore remarried in 1874 to David Nation, a minister in the Cambellite church.[23] In 1889 he was savagely beaten by a gang of hoodlums in Richmond, Texas, an incident that has been reputed to be partly responsible for her anti-liquor fervor. However, the couple didn't get on particularly well and eventually divorced. His injuries contributed to his poor health and may have eventually contributed to his death in 1903.

Nation was active in the WCTU chapter in Medicine Lodge, Kansas, her hometown, and was soon elected county president. She and her coworkers appealed to town officials to close all the local saloons — which were illegal under the law — but their requests were generally ignored. As a result, in June of 1900, at age 54, Nation started the most visible part of her temperance career after she claimed that a voice from above told her to go forth and smash up saloons. She dutifully went twenty miles south to Kiowa, Kansas, and led a raid on O.L. Day's drugstore, which was selling "medicinal alcohol" and patent medicines high in alcohol content.

As part of Nation's "raid," she found a ten-gallon barrel of whiskey and took it out into the street, where she smashed it with a sledgehammer then set the liquid on fire. Day claimed that it was brandy to be used for medicinal purposes only, which was legal, but Nation claimed at the subsequent trial that it was sour-mash whiskey. Nation went on to vandalize several other places in the town of Kiowa that were selling alcohol. She was threatened with arrest for destruction of private property, but the sheriff didn't quite know what to do with her. His problem was that selling whiskey was contrary to Kansas prohibition laws, so if he arrested Nation he would be guilty of condoning liquor sales. So he eventually let her go.

Part of the whole saloon issue was strictly economic. Saloons were needed to attract business to Kiowa and similar towns from railroad men and other local workers and to provide taxes and "fines" to run the municipal government. If the saloons were closed, no money came into the city coffers. In March 1900, for example, Arkansas City had to close its municipal fire department because temperance workers had forced saloons to close and there was no revenue to support it.[24]

Six months later Nation went on another rampage. In December 1900, she and her cohorts raided and smashed up the bar of the Carey Hotel in Wichita, Kansas, doing $3,000 worth of damage to the bar and its stock of liquor, including a valuable "saloon art" painting *Cleopatra at the Bath*. This time the chief of police, George Cubbon, arrested her and put her in jail. He and city officials kept her there through a series of legal maneuvers. She was finally released in January 1901, but nine days later she was back at the head of a brigade of saloon-wrecking women who marched down saloon row in Wichita destroying more bottles. She was arrested and released again. She tried to make her way out of town, followed by a crowd of enthusiastic onlookers, to find new saloons to smash, but she was arrested again before she could leave. Hotheads and agitators in the crowd called for lynching Nation and her fellow conspirators, but the mob backed down at the last moment and she was able to leave.

On February 5, 1901, she smashed up the Senate Bar in Topeka, Kansas, one of the largest saloons in town. She threw the cash register across the room and smashed open several kegs, dousing everyone with beer in the process. In her early raids, she used rocks and iron bars for smashing, but she later found that an axe worked even better for creating this type of destruction. She used this weapon as a symbol and a tool as she continued to campaign vigorously against "the Demon Rum," trying to save men from the evils of liquor. She called her work "hatchetation" and expanded her tools to include three hatchets that she called Faith, Hope, and Charity.[25] Dressed in all black, almost six feet tall, and weighing 175 pounds, she must have presented a formidable appearance as she strode into a saloon at the head of her crusading women. They quickly started in on the bar, bottles, windows, mirrors, and pictures of barroom nudes with their hatchets, destroying whatever they could.

Nation was actually not the first woman to attack saloons and employ violent tactics against them, but she was the most colorful and notorious. Others before her had used hatchets and sledgehammers to destroy drinking places and their contents. One of the earliest saloon-smashing incidents occurred in 1853 when Mrs. Margaret Freeland of Syracuse, New York, went into a local saloon and broke up the bottles and glasses. When asked why she did it, she said that she was driven to it by her husband, who became brutal when he was drunk.[26] Women attacked saloons in Topeka and Lawrence, Kansas, with hatchets as early as 1855 and 1856 during temperance campaigns.

In the 1890s, before Nation started her vigorous opposition to saloons, there were several attacks by women on Kansas saloons. A WCTU member in Kingman, Kansas, smashed several local saloons in April of 1890. In 1891 in Madison, Kansas, the homes of the mayor and a druggist were smashed in protest of illegal drinking. In 1894 a woman in Salina, Kansas, attacked a painting of *Venus at Bath*.[27] In August of 1897, several saloons were damaged during similar raids.

In 1901 Thomas Edison produced a short (one minute) comedy movie called *Kansas Saloon Smashers*. The gist of the plot is that several men are drinking in a Kansas saloon when a group of tall, middle-aged women dressed in black burst into the room and start smashing everything in sight. In retaliation, the saloon-keeper sprays the women down with a stream of seltzer water, then a policeman enters and kicks everybody out. Edison produced a more personal attack on Nation in two-minute movie called *Why Mr. Nation Wants a Divorce*. As the story opens, "Mr. Nation" appears, trying to soothe a crying baby and another child. Finally he becomes frustrated and drinks out of a bottle of whiskey. Just as he does, a tall actor in a black dress comes in, grabs the bottle and breaks it and starts whacking Mr. Nation around in the best tradition of the Three Stooges.

Nation continued what she considered to be her work in spite of criticism.

She was jailed in Los Angeles and San Francisco for causing damage in saloons. In 1903 she appeared in New York in a special version of *Ten Nights in a Barroom*, performing twice a day. The plot was altered to include a special saloon scene where she smashed up bottles on the set. She called her version of the play *Hatchetation*. She continued her outlandish campaign and attracted followers who practiced her techniques in their own communities. She and her followers prayed outside saloons, broke bottles and barrels, and railed against the saloon owners. She started two anti-liquor publications, appropriately called the *Smasher's Mail* and the *Hatchet*, which were intended to spread the word to her faithful followers. In 1904 she wrote an autobiography titled *The Use and Need of the Life of Carry A. Nation*. Her invective included descriptions such as "besotted," "law-breaking," "booze-sodden," "soul-killing," and "filth-smeared spawn of the Devil." Not all of this worked. Eventually even people in her home state of Kansas tired of the spectacle and didn't pay much attention to her. Some saloons even flourished and their business grew as a result of the publicity after having been raided by Nation. One saloon proudly claimed "All Nations Welcome But Carry." In all, she was jailed thirty-three times for a total of 170 days. She went on to St. Louis, Chicago, Detroit, New York, and Europe. When she tried her tactics in the eastern U.S., though, she was usually charged with destruction of private property.

Finally Nation became a parody of herself, as her followers expected her to smash saloons in ever more vigorous fashion. She was treated as more of a joke and was the subject of satirical popular contemporary cartoons. To raise money to finance her activities, she posed for publicity pictures carrying a hatchet, touted pictures of herself, and sold souvenir pins shaped like miniature hatchets. To promote her campaign, she lectured in music halls, burlesque houses, vaudeville shows, and on off–Broadway stages. As one example, she traveled and preached with the *Through the Centre of the Earth Burlesque Company*. Her part was titled "Hell Is No Joke," which was introduced by "a chorus of twenty-five maidens in much abbreviated skirts."[28] She attracted large crowds of people, both supporters and detractors, to her speeches, but she effectively became an entertainer in her efforts to continue promoting her cause. She eventually appeared in carnival sideshows, which further tended to diminish her credibility. Even though the WCTU had helped to launch her career, they did not claim her as one of their own. They felt that they could not endorse her actions, which tended to be more sensational than effective.

Nation was taunted as a crank, a lunatic, demented, psychotic, and hysterical. In spite of this negative image, she was a mother and a wife, fought for women's rights, and set up a home for the elderly and a school for children. In 1909 she bought several homes in Eureka Springs, Arkansas. She named one of them "Hatchet Hall" and used it to house female victims of alcoholic husbands and fathers. Though she was fanatically anti-liquor, she also had other motley targets. She believed in sex education, opposed wife-beating, and championed equal rights for women. On the other side of the coin, she unleashed torrents of abuse against tobacco, immodest fashions, kissing, judges, corsets, and fraternal societies.

In August 1906, she went on a lecture tour that included Denver. The *Denver Post* reported that she was accompanied by a crowd that was estimated to be over 7,000 strong as she marched towards Market Street in a campaign against the red light district. These hangers-on were apparently hoping for one of her usual fiery spectacles. Some of her inflammatory rhetoric that was directed against men in the audience was couched in her usual flowery style: "You are to blame for making these women what they are, low and indiscriminate! Diseased and prurient men! You men, I can hear your libidinous jokes and coarse flings at me. Hell yawns for you."[29] She went to jail for inciting a riot.

Not everybody was in favor of Carrie Nation's tactics. On January 25, 1910, she campaigned in Butte, Montana, but was reported to be "spectacularly unsuccessful." Not all the residents were amused when she declared the town to be "America's cesspool of alcohol, tobacco, and sinful women."[30] When she went into one saloon with the intention of destroying it, she was met by May Maloy, the proprietress, who was a young, strong woman. She beat Nation up and threw her out.

The following year Nation collapsed on the speaker's platform during an anti-liquor address in St. Louis, probably from a stroke. She remained bedridden and died from heart failure on June 9, 1911, at age 64.

Whether she was viewed as a crank or a savior, her anti-liquor crusades and unorthodox behavior focused attention on the issue of temperance. The WCTU officially disapproved of her hatchetation behavior, and other crusading groups did not want to be associated with her for fear that they would get the same reputation. The WCTU gave her the impetus to start, but they found her ways a little too radical and could not endorse her activities. But they could not condemn her either as she gave their cause plenty of publicity. Though many think that she was an aberration, she did raise the level of attention to the cause of temperance.

THE ANTI-SALOON LEAGUE

Another of the significant temperance groups was the Anti-Saloon League, founded on May 24, 1893, by a Congregational minister named Howard Hyde Russell. By 1895 the Anti-Saloon League was the most efficient temperance group and became the prime mover of the temperance cause.

Compared to the WCTU, the Anti-Saloon League was single-minded, was not affiliated with any political party, and did not endorse any particular religion. It grew to be the most successful single-issue organization in American history, as it targeted only the saloon. The league was very active, with a membership that expanded into the millions. Its stated objective was to clean up "drunkenness, gambling, and fornication." In practice, their campaign went after drinking, assuming that control of saloons would lead to control or abolishment of the other two. Later they joined forces with the American Medical Association and the American Pharmaceutical Association to go after drugs.

The Anti-Saloon League tried to work within the existing system to limit the consumption of alcohol through tactics such as licensing drinking establishments. Their motto was "The Saloon Must Go!" And admittedly, by the time they were a dominant force to be reckoned with most saloons were not very elegant establishments.

The Anti-Saloon League was probably one of the effective organizations responsible for getting prohibition laws passed, but Carrie Nation received the focus of the publicity and forced national attention on the issue.

OTHER SUPPORT FOR TEMPERANCE

The temperance cause received support from various other sources. One was anti-alcohol political cartoons in magazines and newspapers of the time. Typical cartoon strips started by showing a well-dressed person sipping a drink. As the cartoon panels progressed, the man became a drunk, a thief, a wife-beater, or maybe all three. By the last of the panels he was depicted as a hopeless drunk.

Popular temperance songs made the rounds, with people singing lyrics to ditties such as "Drink Nothing, Boys, but Water," "Father, Bring Home Your Money Tonight," and the "Lament of the Widowed Inebriate." The lyrics of one old temperance song were:

> No matter what anyone says,
> No matter what anyone thinks,
> If you want to be happy the rest of your life,
> Don't marry a man if he drinks![31]

Temperance promoters frequently traveled the lecture circuit in the Old West, though the tone of the meetings often became more like vaudeville antics, with an actor doing dramatic impersonations, including that of a drunkard. Anti-liquor sentiments were fanned by rhetoric from the podium such as "Crawl from the slimy ooze, ye drowned drunkards, and with suffocation's blue and lurid lips speak out against the drink!" A similar fiery (literally) exhortation was, "Snap your burning chains, ye denizens of the pit, and come up sheeted in the fire, dripping with the flames of hell, and with

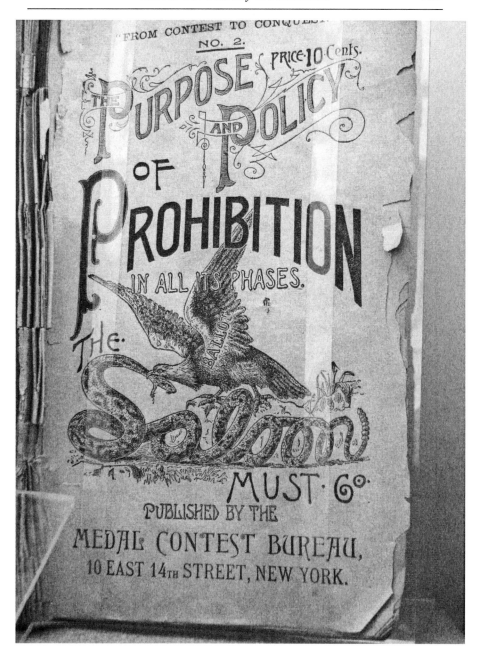

The journey towards Prohibition was rapidly propelled to its destination by temperance lectures, books, sermons, plays, and songs. This magazine is an example of one of the many temperance tracts that flourished to promote the evils of drink and the benefits of abstinence (author's collection).

your trumpet tongues testify against the deep damnation of the drink!"[32] Audiences loved it.

Other attacks on liquor came from literature and the theater. One of the most successful temperance plays was William H. Smith's *The Drunkard; or, The Fallen Saved*. This Victorian potboiler about the evils of drink was first produced in 1844. The essential plot follows Edward Middleton as he succumbs to the evil of drink and descends into the world of the drunkard, leaving his wife sewing shirts by the light of a candle to earn enough money to feed her child a crust of bread. A high point for voyeuristic Victorian audiences was that the lead actor had to writhe around on the floor and scream as he portrayed the character's suffering during an attack of delirium tremens.

In today's terms, the play was filled with melodramatic Victorian cliches. For example, the tavern-keeper taunts the down-and-out hero with "Ha! Ha! What has brought you to this beastly condition, young man?" The hero replies, "You! Rum! Eternal curses on you! Had it not been for your infernal poison shops in our village, I had still been a man — the foul den, where you plunder the pockets of your fellows, where you deal forth death in tumblers, and from whence goes forth the blast of ruin over the land, to mildew the bright hopes of youth, to fill the widow's heart with agony, to curse the orphans, to steal the glorious mind of man, to cast them from their high estate of honest pride, to make them such as — me!"[33] By the end, however, the Victorian morality message had triumphed. The protagonist takes the pledge, stops drinking, and is restored happily to his wife and family. The play was so popular that it ran for 130 consecutive nights at P.T. Barnum's Boston Museum.

Another highly influential temperance play was based on Timothy Shay Arthur's book, *Ten Nights in Bar-room and What I Saw There*. Published in 1854, the book was an immediate success and sold millions of copies. The novel was turned into an even more successful play by William W. Pratt and opened in New York in 1858 with the simpler title of *Ten Nights in a Barroom*. It became one of the most successful plays in America. The play follows the fall of Joe Morgan into "vile and debased drunkenness," which is partly responsible for the death of his young daughter Little Mary. The staging also includes the obligatory Victorian audience-pleaser of the main character portraying an attack of the DT's. The resolution of the plot is that he becomes a teetotaler and is reunited with his wife.

Both of these plays were strongly supported by the Woman's Christian Temperance Union and the Anti-Saloon League and they continued to be presented at temperance meetings and in medicine shows until well after the turn of the century.

In the world of books, the National Temperance Society and Publication House published books with titles such as *The Rum Fiend, and Other Poems* by William H. Burleigh and *How Could He Escape?* by Mrs. J. McNair Wright, which was described in the publisher's advertising: "It shows the terrible effects of even one glass of intoxicating liquor upon the system of one unable to resist its influences." Another volume published by the same company was *The Temperance Doctor* by Miss Mary Dwinell Chellis. The publisher's description included, "In it we have graphically depicted the sad ravages that are caused by the sad use of intoxicating beverages."[34] Other temperance groups promoted the same types of books.

Another example from the world of temperance literature is Frederick Powell, who won a monetary prize in a contest for his essay on temperance titled "Bacchus Dethroned." One can see why with this quote: "The vice of intemperance is a most disgusting and demoralizing one and leads to every species of abomination and crime." The author goes on to emphasize his point: "Intemperance is the most loathsome and ruinous of vices."[35]

Powell continued in several strong statements about the corruption of women: "As we gaze on this diseased and degraded sisterhood ... we are led to inquire, Whence came they? And the answer is too clear to be mistaken. They are, for the most part, the product of our Ruinous Drink System. It is in the public house that many of them receive their first taint. The social glass blunts their moral perceptions, and throws them off their guard, and thus they become an easy prey to the wiles of the seducer."[36] (Again, the ever-abiding concerns about women's morals by others.) His description of prostitutes is even more depressing: "In a very short time, a few months in some, a few years in others, their bloom and beauty fade, and they become either bloated and blaspheming monsters, with every womanly attribute eradicated, or poor emaciated and diseased outcasts, homeless and hopeless."[37]

Another example typical of the anti-liquor propaganda was a lithograph by Nathaniel Currier titled *The Drunkard's Progress* and produced in 1846. This charts the progress of a "typical" drunkard in the shape of an arch, showing a series of illustrated steps up one side of the arch that rise to a peak, and then his fall down the other side into poverty and disease, and his eventual death. The First Step on this mythical road to ruin is labeled "A Glass with a Friend," who is a man or a woman, depending on the particular version of the lithograph. The Second Step upwards is "A Glass to Keep the Cold Out," which shows him drinking with an unidentified woman. Step Three is "A Glass Too Much," which shows him drunk and leaning up against a wall. Step Four, "Drunk and Riotous," shows him being hauled away by a policeman. Step Five, at the peak of the arch, is "The Summit Attained. Jolly Companions. A Confirmed Drunkard," showing him drinking with a group of companions.

Step Six, starting down the other side of the arch, is labeled "Poverty and Disease," as he presumably descends into those conditions. Step Seven, "Forsaken by Friends," shows him all alone, dressed in rags for clothing. Step

Eight is "Desperation and Crime," as he robs another man. And finally, Step Nine is "Death by Suicide," showing him blowing his brains out. Underneath the arch is a representation of his melancholy wife and child standing by as their house burns down.[38]

Many famous figures spoke out against the perceived evils of alcohol. Henry David Thoreau said, "Water is the only drink for a wise man." On the other hand, perhaps there was some truth in the matter, humorist Mark Twain, with his tongue stuck firmly in his cheek, commented, "Water, taken in moderation, cannot hurt anybody." William Jennings Bryan made a speech in 1916 on behalf of banning liquor "because its evil influences cannot be confined." He went on to say, "Alcohol is a poison which weakens the body, impairs the strength of mind, and menaces morals." To promote the principles of temperance he served only water and unfermented grape juice at an official state luncheon in 1913.

Some tried scientific reason as another method of attack. Even though his argument was circumspect, Richmond Hobson, in *Alcohol and the Human Race*, stated, "I was startled to find, almost at the outset, that alcohol is not a product built up from grain, grapes and other food materials, but is the toxin of yeast or ferment germs, which, after devouring the food materials, excrete alcohol as their waste product. Though abstemious myself, the thought that intoxicating liquors were really built up of the excretions of living organisms removed all glamour from the cup, and produced a reaction of loathing."[39]

Temperance promoters loved to emphasize the point that alcohol was the "excrement of the fungi that is yeast," which made drink sound most unappealing. It is true that alcohol is a metabolic by-product of a microscopic fungus (the yeast family) that feeds on sugar, but this is in the same sense that carbon dioxide is an excretion from the breathing process of mammals and is part of the exhalation from human lungs.

In spite of all this, not everyone was in favor of prohibition nor were they temperance advocates. In Colorado City, Colorado, a fire that broke out in 1907 threatened many of the saloons. Spectator the Rev. Duncan Lamont, in a burst of enthusiastic fervor, waved his arms in the air and shouted out loud, "Our prayers have been answered!" Some of the firemen were not so enthusiastic and turned their fire hoses on him. As the night air was below freezing, he had to be carried away encased in a covering of ice.[40]

FROM DRINK TO DRUGS

The social stigma of women consuming alcohol led many to the more acceptable use of opium in the guise of medicine. Perversely, many of the women who became temperance supporters and denounced the drinking habits of men were habitual opium users. They prided themselves on being teetotalers, but staunchly believed in the healthy use of patent medicines and health tonics, dosing themselves with pills and potions containing morphine and opium. One druggist from Boston who was queried about opium purchases at his dispensary reported that he had "but one customer and that a noted Temperance lecturer."[41]

Physician F.E. Oliver, author of the report on opium that was issued by the Massachusetts State Board of Health, believed that the temperance movement in New England had caused a significant increase in addicts. He said, "It is a significant fact that both in England and in this country, the total abstinence movement was almost immediately followed by an increased consumption of opium."[42]

Postscript

As the late 1800s continued into the early 1900s, two major changes affected the use of alcohol and drugs in the Old West. One was that the Temperance Movement finally had a major success with the passing of legislation in 1917 that led to national prohibition of the sale of alcoholic drinks. The other was that the government acknowledged the seriousness of the issues of addiction and took steps to limit public access to narcotic drugs.

The Rise and Fall of Prohibition

The Eighteenth Amendment to the Constitution of the United States passed in 1917, was ratified in 1919, and took effect in 1920. To the surprise of the "wets" the amendment was ratified with unprecedented speed by thirty-six states in less than fourteen months.

The details of the implementation of Prohibition were spelled out in the National Prohibition Act, popularly known as the Volstead Act, which was sponsored by Minnesota Representative Andrew John Volstead and passed in October of 1919. The legislation was vetoed by President Woodrow Wilson, but his veto was overridden by Congress. Prohibition — the so-called Noble Experiment — became law on January 16, 1920. Rebellion against the new regulation was immediate. Within one minute of the Volstead Act going into effect, six armed bandits stole $100,000 worth of medicinal whiskey from a train in Chicago.[1]

The fond expectations of prohibition supporters were that banning the manufacture and sale of alcohol would result in social harmony, reduced crime, and enhanced productivity. Instead, drinking continued, fueled by liquor smuggling (rumrunning) and the manufacture of bootleg alcohol, both of which resulted in a predictable increase in serious crime.

The Volstead Act allowed the continued possession of alcoholic beverages that had been purchased before July 1, 1919. Drinking liquor was still legal, but making and selling it was not. As a result, many individuals and businesses laid in plenty of alcoholic beverages before the law went into effect, which resulted in large-scale hoarding of stocks of liquor.

One man who was farsighted was Spencer Penrose, who owned the lavish Broadmoor Hotel resort in Colorado Springs, Colorado. In 1919, anticipating Prohibition, he purchased 2,400 cases of some of the finest and rarest liquor from Europe and America and put it in storage in New York. He purchased a further 1,000 cases for his private wine cellar in Colorado. When Prohibition was repealed, he shipped the liquor from New York to Colorado in two boxcars and stored it in his cellar. Needless to say, he employed burglar alarms and a full-time security guard to protect it.[2]

The Volstead Act exempted sacramental wine and liquor prescribed by a physician that was used for medicinal purposes. The act also allowed the manufacture of wine and cider at home — up to 200 gallons a year — but banned the sale or commercial manufacture of alcoholic beverages under any

Though temperance supporters hoped that Prohibition would dry up supplies of alcohol and make the country a better place to live, illegal booze continued to flow and whiskey as a "medicine" was commonly available with a doctor's prescription (author's collection).

conditions. The distillation of industrial alcohol was allowed, as was home brewing and making cider. The result was a predictable increase in home manufacturing and in bootlegging. In 1925, during the height of Prohibition, enforcement agents seized 29,087 illegal stills and arrested over 76,000 people.[3]

Suddenly drinking, which had been viewed only a few years earlier as a weakness in men and the destroyer of the Victorian hearth and home, became all the fashion and a symbol of defiance of the government. Making "whiskey" at home was easy. Shops did not sell banned products or encourage people to produce alcohol against the law, but information and supplies for making alcohol were readily and legally available. The residents of the Old West responded valiantly. In 1921, federal officials estimated that Butte, Montana, led the nation in per capita consumption of illicit alcohol.[4]

Apart from the increase in crime associated with bootlegging and rum-running, and the resentment of much of the general population against banning alcoholic drinks, one of the major problems with Prohibition was unemployment. The liquor industry had been big business. At the time Prohibition went into effect, the United States had 178,000 saloons, 1,200 breweries, and over 500 distilleries.[5] Prohibition put workers in these industries into the unemployment lines. The law also forced most saloons out of business. In Denver alone, two breweries and 400 saloons closed their doors. Some were torn down, some became restaurants or stores, and some turned to serving soft-drinks and ice cream or became billiard parlors in order to survive. On top of this, the federal government lost large amounts of tax revenue.

One of the primary downfalls of Prohibition was purely economic. A substantial issue was the financing of federal agents to police Prohibition, the cost of which was far greater than the initial optimistic estimates due to the spiraling increase in crime associated with the manufacture and distribution of illegal liquor. A second issue was the huge loss of tax revenue on alcohol for the government. A third was the loss of revenue and jobs for farmers who grew corn, barley, hops, and the other crops that were turned into alcohol. And, finally, there was the huge economic impact on the country from the loss of jobs in the brewing and distilling industries. Another, perhaps more serious, issue that was another of the unintended consequences of Prohibition was public health. Banning alcohol predictably led to an increase in bootleg liquor. With no controls on who made it or how it was made, much of the "bathtub gin" type of liquor was extremely dangerous to drink.

Corn mash was available legally. It had only to be heated in a kettle to 180°F and the resulting vapor collected to get 100 percent (200 proof) alcohol. This was so strong that it was deadly to drink, so something had to be added to cut the strength and create bootleg "booze." Chemicals that were added to "improve" the flavor, to give it some "kick," or to make the amount of bootleg alcohol go further (as in the previous saloon days of the Old West) were often poisonous. A common additive was methanol antifreeze drained from automobile radiators. Bootleggers claimed that the rust that was often in it was supposed to make a flavorful additive.[6] Other dangerous alcohol-based additives were aftershave, embalming fluid, mouthwash, hair tonic, creosote, paint thinner, and denatured alcohol.[7]

Another lethal beverage was "Jake," which was 90 percent fluid extract of Jamaica Ginger with wood alcohol added. This nasty drink caused the eventual paralysis of the drinkers' hands and feet, and left their legs flopping out of control when they walked. In 1930 the Prohibition Bureau estimated that Jake had paralyzed 15,000 people.[8] The desire for an inebriated sensation through alcohol was so high that farmhands in the Midwest reputedly drank the liquid drained from the bottom of silos where silage had fermented over the years.[9]

The attempt to force Prohibition on the drinking public ended in failure and was repealed by the Twenty-First Amendment to the United States Constitution. Prohibition lasted for almost fourteen years. It ended officially on December 5, 1933.

A Change in Drug Laws

The turn of the century and the end of the Victorian era coincided with the end of the opium trade with China. As the twentieth century dawned, narcotic drugs were freely available from drugstores and other suppliers of medicines. They could also be purchased by mail order from the manufacturer. But a second major result of the temperance movement was increasing legislation to curb the use of opium and other opiate derivatives.

In 1905, the same year that opium and morphine were the fourth best-selling pharmaceuticals in the United States, Congress created a special committee to evaluate the number of users of cocaine and opium.[10] Among its conclusions was that 200,000 people (0.5 percent of the total population) were addicted. In addition, the report noted that opium and morphine users were generally not the drug fiends of the fervent antidrug campaign, but middle-aged men and women who were well-integrated socially and at work and who had started using drugs under medical supervision. Most had used them for a decade or more.

In 1919 another Congressional committee estimated the number of drug users to be 238,000. This figure did not show the huge rate of increase that alarmists had predicted and was actually lower than the rate of growth of the population. But to opponents this number appeared to be "monstrous."[11] As an additional encouraging note, the report mentioned no cases of accidental overdose (suicides excepted), or encouragement of crime among users. Much of the exaggerated fear of opium in the United States was due to prejudices against the opium-smoking Chinese of the West Coast. Smoking opium was viewed as contrary to the American way of life and as a filthy Oriental habit, even though it also held a romantic vicarious thrill of the danger of illegal use.

Contemporary attitudes towards opium addiction bordered on the hysterical. Figures were manipulated and statistics were grossly exaggerated.[12] Typical was a pamphlet written by Richmond Hobson for the International Narcotic Education Association. As part of an inflated propaganda campaign against drugs, he claimed that there were four million users in the United States, even though the federal government estimated only between 100,000 and 200,000. According to him, the danger of drugs lurked everywhere. At one point Hobson even urged women to have their face powder checked for traces of heroin.[13] The Pure Food and Drug Act passed in 1906 included regulations on the labeling of products containing alcohol, opiates, and cocaine. This new law now required disclosure of the ingredients that were in patent medicines.

The dangerous and addictive nature of opium resulted in a worldwide effort to try to control it; however, a meeting of the International Opium Commission in 1909 did not accomplish much. The opium trade was too lucrative and the tax revenues too substantial in the economies of some countries for many governments to want to do much. Everyone was protective of their own opium interests. Because of high import duties, however, many suppliers preferred to smuggle drugs into a country instead of bringing them legally.

In 1909 the United States government passed the Smoking Opium Exclusion Act, which prohibited the importation, possession, and use of smoking-grade opium except for pharmaceutical purposes. As a consequence, users were forced to switch from smoking to hypodermic or oral use of drugs because this method was still available and was cheaper. Smuggled opium was still available. Smuggling, however, increased the price of opium, as well as heroin and morphine, which were more addicting though less expensive. Even the Chinese who usually smoked opium were forced by the economics of the situation to use heroin and morphine.[14]

In 1914, the Harrison Narcotic Act was sponsored by Representative Francis Burton Harrison to control the medicinal use of opium, morphine, heroin, and cocaine.[15] The act did not prohibit narcotics, but it required every manufacturer, distributor and possessor of cocaine, morphine, and opium, including doctors and pharmacists, to register with the Department of the Treasury, to pay taxes, and to keep records of all the narcotics that they prescribed or dispensed. Patients who used potentially harmful narcotic drugs were required to have a prescription. The legislation was aimed at eliminating all nonmedical use of these drugs, but some of this good intent backfired in the 1920s, when almost 30,000 doctors and 8,000 pharmacists ended up in jail for prescribing or selling opium and morphine to undercover policemen posing as addicts.[16]

By 1923, most narcotic substances (including heroin and morphine) were banned from over-the-counter sales. But even with the enforcement of antidrug laws, those with money could still obtain opium from their family physician. So the middle and upper classes who could afford drugs continued to obtain them, while the poor paid even higher prices that were driven up by regulation and the resultant smuggling of illicit drugs.

In Perspective

The second half of the nineteenth century was a time of unprecedented change in America and in the Old West. The western half of the United States matured from vast open spaces populated only by Native American tribes and a few white fur trappers to flourishing large population centers, such as Denver, Leadville, Salt Lake City, Tombstone, and San Francisco. During this time, the use of alcohol and opium had a substantial, but often unrecognized, influence on the behavior of the flood of settlers who emigrated to the West to farm, raise cattle, mine, cut timber, and build the transcontinental railroad. Both drugs were used in various ways and became an integral part of their lives.

Alcohol served as a solace for lonely young men who worked at the back-breaking hard work that was required to tame the Western frontier. But it was also the impetus for many of the quarrels and fights that the legend of the cowboy made famous. Alcohol and saloons — along with gambling and loose women — were responsible for much of the lore that created the popular vision of the Old West as a wild-and-woolly legend. Alcohol was also part of the shabby treatment that was often the lot of American Indians.

Opium as a medicine came to the West with the early pioneers, who used it to relieve their aches and pains and to successfully treat the symptoms of the dysentery that was widespread. But opium also created the lore of sinister Chinese opium dens. Unrecognized opium addiction was the fate of many who used the drug, whether knowingly or unknowingly from legitimate medical treatment or through patent medicines.

As addictive drugs, both alcohol and opium had a negative influence on many individuals and households. What started out with serious social concerns about drugs and whiskey in the 1850s festered through the last half of

the century, culminating in the early part of the twentieth century with Prohibition and the government control of narcotic drugs. Though neither of
these regulations was particularly successful, they brought an end to the free-
and-easy flow of alcohol and the over-the-counter purchase of narcotic drugs.
This at least lessened the influence of the two and relegated them to part of
the colorful fabric that makes up the history of the Old West.

Appendix I:
Apothecaries' Weights
and Measures

Apothecaries' Weights

1 grain = 60 milligrams*
20 grains = 1 scruple
3 scruples = 1 drachm (modern spelling *dram*) = 60 grains
8 drachm = 1 ounce = 480 grains
12 ounces = 1 apothecaries' pound = 5,760 grains†
16 ounces = 1 avoirdupois pound (English and American system) = 7,000 grains

*One grain was originally defined as the weight of a ripe grain of wheat.
†This is the same as the troy pound used to weigh precious metals.

Apothecaries' Liquid Measures

60 minims = 1 fluid drachm (dram) = 60 drops
8 fluid drachms = 1 fluid ounce
16 fluid ounces = 1 pint
1 teaspoon = 1 fluid drachm = ⅛ fluid ounce
1 tablespoon is approximately 4 teaspoons = 4 fluid drachms = ½ fluid ounce

Appendix II:
Common 19th Century
Medicines

Blue mass: see *Calomel*

Calomel: Mercurous chloride (chloride of mercury, also called horn mercury or sweet mercury), also known as "blue mass"; used for purging the bowels.

Carbolic acid: Also known as phenol, a substance derived from the distillation of coal tar; used as a general disinfectant, as a douche by ladies of the night to prevent venereal disease, and by prostitutes to commit suicide.

Castor oil: An unpleasant-tasting oil made from the beans of the castor plant (*Ricinus communis*); used as a laxative.

Cocaine: A drug obtained from the coca plant (*Erythroxylon coca*) that grows in Peru; used as a local anesthetic.

Colocynth: The pulp of the fruit from the plant *Citrullos colocynthis*; used as a dramatic purgative.

Croton oil: An oil made from the ripe seeds of the croton plant (*Croton tiglium*) grown in Ceylon (now Sri Lanka) and China; used as a dramatic purgative.

Dover's powder: A mixture of opium, ipecac, and sugar of milk (lactose); used as a sedative or to produce sweating.

Heroin: Diacetyl morphine, a highly addictive narcotic derived from morphine; used for the treatment of asthma or a cough. (The Narcotics Control Act of 1956 made the acquisition, possession, or transportation of heroin illegal.)

Ipecac: A medicine derived from the dried root of the South American plant *Cephaelis ipecacuanha*; used to induce vomiting and to promote sweating.

Jalap: Derived from the root of the Mexican plant *Convolvulus jalapa*; used as a dramatic and explosive purgative.

Laudanum: An alcohol solution of opium, also called tincture of opium; used as a sedative, a painkiller, and to check diarrhea.

Mercury: A heavy, poisonous metallic element that is liquid at room temperature; often used as calomel (mercurous chloride) as a purgative.

Morphine: One of the most important alkaloids derived from opium; used to control severe pain.

Opium: The parent of laudanum and morphine, made from the dried juice of the poppy plant, *Papaver somniferum*, from the Far East; used for the control of pain and to check diarrhea.

Paragoric: Laudanum (tincture of opium) mixed with camphor; used to soothe teething babies and to check diarrhea in children.

Quinine: Also known as Peruvian bark or Jesuit bark, quinine is a bitter substance derived from the bark of the *Cinchona* family of trees that grow in South America; used primarily as a preventative for malaria, but also used to reduce fevers and relieve pain.

Tartar emetic: White, poisonous, metallic-tasting crystals of antimony and potassium tartarate; used to induce vomiting.

Whiskey: Ethyl alcohol (ethanol) with various colorings and flavorings; used as a universal treatment for many ailments in the Old West. Whiskey was sometimes combined with quinine for the prevention of malaria.

Chapter Notes

Preface

1. The term "Victorian" used here includes the social and moral climate that existed during the last half of the nineteenth century. Queen Victoria was on the British throne from 1837 to 1901.

2. Powell, *Bacchus Dethroned*, 161.

3. Kerr, *Inebriety*, 236.

4. Harris, *This Drinking Nation*, 15.

5. These dates are arguable. Much of the expansion and settlement of the Old West took place after the 1840s and the cross-country treks of the early pioneers along the Oregon and California trails. Depending on the particular historian, the end of this expansion and colonization came either with the end of the Indian Wars between the U.S. Army and the Sioux Indians at the battle of Wounded Knee, South Dakota, in 1890; or when Frederick Jackson Turner and the U.S. Census Bureau stated that the American frontier was gone in 1890; or when Arizona, the last of the territories in the Old West, gained statehood in 1912.

6. Noel, *The City and the Saloon*, 126.

Chapter One

1. Secrest, *Hell's Belles*, 89.

2. Holland, *The Joy of Drinking*, 59.

3. Bordin, *Woman and Temperance*, 5.

4. "Alkali" was a generic name for strong salts of sodium and potassium that were poisonous if they were present in high enough concentration in the water.

5. Unrau, *White Man's Wicked Water*, 34.

6. Gateley, *Drink*, 274.

7. Clappe, *The Shirley Letters*, 59.

8. Brutal temperatures as low as -80°F were recorded near Dawson in the winters of 1897 and 1898.

9. This one-minute movie was actually filmed in Thomas Edison's "Black Maria" studio in West Orange, New Jersey.

10. Nadeau, *Fort Laramie and the Sioux Indians*, 33.

11. Ibid., 38.

12. Ibid.

13. Unrau, *White Man's Wicked Water*, 34.

14. Nadeau, *Fort Laramie and the Sioux Indians*, 35.

15. Ibid., 36.

16. Lavender, *Bent's Fort*, 172.

17. Hugh Evans, "Journal of a Dragoon Campaign of 1835," *Mississippi Valley Historical Review* (September 1927), 271.

18. Lavender, *Bent's Fort*, 159–160.

19. Nadeau, *Fort Laramie and the Sioux Indians*, 33.

20. Unrau, *White Man's Wicked Water*, 10.

21. Ibid., 47.

22. Dasgupta, *The Science of Drinking*, 3.

23. Holland, *The Joy of Drinking*, 14.

24. In the mysterious world of the chemist, ethanol is part of a family of organic chemicals that consist of a string of carbon atoms connected to hydrogen atoms and one hydroxyl (-OH) group. The specific type of alcohol depends on the number of carbon atoms in the backbone of its chemical formula. Ethanol is a relatively simple alcohol, containing two carbon atoms; its chemical formula is C_2H_5OH.

25. Modern production methods synthesize methanol from methane gas.

26. This is still performed by some primitive native Indian cultures in South America.

27. Erdoes, *Saloons of the Old West*, 95.

28. Carr, *A Yankee Trader*, 177.

29. Ibid., 183–184.

30. Alcohol boils and evaporates at about 180°F, whereas water boils at 212°F at sea level.

31. Gateley, *Drink*, 216.

32. West, *The Saloon on the Rocky Mountain Mining Frontier*, 106.

33. Edwards, *Alcohol: The World's Favorite Drug*, 50.

34. Craig MacAndrew and Robert B. Edgerton, *Drunken Comportment: A Social Explanation* (Chicago: Aldine, 1968), 9.

35. Drinking is even today implicated in a large number of violent (including sexual) assaults.

36. Clappe, *The Shirley Letters*, 104.

37. Dasgupta, *The Science of Drinking*, 92.

38. Many of these same dangerous ingredients were added to bootleg booze during the later Prohibition era of the 1920s. One of the more disgusting additives to Prohibition liquor was manure, which must have given the alcohol a very peculiar taste indeed.

39. T.E. Van Evra, "One Man's Experience in Early Leadville," *Trail*, December 1918, pp. 20–23.

40. In modern times moonshiners add cooking oil (called by them "beading oil") or lye to whiskey of poor quality to make it seem that their product has a high proof.

41. Faulk, *Tombstone*, 97.

42. Yes, believe it or not, the bilious-looking liquid from the gall bladder of an ox.

43. Sage Rufus, *Wild Scenes in Kansas and Nebraska, and the Rocky Mountains, Oregon, California, New Mexico, Texas, and the Grand Prairies; or Notes by the Way...* (Philadelphia: G.D. Mille, 1855), 132–133.

44. Sarsaparilla was a carbonated drink with an acrid, sweet taste, flavored with an extract from the dried roots of a group of climbing vines found in tropical Central America.

45. Two of the more interestingly named ones from England that pique the imagination were Cuckold's Comfort and Ladies' Delight.

46. Dabney, *Mountain Spirits*, xv.

Chapter Two

1. Santella, *Opium*, 17.

2. Escohotado, *A Brief History of Drugs*, 62.

3. Santella, *Opium*, 16.

4. Musto, *Drugs in America*, 215.

5. Poppy seeds do, however, contain tiny amounts of morphine and codeine. In spite of this harmless amount, an individual can fail a drug test if he has previously eaten food that contains poppy seeds, such as poppy seed cake or muffins.

6. Santella, *Opium*, 8.

7. Ibid., 9.

8. Booth, *Opium*, 15.

9. Ibid., 103–104.

10. Bergersen and Krug, *Pharmacology in Nursing*, 235.

11. Santella, *Opium*, 27.

12. At one time, the tax on all this tea provided 10 percent of the British government's entire revenue (Beeching, *The Chinese Opium Wars*, 29).

13. Booth, *Opium*, 112.

14. Al Rose, *Storyville, New Orleans* (Tuscaloosa: University of Alabama Press, 1974), xii.

15. Bill Bryson, *At Home* (New York: Anchor, 2011), 449.

16. David E. Owen, *British Opium Policy in China and India* (New Haven: Yale University Press, 1934), vii.

17. Santella, *Opium*, 31.

18. Adam Hart-Davis, *What the Victorians Did for Us* (London: Headline, 2001), 154.

19. Sutcliffe and Duin, *A History of Medicine*, 50. It is difficult to ferret out the correct number, and various sources report a wide range of figures. Santella says that by 1830 Britain was consuming 22,000 pounds of opium a year (Santella, *Opium*, 13). Booth says that shipments to Britain went from 91,000 pounds in 1830 to 280,000 pounds in 1860 (Booth, *Opium*, 51). In any case, it was a very large amount.

Chapter Three

1. Gateley, *Drink*, 269.

2. Moerman, *Native American Medicinal Plants*, 52.

3. Winfred Blevins, *Dictionary of the American West* (New York: Facts on File, 1993), 365.

4. Moerman, *Native American Medicinal Plants*, 169.

5. Ibid., 173.

6. de Ropp, *Drugs and the Mind*, 50.

7. Mescaline is better known to the chemist as 3,4,5-trimethoxy-phenyl-ethylamine.

8. Steele, *Bleed, Blister and Purge*, 41.

9. MacAndrew and Edgerton, *Drunken Comportment*, 101.

10. Erdoes, *Saloons of the Old West*, 96–98.

11. The term "lightning" had been used as early as 1858 in San Francisco for strong, raw liquor, but in the Old West the term was generally reserved to describe the powerful variety brewed in Taos and other raw liquors of the frontier. The term lives on in the contemporary name "white lightning."

12. Nancy Fitzhugh Norton, "Christmas in

Denver in 1859," *The Trail*, December 1920, pp. 12–13.

13. The buildings have been re-created on the original site as part of a historical museum in modern downtown Pueblo, Colorado.

14. Ralph C. Taylor, *Colorado: South of the Border* (Denver: Sage, 1963), 113.

15. The Taos Rebellion, during which even New Mexico governor Charles Bent was killed, was sparked by a fear in some residents that annexation of New Mexico by the United States during the Mexican War (1846–1848) would lead to an outlawing of their Catholic religion, banning of the Spanish language, and a loss of their land rights. A more subtle motivation for the attack on Turley's mill may have been resentment over the negative effects of American whiskey on the local Indian population.

16. Erdoes, *Saloons of the Old West*, 87.

17. Clappe, *The Shirley Letters*, 41.

Chapter Four

1. Santella, *Opium*, 45.

2. Parkman, *The Oregon Trail*, 317–318.

3. Gardner, *The Domestic Physician*, 122. Tenesmus is the medical name for a spasmodic sharp pain in the bowels that accompanies an urgent desire to empty them.

4. Gardner, *The Domestic Physician*, 122.

5. James and Raymond, *Comstock Women*, 108.

6. Booth, *Opium*, 69.

7. Hodgson, *In the Arms of Morpheus*, 79.

8. The three major classes of natural opiates in the body are called endorphins, enkephalins, and dynorphins, first discovered in 1974. These are called "endogenous opiates," or opium-like substances, that exist inside the body. The word "endorphin" comes from a contraction of "endogenous" and "morphine." It has been suggested that these substances are involved in the so-called runner's high that creates a sensation of euphoria and happiness after extended strenuous exercise. Opium and morphine are called "exogenous opiates" because they are introduced from outside the body; however, more recent studies have shown that some human body tissue is capable of producing morphine itself.

9. Sanberg and Bunsey, *Prescription Narcotics*, 40.

10. Haller and Haller, *The Physician and Sexuality in Victorian America*, 276.

11. Booth, *Opium*, 28.

12. Child, *The Family Nurse*, 102.

13. Ibid., 95.

14. Learned men of the time wrote scientific treatises and medical papers in Latin, which was considered to be the language of scholars. Many of them gave themselves Latin names.

15. Musto, *Drugs in America*, 184.

16. Child, *The Family Nurse*, 107.

17. Kenneth L. Holmes, *Covered Wagon Women: Diaries and Letters from the Western Trails, 1840–1890*, vol. 9 (Spokane: Arthur H. Clark, 1990), 85–86.

18. A poultice was a hot, moist paste that was used to relieve congestion or pain. It was applied over the skin, then covered with a linen cloth or towel.

19. Phthisis was the term used for a wasting disease caused by lung problems. "Miner's phthisis," for example, was a lung disease caused by inhaling rock dust in the mines. The term was commonly linked with various forms of tuberculosis.

20. Lake, *Wyatt Earp*, 197.

21. Bat Masterson, "Famous Gunfighters of the Western Frontier," *Human Life*, May 1907, 5.

22. Child, *The Family Nurse*, 9.

23. Bergersen and Krug, *Pharmacology in Nursing*, 235.

24. Child, *The Family Nurse*, 96.

25. A cathartic was a medicine that produced a series of violent bowel evacuations, often accompanied by pain and cramping. This was similar to a laxative but more turbulent in action.

26. F.E. Oliver, *The Use and Abuse of Opium*, Massachusetts State Board of Health, Third Annual Report (Boston: Wright and Potter, 1872), 162–177.

27. A general anesthetic (such as chloroform) puts the patient to sleep; a local anesthetic (such as cocaine) blocks pain from a small area of the body (as in a toothache or severe skin laceration) while the patient is awake.

28. O'Neal, *Encyclopedia of Western Gunfighters*, 63.

29. Wilbur, *Civil War Medicine*, 108.

30. Ibid., 109.

31. Booth, *Opium*, 73.

32. Bollet, *Civil War Medicine*, 90.

33. Ibid., 284.

34. G.W. Adams, "Confederate Medicine," *Journal of Southern History* (1940), 6, 151–188.

35. "Bilious" was a generic term for any nebulous illness thought to be caused by a disordered liver, resulting in constipation, headache, and a loss of appetite.

36. Straubing, *In Hospital and Camp*, 5.
37. Holland, *The Joy of Drinking*, 6–7.
38. Edwards, *Alcohol: The World's Favorite Drug*, 168.
39. Extracted from copies of handwritten notes from an anonymous doctor's patient treatment records in New London, Connecticut.
40. Edwards, *Alcohol: The World's Favorite Drug*, 168.

Chapter Five

1. Chinese immigrants arrived on the West Coast in the late 1840s and steadily increased in numbers over the next several decades. Japanese men, however, did not commonly appear until the 1890s.
2. Booth, *Opium*, 194.
3. James and Raymond, *Comstock Women*, 97.
4. Booth, *Opium*, 176.
5. Ibid., 199.
6. Anthony J. Lorenz, "Scurvy in the Gold Rush," *Journal of the History of Medicine* (October 1957), 473–510.
7. Chang, *The Chinese in America*, 46.
8. Time-Life Books Editors, *The Forty-Niners* (New York: Time, 1974), 106.
9. Morgan, *Wanton West*, 87.
10. Ibid.
11. Goldman, *Gold Diggers and Silver Miners*, 96.
12. Barsness, *Gold Camp*, 234.
13. Miller, *Holladay Street*, 51.
14. Secrest, *Hell's Belles*, 113.
15. Curt Gentry, *The Madams of San Francisco* (New York: Ballantine, 1964), 65.
16. Rutter, *Upstairs Girls*, 5.
17. Morgan, *Wanton West*, 30.
18. Goldman, *Gold Diggers and Silver Miners*, 96.
19. Miller, *Holladay Street*, 52.
20. Black powder is a mixture of sulfur, charcoal, and saltpeter (potassium nitrate).
21. Ambrose, *Nothing Like It in the World*, 198.
22. James and Raymond, *Comstock Women*, 96.
23. Bruns, *Desert Honkytonk*, 132.
24. Accounts of the Chinese in these turf wars generally identify opposing groups only as "Cantons" and "Hong Kongs." These names were not necessarily the true basis of the social origin of the participants but rather were general geographical names that included various groups and origins.

25. Carr, *A Yankee Trader*, 136–141.
26. Bruns, *Desert Honkytonk*, 133.
27. Myers, *The Last Chance*, 76–77.
28. G. Edward White, *The Eastern Establishment and the Western Experience: The West of Frederic Remington, Theodore Roosevelt, and Owen Wister* (New Haven, 1968), 57, 109.
29. Asbury, *The Barbary Coast*, 157.
30. Barsness, *Gold Camp*, 233.
31. Ibid.
32. Time-Life Books Editors, *The Miners* (New York: Time, 1976), 109.
33. Morgan, *Skid Road*, 86.
34. Chang, *The Chinese in America*, photo section 2.
35. The first use of the derisive name "heathen Chinee" for Chinese immigrants is generally attributed to newspaperman Bret Harte in his popular poem *Plain Language from Truthful James*. The poem was first published in *Overland Monthly* in September 1870 and later brought to the stage by Harte and Mark Twain.
36. Bird, *Bordellos of Blair Street*, 73.
37. Twain, *Roughing It*, 105.
38. Blair, *Leadville*, 61.
39. Parker, *Deadwood*, 65.
40. Ibid., 78.
41. Chang, *The Chinese in America*, 44.
42. Steele, *Bleed, Blister and Purge*, 104.
43. Dorsett, *The Queen City*, 103.
44. Morgan, *Wanton West*, 86, 231.
45. Ibid., 87.
46. Ibid., 94.
47. McCunn, *An Illustrated History of the Chinese in America*, 79.
48. Lucius Beebe and Charles Clegg, *The American West* (New York: E.P. Dutton, 1955), 319.
49. Ambrose, *Nothing Like It in the World*, 150.
50. McCunn, *An Illustrated History of the Chinese in America*, 43.
51. Dorsett, *The Queen City*, 102.
52. Whiteside, *Menace in the West*, 3.

Chapter Six

1. *Tri-Weekly Miner's Register*, January 6, 1863.
2. Noel, *The City and the Saloon*, 88.
3. Lake, *Wyatt Earp*, 33.
4. Lavender, *Bent's Fort*, 351.
5. Schoenberger, *The Gunfighters*, 2.
6. Ibid., 13.
7. *Ellsworth Reporter*, August 21, 1873.
8. Schoenberger, *The Gunfighters*, 167.

9. Lake, *Wyatt Earp*, 57.

10. Billings, *Hardtack and Coffee*, 140.

11. Straubing, *In Hospital and Camp*, 3.

12. P.M. Ashburn, *A History of the Medical Department of the United States Army* (Boston: Houghton Mifflin, 1929), 121.

13. Lawrence A. Frost, *General Custer's Libbie* (Seattle: Superior, 1976), 177.

14. Wyoming Department of State Parks and Cultural Resources, *Fort Fetterman*, undated pamphlet.

15. The sutler was a storekeeper franchised to sell various goods and provisions on an army post. This function was later replaced by the post exchange (PX).

16. Ashburn, *A History of the Medical Department of the United States Army*, 102.

17. Unrau, *White Man's Wicked Water*, ix.

18. Rickey, *Forty Miles a Day on Beans and Hay*, 204.

19. Billings, *Hardtack and Coffee*, 140.

20. Elizabeth B. Custer, *Tenting on the Plains, or General Custer in Kansas and Texas* (Norman: University of Oklahoma Press, 1994), 257.

21. Herman J. Viola, ed., *The Memoirs of Charles Henry Veil: A Soldier's Recollections of the Civil War and the Arizona Territory* (Waterville, ME: Thorndike, 1993), 241–244.

22. Robert M. Utley, ed., *Life in Custer's Cavalry: Diaries and Letters of Albert and Jennie Barnitz, 1867–1868* (Lincoln: University of Nebraska Press, 1977), 139.

23. Unrau, *White Man's Wicked Water*, 7.

24. Ibid., ix.

25. Rickey, *Forty Miles a Day on Beans and Hay*, 159.

26. Eales, *Army Wives on the American Frontier*, 133.

27. Unrau, *White Man's Wicked Water*, 7.

28. Thompson, *Lake City*, 42.

29. Secrest, *Hell's Belles*, 112.

30. West, *The Saloon on the Rocky Mountain Mining Frontier*, 2.

31. Furnas, *The Life and Times of the Late Demon Rum*, 82.

32. Craig MacAndrew and Robert B. Edgerton, *Drunken Comportment: A Social Explanation* (Chicago: Aldine, 1968), 2.

33. Furnas, *The Life and Times of The Late Demon Rum*, 82–83. Introduced to the United States in 1832, phrenology was the practice of studying the shape and bumps on a person's head and using this information to describe that person's characteristics, virtues, and vices. On this basis, newspaperman Horace Greeley felt that in order to avoid train accidents railroad workers should be hired based on the configuration of their heads.

34. Morgan, *Yesterday's Addicts*, 8. A similar problem existed in Australia. In 1890, 17,684 pounds of opium were imported, of which only 400 pounds were for medicinal use (Booth, *Opium*, 178).

35. Haller and Haller, *The Physician and Sexuality in Victorian America*, 275; Terry and Pellens, *The Opium Problem*, 50–51.

36. Terry and Pellens, *The Opium Problem*, 50–51.

37. Haller and Haller, *The Physician and Sexuality in Victorian America*, 278.

38. C.W. Earle, "The Opium Habit," *Chicago Medical Review* 2 (1880), 443–444.

39. F.E. Oliver, *The Use and Abuse of Opium*, Massachusetts State Board of Health, Third Annual Report (Boston: Wright and Potter, 1872), 170–177.

40. Bollet, *Civil War Medicine*, 241.

41. *Territorial Enterprise*, February 19, 1872.

42. Kerr, *Inebriety*, 234.

43. Haller and Haller, *The Physician and Sexuality in Victorian America*, 280.

44. Ibid., 173.

45. Ibid.

46. William W. Sanger, *The History of Prostitution* (New York: Harper, 1858), 488.

47. Williams, *The Red Light Ladies of Virginia City*, 22.

48. *Denver Times*, October 3, 1891.

49. Haller and Haller, *The Physician and Sexuality in Victorian America*, 230.

50. Martha L. Hildreth and Bruce T. Moran, eds., *Disease and Medical Care in the Mountain West: Essays on Region, History, and Practice* (Reno: University of Nevada Press, 1997), 95–109.

51. George Wood, *A Treatise on Therapeutics and Pharmacology, or Materia Medica* (Philadelphia: Lippincott, 1868), 726.

52. H.H. Kane, *Opium Smoking in America and Abroad* (New York: G.P. Putnam's, 1881).

53. Musto, *Drugs in America*, 217.

54. Florence Dakin, Ella M. Thompson and Margaret LeBaron, *Simplified Nursing* (Philadelphia: J.B. Lippincott, 1956), 709.

55. Powell, *Bacchus Dethroned*, 77.

56. Secrest, *Hell's Belles*, 112.

57. Burnham, *Bad Habits*, 115–116.

58. Furnas, *The Life and Times of the Late Demon Rum*, 183.

59. Dary, *Frontier Medicine*, 266.

60. Ibid.

61. Furnas, *The Life and Times of the Late Demon Rum*, 182.

62. Haller and Haller, *The Physician and Sexuality in Victorian America*, 288.

Chapter Seven

1. Barrows and Room, *Drinking*, 113.
2. Robert L. Brown, *Ghost Towns of Colorado: Past and Present* (Caldwell, ID: Caxton, 1981), 208.
3. Owen White, *Out of the Desert: The Historical Romance of El Paso* (McMath, 1923), 50.
4. West, *The Saloon on the Rocky Mountain Mining Frontier*, 134.
5. MacKell, *Brothels, Bordellos, and Bad Girls*, 200.
6. Dennis Drabelle, *Mile-High Fever: Silver Mines, Boom Towns, and High Living on the Comstock Lode* (New York: St. Martin's, 2009), 84.
7. Brown, *Saloons of the American West*, 71.
8. Adobe was a popular building material in the Southwest because it was readily available — and cheap. Adobe bricks, also called "dobie," "adobys" or "Spanish brick," were unfired bricks made of local mud, with straw as a binder, that were dried in the sun. They were typically about twelve inches long, ten inches wide, and four inches thick.
9. West, *The Saloon on the Rocky Mountain Mining Frontier*, 43.
10. Brown, *Saloons of the American West*, 17.
11. Dykstra, *The Cattle Towns*, 103.
12. Parker, *Deadwood*, 72.
13. George Cushman, "Abilene, First of the Kansas Cowtowns," *Kansas State Historical Society Quarterly* 9, no. 3 (August 1940), 244.
14. Benjamin E. Lloyd, *Lights and Shades in San Francisco* (San Francisco: A.L. Bancroft, 1876), 182–183.
15. Secrest, *Hell's Belles*, 102.
16. Rosa, *They Called Him Wild Bill*, 137.
17. West, *The Saloon on the Rocky Mountain Mining Frontier*, xiv.
18. Thompson, *Lake City*, 41.
19. Asbury, *The Barbary Coast*, 116.
20. MacKell, *Red Light Women of the Rocky Mountains*, 248.
21. Secrest, *Hell's Belles*, 101.
22. Morgan, *Wanton West*, 45.
23. Noel, *The City and the Saloon*, 35.
24. Pat Jahns, *The Frontier World of Doc Holliday* (New York: Hastings House, 1957), 66.
25. West, *The Saloon on the Rocky Mountain Mining Frontier*, 115.
26. Asbury, *The Barbary Coast*, 113.
27. Bennett, *Old Deadwood Days*, 105.
28. Monahan, *The Wicked West*, 34.
29. Morgan, *Wanton West*, 246.
30. Brown, *Saloons of the American West*, 102.
31. MacKell, *Red Light Women of the Rocky Mountains*, 270.

Chapter Eight

1. H.H. Kane, "American Opium Smokers," *Harper's Weekly*, September 24, 1881, 646.
2. Ibid.
3. Parkhill, *The Wildest of the West*, 110.
4. The *National Police Gazette*, more commonly known as the *Police Gazette*, was founded in 1845 and achieved great popularity in the late 1800s. It was an illustrated tabloid-type publication that specialized in lurid coverage of murders, events in the Wild West, and scandalous events involving women.
5. Mary M. Mathews, *Ten Years in Nevada; or, Life on the Pacific Coast* (Lincoln: University of Nevada Press, 1985), 250.
6. Kane, "American Opium Smokers," *Harper's Weekly*, 646.
7. Ibid.
8. Arthur C. Doyle, *The Complete Sherlock Holmes* (Garden City: Doubleday, 1960), 230–231.
9. Mathews, *Ten Years in Nevada; or, Life on the Pacific Coast*, 250.
10. Secrest, *Hell's Belles*, 117.
11. Santella, *Opium*, 45.
12. Booth, *Opium*, 211.
13. Sax Rohmer, *The Mystery of Dr. Fu-Manchu* (London: Methuen, 1953), 38.
14. Ibid., 38–39.
15. Ibid., 40.
16. The novel was unfinished when Dickens died in 1870 felled by a massive stroke. This left many loose ends. The most popular theory is that Drood was murdered by his uncle, Jasper, in a delirium induced by Jasper's opium smoking.
17. Twain, *Roughing It*, 109–110.
18. The Barbary Coast in San Francisco was named for the area in Northern Africa that stretched from Tripoli to Morocco, which was notorious for its pirates and thieves. In San Francisco, the namesake Barbary Coast was located just north of Portsmouth Square and centered between Stockton and Montgomery streets. It was lined with saloons, gambling dens, low-class variety theaters, and houses of prostitution. The main area extended for three blocks or so along Pacific Street, known locally at the time as "Terrific Street."

19. Asbury, *The Barbary Coast*, 156.
20. Benjamin E. Lloyd, *Lights and Shades in San Francisco* (San Francisco: A.L. Bancroft, 1876), 182–183.
21. Asbury, *The Barbary Coast*, 204.
22. Bennett, *Old Deadwood Days*, 28.
23. Terry and Pellens, *The Opium Problem*, 50–51.

Chapter Nine

1. Terry and Pellens, *The Opium Problem*, 50–51.
2. Addiction can be defined as domination by a drug habit.
3. The word "injection" literally means to force a fluid into the body by means of a syringe. Before the use of hypodermic injections, the medical term "injection" referred to an enema. *Hypo* means "below" and *dermis* is "skin," so "hypodermic" literally means "under the skin."
4. Booth, *Opium*, 71.
5. Child, *The Family Nurse*, 138.
6. Bollet, *Civil War Medicine*, 239.
7. Much of this was not new but had been lost or forgotten over time. The writings of Theophrastus in the third century B.C. describe the administration of opium either through punctures in the skin or by inhalation of the vapor.
8. Musto, *Drugs in America*, 206.
9. Asbury, *The Barbary Coast*, 113–114.
10. Escohotado, *A Brief History of Drugs*, 66.
11. Opium is still used medically today under limited conditions, but its administration is typically short-term so that medically induced dependence is rare.
12. Sutcliffe and Duin, *A History of Medicine*, 51.
13. Beeching, *The Chinese Opium Wars*, 178.
14. Santella, *Opium*, 45.
15. Bergersen and Krug, *Pharmacology in Nursing*, 243–244.
16. Kerr, *Inebriety*, 235.
17. *British and Foreign Medical Review* 4, p. 394, quoted in Powell, *Bacchus Dethroned*, 79.
18. Haller and Haller, *The Physician and Sexuality in Victorian America*, 276.
19. *British and Foreign Medical Review* 4, p. 394, quoted in Powell, *Bacchus Dethroned*, 79.
20. John A. Hawkins, *Opium: Addicts and Addictions* (Danville, VA: John A. Hawkins, 1937), 152–153.

21. Holland, *The Joy of Drinking*, 15.
22. Hodgson, *In the Arms of Morpheus*, 71.
23. Musto, *Drugs in America*, 188.
24. Al Rose, *Storyville, New Orleans* (Tuscaloosa: University of Alabama Press, 1974), 94.
25. Booth, *Opium*, 192.
26. William A. Hammond, "Coca: Its Preparations and Their Therapeutical Qualities, with Some Remarks on the So-Called Cocaine Habit," *Virginia Medical Monthly* (November 1887), 598–610.
27. Alexander Lambert, "The Obliteration of the Craving for Narcotics," *Journal of the American Medical Association* 53, no. 13 (1909), 985–989. Other treatments followed similar techniques of purging to flush out the "poisons." For a more detailed review of treatments see Terry and Pellens, *The Opium Problem*, 517–628.
28. Booth, *Opium*, 94.
29. Advertising for Keeley's sanitarium treatment in Armstrong and Armstrong, *The Great American Medicine Show*, 47.
30. Rose and Cherpitel, *Alcohol*, 19–20.
31. J.B. Mattison, "Opium Antidotes and Their Vendors," *Journal of the American Medical Association* 7 (1886), 569–570.
32. Rose and Cherpitel, *Alcohol*, 19–20.
33. Mattison, "Opium Antidotes and Their Vendors," 569–570.
34. Rose and Cherpitel, *Alcohol*, 21.
35. One modern treatment for addicts uses methadone, which was first synthesized in the 1940s. Methadone blocks morphine and heroin from working and is considered easier to withdraw from than the other two. While similar to morphine in its effects and perhaps less addictive than morphine, methadone still carries the risks of substituting one type of addiction for another. One plus is that methadone is taken by mouth, which eliminates the ritual reinforcement that is part of a hypodermic drug habit. The theory of use is that the dosages of methadone are decreased until they are stopped altogether. Modern addicts, however, say that it does not necessarily work that easily.
36. Booth, *Opium*, 77. Bayer Laboratories was originally a small dye factory but eventually became a giant in the chemical world because of its manufacture and marketing of heroin and aspirin. Aspirin (acetylsalicylic acid) had been known since the 1830s but was not mass produced by Bayer until 1900. After it became commonly available, aspirin took the place of morphine and opium for lesser aches and pains.

37. Rutter, *Upstairs Girls*, 10.

38. Owen, *British Opium Policy in China and India*, 3–4.

39. Haller and Haller, *The Physician and Sexuality in Victorian America*, 293.

40. This drifting away into sleep and nothingness was probably better for the victim than the common alternatives of drinking strychnine or the antiseptic carbolic acid. The women who made these latter choices usually lingered in agony for hours before dying.

41. MacKell, *Brothels, Bordellos, and Bad Girls*, 77.

42. Morgan, *Wanton West*, 34.

43. MacKell, *Red Light Women of the Rocky Mountains*, 28. Jamaica ginger was a highly toxic substance used as a substitute for alcohol in bootleg booze.

Chapter Ten

1. West, *The Saloon on the Rocky Mountain Mining Frontier*, 3.

2. Jerome C. Smiley, *History of Denver* (Denver: Times-Sun Publishing, 1901), 293.

3. Noel, *The City and the Saloon*, 10.

4. William McGlove produced the first beer in California in 1837, but not much was drunk until after the Mexican War.

5. Marshall Sprague, *Newport in the Rockies: The Life and Good Times of Colorado Springs* (Denver: Sage, 1961), 317–318.

6. Ibid., 226.

7. Noel, *The City and the Saloon*, 30.

8. Barrows and Room, *Drinking*, 17.

9. Rose and Cherpitel, *Alcohol*, 23.

10. MacKell, *Brothels, Bordellos, and Bad Girls*, 119, 227.

11. Ibid., 106.

12. Secrest, *Hell's Belles*, 264.

13. Russell, *The Lives and Legends of Buffalo Bill*, 303.

14. Dasgupta, *The Science of Drinking*, 23.

15. Holland, *The Joy of Drinking*, 104.

16. Ibid., 100.

17. Max H. Pittler, Joris Verster and Edzard Ernst, "Interventions for preventing or treating alcohol hangover: systematic review of randomised controlled trials," *British Medical Journal* 331 (2005), 1515.

18. Rose and Cherpitel, *Alcohol*, 139.

19. Powell, *Bacchus Dethroned*, 161.

20. Crowley, *Drunkard's Progress*, 102.

21. Ibid., 144–145.

22. West, *The Saloon on the Rocky Mountain Mining Frontier*, 23.

23. Parker, *Deadwood*, 160.

24. Eales, *Army Wives on the American Frontier*, 102.

25. "Brimstone" was an early chemist's term that literally meant "burning stone," an element known to the modern chemist as sulfur.

26. Powell, *Bacchus Dethroned*, 161.

27. For a collection of these bizarre incidents see Charles H. Fort, *The Books of Charles Fort* (New York: Henry Holt, 1941), 656–657, 661–663, 927–930.

28. Furnas, *The Life and Times of the Late Demon Rum*, 189.

29. Macnish, *The Anatomy of Drunkenness*.

30. Jerome C. Smiley, *History of Denver* (Denver: Times-Sun Publishing, 1901), 293.

31. Noel, *The City and the Saloon*, 75.

32. *Wichita Eagle*, January 4, 1877.

33. Leon Metz, *John Selman: Texas Gunfighter* (New York: Hastings House, 1966), 70–71.

34. Richard E. Holben, "Badman Saloonkeeper," *Pioneer West*, February 1972, 14–18.

35. This was what was reported in the *Kansas Daily Tribune*, September 30, 1869. On the other hand, author Joseph Rosa has stated that several of the facts were misrepresented by the local newspaper. His research shows that the man's name was Strawhun and that the location was John Bitter and Company's Leavenworth Beer Saloon (Rosa, *They Called Him Wild Bill*, 147). Nash says that the name was Strawhim or Strawan, the date was September 27, and the saloon was John Bitter's Leavenworth Beer Saloon (Nash, *Encyclopedia of Western Lawman and Outlaws*, 295). These are small differences, but they point out the difficulties in tracking down the facts in historical research.

36. Rosa, *They Called Him Wild Bill*, 253.

37. O'Neal, *Encyclopedia of Western Gunfighters*, 189.

38. Ibid., 100.

39. Bennett, *Old Deadwood Days*, 160–161.

40. Erdoes, *Saloons of the Old West*, 49.

41. Blair, *Leadville*, 78.

42. Nash, *Encyclopedia of Western Lawman and Outlaws*, 303.

43. MacKell, *Red Light Women of the Rocky Mountains*, 78.

44. Sanford C. Gladden, *Ladies of the Night* (Boulder: privately published, 1979), 28.

45. Joseph Cook, *Diary and Letters* (Laramie: Laramie Republican, 1919), 12.

46. Thompson, *Lake City*, 41–42.

47. Powell, *Bacchus Dethroned*, 77.

48. Palmer, *Inebriety*, 59.

49. Ibid., 62.

50. Ibid., 98.

51. Ibid., 97.

52. Ibid., 109.

53. Secrest, *Hell's Belles*, 112.

54. Janet Staiger, *Bad Women: Regulating Sexuality in Early American Cinema* (Minneapolis: University of Minnesota Press), 1995, 44.

55. Agnew, *Entertainment in the Old West*, 45–46.

56. Craig MacAndrew and Robert B. Edgerton, *Drunken Comportment: A Social Explanation* (Chicago: Aldine, 1968), 8.

Chapter Eleven

1. Thompson, *Lake City*, 21.

2. Rose and Cherpitel, *Alcohol*, 22.

3. Benjamin Rush, *An Inquiry into the Effects of Ardent Spirits upon the Human Body and Mind, with an Account of the Means of Preventing, and of the Remedies for Curing Them* (1823; Whitefish: Kessinger, 2010).

4. Musto, *Drugs in America*, 28.

5. Furnas, *The Life and Times of the Late Demon Rum*, 39–40.

6. Musto, *Drugs in America*, 9.

7. Gardner and Aylworth, *The Domestic Physician*, 59.

8. Holland, *The Joy of Drinking*, 75.

9. Furnas, *The Life and Times of the Late Demon Rum*, 209.

10. Noel, *The City and the Saloon*, 84.

11. Furnas, *The Life and Times of the Late Demon Rum*, 193.

12. Powell, *Bacchus Dethroned*, 17.

13. Furnas, *The Life and Times of the Late Demon Rum*, 80.

14. Ibid., 81.

15. Thompson, *Lake City*, 21.

16. Furnas, *The Life and Times of the Late Demon Rum*, 82.

17. Ibid., 80.

18. Edwards, *Alcohol: The World's Favorite Drug*, 79.

19. Burns, *The Spirits of America*, 118.

20. Ibid.

21. Morgan, *Wanton West*, 243.

22. Barrows and Room, *Drinking*, 223.

23. The Cambellites, an offshoot of the Baptists, were the followers of Thomas and Alexander Campbell, whose teachings started several other Protestant denominations. The Cambellites' guide was the strict interpretation of the Christian Testament.

24. Grace, *Carry A. Nation*, 148.

25. Furnas, *The Life and Times of the Late Demon Rum*, 295.

26. Ibid., 235.

27. Grace, *Carry A. Nation*, 145.

28. Ibid., 218.

29. Ibid., 247.

30. Morgan, *Wanton West*, 157.

31. Furnas, *The Life and Times of the Late Demon Rum*, 213.

32. Ibid., 155.

33. Frank Rahill, *The World of Melodrama* (University Park: Pennsylvania State University Press, 1967), 244.

34. From advertising material in the back pages of Powell, *Bacchus Dethroned*.

35. Powell, *Bacchus Dethroned*, 13.

36. Ibid., 42.

37. Ibid.

38. Crowley, *Drunkard's Progress*, first illustration after page 96.

39. Richmond P. Hobson, *Alcohol and the Human Race* (New York: Fleming H. Revell, 1919), 7–10.

40. MacKell, *Brothels, Bordellos, and Bad Girls*, 202–203.

41. F.E. Oliver, *The Use and Abuse of Opium*, Massachusetts State Board of Health, Third Annual Report (Boston: Wright and Potter, 1872), 170–177.

42. Ibid., 162–177.

Postscript

1. Gateley, *Drink*, 373.

2. Marshall Sprague, *Newport in the Rockies: The Life and Good Times of Colorado Springs* (Denver: Sage, 1961), 347.

3. Dabney, *Mountain Spirits*, xiv.

4. Morgan, *Wanton West*, 252.

5. Harris, *This Drinking Nation*, 86.

6. Burns, *The Spirits of America*, 219.

7. Denatured alcohol is ethanol mixed with substances such as wood alcohol, pyridine, sulfuric acid, soap, or benzene to make it unfit for human consumption as beverage alcohol but still allows it to be used for industrial purposes.

8. Burns, *The Spirits of America*, 221–222.

9. Ibid., 221.

10. Hodgson, *In the Arms of Morpheus*, 77.

11. Ibid., 81.

12. Booth, *Opium*, 198.

13. Richmond P. Hobson, *Mankind's Greatest Affliction and Gravest Menace* (Los Angeles: International Narcotic Education Association, 1928), 271.

14. Booth, *Opium*, 198.

15. The Supreme Court deliberated the constitutionality of the act for the next five years before deciding it was acceptable.

16. Hodgson, *In the Arms of Morpheus*, 77.

Bibliography

Adams, George W. *Doctors in Blue*. New York: Henry Schuman, 1952.

Agnew, Jeremy. *Brides of the Multitude: Prostitution in the Old West*. Lake City, CO: Western Reflections, 2008.

_____. *Entertainment in the Old West: Theater, Music, Circuses, Medicine Shows, Prizefighting and Other Popular Amusements*. Jefferson, NC: McFarland, 2011.

_____. *Medicine in the Old West: A History, 1850–1900*. Jefferson, NC: McFarland, 2010.

Ambrose, Stephen E. *Nothing Like It in the World: The Men Who Built the Transcontinental Railroad, 1863–1869*. New York: Simon & Schuster, 2000.

Armstrong, David, and Elizabeth M. Armstrong. *The Great American Medicine Show*. New York: Prentice-Hall, 1991.

Asbury, Herbert. *The Barbary Coast*. New York: Pocket Books, 1947.

_____. *Carry Nation*. New York: Alfred A. Knopf, 1929.

Barnhart, Jacqueline B. *The Fair but Frail: Prostitution in San Francisco, 1849–1900*. Reno: University of Nevada Press, 1986.

Barrows, Susanna, and Robin Room, eds. *Drinking: Behavior and Belief in Modern History*. Berkeley: University of California Press, 1991.

Barsness, Larry. *Gold Camp: Alder Gulch and Virginia City, Montana*. New York: Hastings House, 1962.

Beebe, Lucius, and Charles Clegg. *The American West*. New York: E.P. Dutton, 1955.

Beeching, Jack. *The Chinese Opium Wars*. New York: Harcourt Brace Jovanovich, 1975.

Bennett, Estelline. *Old Deadwood Days*. New York: Charles Scribner's Sons, 1935.

Bergersen, Betty S., and Elsie E. Krug. *Pharmacology in Nursing*. St. Louis: C.V. Mosby, 1966.

Billings, John D. *Hardtack and Coffee: The Unwritten Story of Army Life*. Lincoln: University of Nebraska Press, 1993.

Bird, Allan G. *Bordellos of Blair Street*. Pierson, MI: Advertising, Publications & Consultants, 1993.

Blair, Edward. *Leadville: Colorado's Magic City*. Boulder: Pruett, 1980.

Bollet, Alfred J. *Civil War Medicine: Challenges and Triumphs*. Tucson: Galen, 2002.

Booth, Martin. *Opium: A History*. New York: St. Martin's, 1996.

Bordin, Ruth. *Frances Willard: A Biography*. Chapel Hill: University of North Carolina Press, 1986.

_____. *Woman and Temperance: The Quest for Power and Liberty, 1873–1900*. New Brunswick: Rutgers University Press, 1990.

Breeden, James O., ed. *Medicine in the West*. Manhattan, KS: Sunflower University Press, 1982.

Brown, Robert L. *Saloons of the American West*. Silverton, CO: Sundance, 1978.

Bruns, Roger A. *Desert Honkytonk: The Story of Tombstone's Bird Cage Theatre*. Golden, CO: Fulcrum, 2000.

Burnham, John C. *Bad Habits: Drinking, Smoking, Taking Drugs, Gambling, Sexual Misbehavior, and Swearing in American History*. New York: New York University Press, 1993.

Burns, Eric. *The Spirits of America: A Social History*. Philadelphia: Temple University Press, 2004.

Butler, Anne M. *Daughters of Joy, Sisters of Misery*. Urbana: University of Illinois Press, 1987.

Carr, Mary S. *A Yankee Trader in the Gold Rush: The Letters of Franklin A. Buck*. Boston: Houghton Mifflin, 1930.

Chang, Iris. *The Chinese in America: A Narrative History*. New York: Viking, 2003.

Child, Lydia M. *The Family Nurse; or, Companion of the American Frugal Housewife*. Boston: Charles J. Hendee, 1837.

Clappe, Louise A. (Dame Shirley). *The Shirley Letters from the California Mines, 1851–1852*. New York: Alfred A. Knopf, 1949.

Crowley, John W. *Drunkard's Progress: Narratives of Addiction, Despair, and Recovery*. Baltimore: Johns Hopkins University Press, 1999.

Dabney, Joseph E. *Mountain Spirits: A Chronicle of Corn Whiskey*. New York: Charles Scribner's Sons, 1974.

Dakin, Florence, Ella M. Thompson and Margaret LeBaron. *Simplified Nursing*. Philadelphia: J.B. Lippincott, 1956.

Dary, David. *Frontier Medicine: From the Atlantic to the Pacific, 1492–1941*. New York: Alfred A. Knopf, 2008.

_____. *Seeking Pleasure in the Old West*. Lawrence: University Press of Kansas, 1995.

Dasgupta, Amitava. *The Science of Drinking: How Alcohol Affects Your Body and Mind*. Lanham, MD: Rowman & Littlefield, 2011.

Denney, Robert E. *Civil War Medicine: Care and Comfort of the Wounded*. New York: Sterling, 1994.

de Ropp, Robert S. *Drugs and the Mind*. New York: Grove, 1961.

Dorsett, Lyle W. *The Queen City: A History of Denver*. Boulder: Pruett, 1977.

Dykstra, Robert R. *The Cattle Towns*. New York: Alfred A. Knopf, 1968.

Eales, Anne B. *Army Wives on the American Frontier*. Boulder: Johnson, 1996.

Edwards, Griffith. *Alcohol, the World's Favorite Drug*. New York: Thomas Dunne, 2000.

Erdoes, Richard. *Saloons of the Old West*. New York: Alfred Knopf, 1979.

Escohotado, Antonio. *A Brief History of Drugs: From the Stone Age to the Stoned Age*. Rochester: Park Street, 1999.

Faulk, Odie B. *Tombstone: Myth and Reality*. New York: Oxford University Press, 1972.

Feitz, Leland. *Myers Avenue*. Denver: Golden Bell, 1967.

Furnas, J.C. *The Life and Times of the Late Demon Rum*. New York: G.P. Putnam's Sons, 1965.

Gardner, Marlin, and Benjamin H. Aylworth. *The Domestic Physician and Family Assistant*. Cooperstown, NY: H. and E. Phinney, 1836.

Gateley, Iain. *Drink: A Cultural History of Alcohol*. New York: Gotham, 2008.

Goldman, Marion. *Gold Diggers and Silver Miners: Prostitution and Social Life on the Comstock Lode*. Ann Arbor: University of Michigan Press, 1981.

Goodstein, Phil. *The Seamy Side of Denver*. Denver: New Social Publications, 1993.

Grace, Fran. *Carry A. Nation: Retelling the Life*. Bloomington: Indiana University Press, 2004.

Green, Harvey. *The Light of the Home*. New York: Pantheon, 1983.

Groh, George W. *Gold Fever: Being a True Account, Both Horrifying and Hilarious of the Art of Healing (So-Called) During the California Gold Rush*. New York: William Morrow, 1966.

Haller, John S., Jr., and Robin M. Haller. *The Physician and Sexuality in Victorian America*. Urbana: University of Illinois Press, 1974.

Harris, Jonathan. *This Drinking Nation*. New York: Four Winds, 1994.

Hart-Davis, Adam. *What the Victorians Did for Us*. London: Headline, 2001.

Hine, Robert V., and John M. Faragher. *The American West: A New Interpretive History*. New Haven: Yale University Press, 2000.

Hodgson, Barbara. *In the Arms of Morpheus: The Tragic History of Laudanum, Morphine, and Patent Medicines*. Buffalo: Firefly, 2001.

Holland, Barbara. *The Joy of Drinking*. New York: Bloomsbury USA, 2007.

James, Ronald M., and Elizabeth C. Raymond. *Comstock Women: The Making of a Mining Community*. Reno: University of Nevada Press, 1998.

_____. *The Roar and the Silence: A History of Virginia City and the Comstock Lode*. Reno: University of Nevada Press, 1998.

Johnson, Susan L. *Roaring Camp: The Social World of the California Gold Rush*. New York: W.W. Norton, 2000.

Karolevitz, Robert F. *Doctors of the Old West*. Seattle: Superior, 1967.

Kerr, Norman. *Inebriety; or, Narcomania: Its Etiology, Pathology, Treatment and Jurisprudence*. London: Lewis, 1894.

Kuz, Julian E., and Bradley P. Bengtson. *Orthopaedic Injuries of the Civil War*. Kennesaw: Kennesaw Mountain, 1996

Lake, Stuart N. *Wyatt Earp: Frontier Marshal*. New York: Simon & Schuster, 1994.

Lavender, David. *Bent's Fort*. Lincoln: University of Nebraska Press, 1972.

Lyman, George D. *The Saga of the Comstock Lode*. New York: Charles Scribner's Sons, 1934.

MacAndrew, Craig, and Robert B. Edgerton. *Drunken Comportment: A Social Explanation*. Chicago: Aldine, 1968.

MacKell, Jan. *Brothels, Bordellos, and Bad Girls*. Albuquerque: University of New Mexico Press, 2004.

_____. *Red Light Women of the Rocky Mountains*. Albuquerque: University of New Mexico Press, 2009.

Macnish, Robert. *The Anatomy of Drunkenness*. Glasgow: M'Phun, 1834.

McCunn, Ruthanne L. *An Illustrated History of the Chinese in America*. San Francisco: Design Enterprises of San Francisco, 1979

Miller, Brandon M. *Just What the Doctor Ordered: The History of American Medicine*. Minneapolis: Lerner, 1997.

Miller, Max. *Holladay Street*. New York: Signet, 1962.

Miller, Nyle H., and Joseph W. Snell. *Great Gunfighters of the Kansas Cowtowns, 1867–1886*. Lincoln: University of Nebraska Press, 1963.

Moerman, Daniel E. *Native American Medicinal Plants*. Portland: Timber, 2009.

Monahan, Sherry. *The Wicked West: Boozers, Cruisers, Gamblers, and More*. Tucson: Rio Nuevo, 2005

Morgan, H. Wayne, ed. *Yesterday's Addicts: American Society and Drug Abuse, 1865–1920*. Norman: University of Oklahoma Press, 1974.

Morgan, Lael. *Wanton West: Madams, Money, Murder, and the Wild Women of Montana's Frontier*. Chicago: Chicago Review Press, 2011.

Morgan, Murray. *Skid Road*. Seattle: University of Washington Press, 1982.

Musto, David F., ed. *Drugs in America: A Documentary History*. New York: New York University Press, 2002.

Myers, John M. *The Last Chance: Tombstone's Early Years*. New York: E.P. Dutton, 1950.

Nadeau, Remi. *Fort Laramie and the Sioux Indians*. Englewood Cliffs: Prentice-Hall, 1967.

Nash, Jay R. *Encyclopedia of Western Lawman and Outlaws*. New York: Da Capo, 1994.

Noel, Thomas J. *The City and the Saloon: Denver, 1858–1916*. Lincoln: University of Nebraska Press, 1982.

Norton, Nancy Fitzhugh. "Christmas in Denver in 1859." *The Trail*, December 1920.

O'Neal, Bill. *Encyclopedia of Western Gunfighters*. Norman: University of Oklahoma Press, 1960.

Owen, David E. *British Opium Policy in China and India*. New Haven: Yale University Press, 1934.

Palmer, Charles F. *Inebriety: Its Source, Prevention, and Cure*. New York: Fleming H. Revell, 1898.

Parker, Watson. *Deadwood: The Golden Years*. Lincoln: University of Nebraska Press, 1981.

Parkhill, Forbes. *The Wildest of the West*. New York: Henry Holt, 1951.

Parkman, Francis. *The Oregon Trail*. Garden City: Doubleday, 1946.

Pierce, R.V. *The People's Common Sense Medical Advisor in Plain English*. Buffalo: World's Dispensary, 1895.

Powell, Frederick. *Bacchus Dethroned*. New York: National Temperance Society, 1874.

Rickey, Don. *Forty Miles a Day on Beans and Hay: The Enlisted Soldier Fighting the Indian Wars*. Norman: University of Oklahoma Press, 1963.

Rosa, Joseph G. *They Called Him Wild Bill: The Life and Adventures of James Butler Hickok.* Norman: University of Oklahoma Press, 1974.

Rose, Mark E., and Cheryl J. Cherpitel. *Alcohol: Its History, Pharmacology and Treatment.* Center City, MN: Hazelden, 2011.

Russell, Don. *The Lives and Legends of Buffalo Bill.* Norman: University of Oklahoma Press, 1960.

Rutter, Michael. *Upstairs Girls: Prostitution in the American West.* Helena, MT: Farcountry, 2005.

Sanberg, Paul R., and Michael D. Bunsey. *Prescription Narcotics: The Addictive Painkillers.* New York: Chelsea House, 1986.

Santella, Thomas M. *Opium.* New York: Chelsea House, 2007.

Schoenberger, Dale. *The Gunfighters.* Caldwell, ID: Caxton, 1971.

Secrest, Clark. *Hell's Belles: Denver's Brides of the Multitudes.* Aurora: Hindsight Historical Publications, 1996.

Shrikes, Robert H. *Rocky Mountain Medicine.* Boulder: Johnson, 1986.

Smith, Duane A. *Rocky Mountain Mining Camps.* Lincoln: University of Nebraska Press, 1967.

Steele, Volney. *Bleed, Blister and Purge: A History of Medicine on the American Frontier.* Missoula: Mountain Press, 2005.

Straubing, Harold E. *In Hospital and Camp: The Civil War Through the Eyes of Its Doctors and Nurses.* Harrisburg, PA: Stackpole, 1993.

Sutcliffe, Jenny, and Nancy Duin. *A History of Medicine.* London: Morgan Samuel, 1992.

Terry, Charles E., and Mildred Pellens. *The Opium Problem.* New York: Bureau of Social Hygiene, 1928.

Thompson, Thomas G. *Lake City, Colorado: An Early Day Social and Cultural History.* Oklahoma City: Metro, 1974.

Toms, Don. *Tenderloin Tales.* Pierre: State, 1997.

Twain, Mark. *Roughing It.* Vol. 2. New York: Harper & Brothers, 1913.

Unrau, William E. *White Man's Wicked Water: The Alcohol Trade and Prohibition in Indian Country, 1802–1892.* Lawrence: University Press of Kansas, 1996.

Vestal, Stanley. *Queen of the Cowtowns: Dodge City.* New York: Harper, 1952.

Wagner, Heather L. *Alcohol.* Philadelphia: Chelsea House, 2003.

Ward, Geoffrey C. *The West.* Boston: Little, Brown, 1996.

Weber, David J. *The Taos Trappers: The Fur Trade in the Far Southwest, 1540–1846.* Norman: University of Oklahoma Press, 1971.

West, Elliott. *The Saloon on the Rocky Mountain Mining Frontier.* Lincoln: University of Nebraska Press, 1976.

Whiteside, Henry O. *Menace in the West: Colorado and the American Experience with Drugs, 1873–1963.* Denver: Colorado Historical Society, 1997.

Wilbur, C. Keith. *Civil War Medicine, 1861–1865.* Guilford, CT: Globe Pequot, 1998.

Williams, George. *The Red Light Ladies of Virginia City, Nevada.* Dayton, OH: Tree by the River, 1990.

Index

Page numbers in **_bold italics_** indicate pages with illustrations.